Sexualizing Power in Naturalism

Theodore Dreiser and Frederick Philip Grove

Irene Gammel

UNIVERSITY OF CALGARY PRESS

University of Calgary Press
2500 University Drive N.W.
Calgary, Alberta, Canada T2N 1N4

Canadian Cataloguing in Publication Data

Gammel, Irene, 1959–
    Sexualizing power in naturalism

    Includes bibliographical references and index.
    ISBN 1-895176-39-5

    1. Grove, Frederick Philip, 1879–1948—Criticism and
interpretation. 2. Dreiser, Theodore, 1871–1945—Criticism
and interpretation. 3. Naturalism in literature. 4. Sex in
literature. 5. Women in literature. I. Title.
PS8513.R68Z65 1994   C813'.52   C94-910931-2
PR9199.2.G76Z65 1994

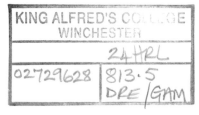

COMMITTED TO THE DEVELOPMENT OF CULTURE AND THE ARTS

Front cover: Henri de Toulouse-Lautrec, *Jane Avril Leaving the Moulin Rouge, 1892.* Wadsworth Atheneum, Hartford, Connecticut. Bequest of George A. Gay.

Printed and bound in Canada by Hignell Printing Ltd.

∞ This book is printed on acid-free paper.

Sexualizing Power in Naturalism

Theodore Dreiser and Frederick Philip Grove

To my parents,

Gertrud and Gerhard Gammel

Contents

Acknowledgements

This book began as a doctoral dissertation at McMaster University, but its roots go back even further. After I had left Germany to study in Canada in 1986, Carl Ballstadt's exploration of the "Literature of the Arrival" introduced me to F.P. Grove, touching some deep cords in my own life of cultural transition. Thus, the research for and writing of this book have helped me come to grips with my own efforts at translating and recontextualizing cultural conventions left behind.

Just as the process of researching this book has created an exciting network of new friends and ideas, so this book as a finished product is an intertextual web, deeply indebted to the stimulus and inspiration of others, whom I would like to thank: Joseph Adamson, Barry Allen, Carl Ballstadt, E.D. Blodgett, James Brasch, Gaby Divay, Gisi Baronin von Freytag-Loringhoven, Elizabeth Epperly, Miriam Gogol, Hans Itschert, Heather Jones, Erhard Linsen, Hans-Jörg Neuschäfer, Mary O'Connor, and Jean Wilson. I am very grateful to Don Mason for his valuable editorial advice and his preparation of the index. My special thanks go to Ed Martin for his generosity in reading and commenting on the early drafts.

Parts of this book have appeared in earlier versions in the following journals: *Canadian Literature*, 135 (Winter 1992), *Ariel: A Review of International English Literature* 23.3 (July 1992), *Studies in Canadian Literature* 17.2 (1992), and *The Canadian Review of American Studies* 22 (Fall 1991). I am grateful for permission to reprint parts of this material. Also, it was the work on a chapter for Miriam Gogol's forthcoming collection of essays entitled *Theodore Dreiser: Beyond Naturalism* (New York: New York UP, 1995) that helped me shape my thoughts on Dreiser's conceptualization of female sexuality. By a twist of fate, my book happens to precede hers by a few months, but I would like to acknowledge that the original material really belongs to her collection.

This book has greatly benefited from the generous support of the World University Service of Canada as well as the T. Glendenning Hamilton Research Grant of the University of Manitoba. Finally, this book has been published with the help of a grant from the Canadian Federation for the Humanities, using funds provided by the Social Sciences and Humanities Research Council of Canada.

Introduction

Naturalism's "gallery of women" includes such diverse figures as the actress-prostitute, the woman yielding passively to "la chair molle," and the sexually active female, whose body becomes a source of contagious disease. Within the boundaries of naturalist fiction, female sexuality is always already problematic and dangerous. Naturalism's treatment of female sexuality in different centuries and countries highlights the underlying gender bias of the genre, but the changes in the representation of its sexualized stock figures also signal the subtle ideological, aesthetic, and cultural shifts in naturalism across temporal and national boundaries. Though naturalism is often seen as a nineteenth-century European literary reaction to the industrial and Darwinian revolution, the twentieth century witnessed a renaissance of naturalist forms in North America at a time when modernism, with its formal and generic experimentations, was about to establish itself as the dominant paradigm of literature. One objective of this study is to examine what made it possible for American and Canadian naturalist forms to carve out a niche for themselves and survive alongside expressionist and modernist art forms. I argue that the "survival" and transformation of European naturalist conventions

1

in a North American context is deeply rooted in the genre's preoccupation with sexuality and power. By appropriating this nineteenth-century naturalist concern, American and Canadian naturalism established itself as a significant art form in the early twentieth century, translating, recontextualizing, and rewriting the conventions of nineteenth-century European forms.

The conventions of European naturalism have most recently been theorized by David Baguley in *Naturalist Fiction: The Entropic Vision* (1990), which I use as a point of departure. Emphasizing naturalism's obsession with sexuality, and especially with female sexuality, Baguley notes that there are "fundamental links between naturalist narratology, physiology and (the sadistic fantasies of some kind of advanced form of) 'Ripperology.'"[1] Amongst others, he points to the Goncourts' *Germinie Lacerteux* (1864) as a representative text: "Germinie, as well as being of the People, is also Woman, another unexplored territory, another 'coin saignant de l'humanité,' probed by the fascinated scrutiny of the male naturalist cum physiologist, a hysterical woman with unrestrained sexual cravings" (*NF* 83). Indeed, from its "official" beginning in the nineteenth century, female sexuality has played a pivotal role in naturalist fiction, which is not to say that male characters are outside the realm of sexuality. The naturalist gallery of sexualized females frequently finds its male counterpart in the prostitute's customer, the womanizer, the fetishist, and the sexually predatory employer. It should come as no surprise, then, that much of the sexualized power inscribed in the naturalist genre is conceptualized in engendered terms. As a general rule, naturalist fiction presents male authors, narrators, and characters looking at, inspecting, and framing female sexuality and the female body. Baguley highlights that European naturalism has an aura of a "club for males only," much of their writing being "about the threat of femininity, the dangers of feminisation" (*NF* 84).

Using Baguley's notion of the naturalist "male club" as a springboard, I want to provide a revisionary – gender-critical – reading of twentieth-century American and Canadian naturalism. This approach is partly indebted to Judith Fetterley's notion of the "resisting reader,"[2] as it resists a reading along the male authors' "intentions." Instead, it aims at exposing naturalism's male complicity in the very sexualization of power

---

1 (Cambridge: Cambridge UP) 83. References will appear in the text, abbreviated *NF*.

2 This notion is discussed in her book of the same name, *The Resisting Reader: A Feminist Approach to American Fiction* (Bloomington: Indiana University Press, 1978).

the genre so ostentatiously highlights in its thematics. Rereading a predominantly male genre, then, means revealing and critiquing the texts' (male) biases, ideologies, and self-contradictions. In this approach, modern French feminist theory with its focus on *écriture féminine*, on female pleasure and the body provides a critical frame to explore naturalism's negative obsession with the female body as a locus of contagion, of either excessive (hysterical, nymphomaniac, and sado-masochistic) or repressed (frigid, hostile, and exploitative) sexuality.

Connected with this gender-critical perspective is a second project, namely, a study of the specific ruptures in naturalism's representation of sexuality as the genre crossed from the nineteenth into the twentieth century. Nineteenth-century European naturalism had established itself as a literature with the right to articulate the "truth" on sexuality; twentieth-century American and Canadian naturalism continued this tradition at a time that witnessed radical changes in sexual behaviour and norms. Naturalism's ideology and aesthetics were undoubtedly shaped by the historical changes that announced the advent of the twentieth century: the large-scale deployment of an urbanite consumer market (that appealed primarily to women and was accompanied by a new pleasure ideology), the arrival of the New Woman (who claimed her sexual and professional rights at the turn of the century), and the ensuing crisis of masculinity (with its defense of traditional forms of male sexuality and power). Thus, twentieth-century naturalism became a field in which these changes in sexual mores were not just translated into literary conventions, but were also debated and negotiated. In this process, naturalism's traditional character types and motifs were recontextualized in new forms and given new ideological twists, at the same time that the genre's boundaries also served as a frame to contain what may have been perceived as women's "excessive" rebellion and threatening demand for change.

With the cultural shift from the nineteenth to the twentieth century, a subtle shift occurred, for instance, in the representation of the prostitute, the "inevitable" female icon of nineteenth-century naturalism. The naturalist prototype for this figure is undoubtedly Zola's title character in *Nana* (1880), who represents the nineteenth-century commercialization of life by selling her sexualized body both as an actress and as a literal prostitute. With the increasing demand for new female sexual rights at the turn of the century, German and Canadian naturalist fiction frequently deconstructs the Nana-figure, drawing attention to its social construction and its misogynistic implications. Furthermore, in twentieth-century American naturalism the literal prostitute is increasingly replaced by the "imaginary prostitute," who makes her living by selling "not the reality of flesh, but its image," to use Angela Carter's polemical words.[3] In Zola's fiction, sex crosses class boundaries (men of all social classes have access to Nana's body), whereas the American treatment of sexuality in Theodore Dreiser's *Sister Carrie* (1900) and Edith Wharton's *The House of Mirth* (1905) place more emphasis on sexuality as a marker of social difference: bourgeois sexuality is much more refined and artistic than proletarian sex. At the same time, sexuality in twentieth-century naturalism is paradoxically also a field of ironic levelling, continually deflating D.H. Lawrence's romanticized version of sex as a quasi-religious force. As an object of abstract, distanced, and scopophilic desire rather than of actual sexual intercourse, the body of the high-class "imaginary" prostitute symbolizes an increasingly more sophisticated consumer economy that works not through suppression and crude exploitation but through pleasurable seduction.

Some of these cultural transitions in naturalism are already anticipated in Zola's middle and late fiction. The twentieth-century emphasis on the displacement of the sexual act into consumer desire is initiated by Zola's *Au Bonheur des Dames* (1883). The representation of the family, another naturalist topic and privileged locus for the inscription of sexuality and power in nineteenth-century French naturalism, undergoes a similar shift under the influence of psychoanalysis. Twentieth-century German, Canadian, and American naturalist fiction shifts its focus from the genetically determined to the Oedipal family, with the different family members enchained in laws of psychological determinism and circles of incestuous obsessions. Often the father figure appears to the rebelling daughter as a repulsive figure of tyrannical power while she is simultaneously chained to his seductive power: he often emerges as the ultimate fantasy love object in her life. If nineteenth-century naturalism is mainly interested in sexual reproduction as a site of a hereditary determination of the next generation, early twentieth-century naturalism focuses its attention on questions of contraception and abortion, the very questions that Zola had started to explore in his late work *Fécondité* (1899). Although the emphasis changes, the sexualization of power continues to be the privileged focus in American and Canadian naturalist fiction.

In order to explore the sexualization of power in twentieth-century naturalism, I have chosen to examine the fiction of two representative authors, Frederick Philip Grove (1879–1948) and Theodore Dreiser (1871–

---

3 Angela Carter, *The Sadeian Woman: An Exercise in Cultural History* (London: Virago, 1990) 67.

1945). This choice allows me to cover the first four decades of the twentieth century and three cultures – German, Canadian, and American. As an immigrant from Germany and as the son of a first-generation German immigrant, respectively, Grove and Dreiser not only shared a common cultural heritage but were canonized as America's and Canada's naturalist figureheads. At first rejected as a naturalist, Dreiser was soon embraced by his readers as America's Zola, especially after the publication of his bestselling novel *An American Tragedy* (1925) (which coincided with the publication of Grove's *Settlers of the Marsh* in Canada). In 1930, Vernon Louis Parrington labelled Dreiser the "Chief of American Naturalists"; in 1941, Oscar Cargill described Dreiser's work as "the very quintessence of Naturalism"; and in 1955, Robert Spiller had Dreiser's naturalism coincide with "America's second literary renaissance."[4] Since the 1970s, there have also been studies examining the extent to which Dreiser moves "beyond naturalism," emphasizing that Dreiser's writing is different from Zola's naturalism.[5] Such studies, although they have made significant contributions, frequently depart from a static notion of naturalism, one that simply equates naturalism with Zola's hereditary determinism. Reconceptualizing naturalism as a dynamic, continually changing genre, I propose a careful examination of the transformations naturalism has undergone in Dreiser's American and Grove's Canadian fiction.

In Part 1, I will examine the changes and ruptures in the genre's concern with sexuality and power. My argument on naturalism's sexualization of power takes as its starting point Michel Foucault's theory that in Western society, power and sexuality are deeply enmeshed with each other, condition and support each other. In *The History of Sexuality* (1976), the French historian has argued that sexuality – an historical construct – does not exist before, but is constructed in, culture. Although this point is opposed to naturalism's traditional vision of sexuality as an innate drive that precedes language and culture, it clearly intersects with naturalism's social determinism. Tracing the Western "history of sexuality," Foucault has raised the question why there is such an obsession

---

4 Vernon Louis Parrington, "1860–1920: The Beginnings of Critical Realism in America," *Main Currents in American Thought*, vol. 3 (New York: Harcourt, Brace, 1930) 354; Oscar Cargill, *Intellectual America: Ideas on the March* (New York: Macmillan, 1941), 107; Robert E. Spiller, *The Cycle of American Literature: An Essay in Historical Criticism* (1955; New York: Mentor with Macmillan, 1956), 162.

5 See, for example, Paul Orlov's "The Subversion of the Self: Anti-Naturalistic Crux in *An American Tragedy*," *Modern Fiction Studies* 23 (1977–78): 457–72. Also Miriam Gogol's forthcoming collection of essays is entitled *Theodore Dreiser: Beyond Naturalism* (New York: New York UP, 1995).

in Western societies to put sexuality into discourse in science and medicine, juridical and bureaucratic apparatuses. Foucault's answer is baffling in its simplicity and unconventionality: sexuality has become the "arm of power" through which controls are exerted over the individual and social body. Far from repressing sexuality, the social agencies of power make use of sexuality, by concerning themselves with the health and well-being of the individual and social body. No longer purely repressive, power seduces, co-opts, and requires its victim's complicity and assent.

From the vantage point of Foucault's "history of sexuality," naturalist fiction emerges as both a product of social assumptions about sexuality and a cultural agent that actively participates in the construction and perpetuation of dominant scientific models on sexuality. Foucault has identified the hereditary-degenerescence model as the dominant scientific theory in the nineteenth century, and it is this very model (best encapsulated in the social and moral decline of Émile Zola's Rougon-Macquart family) that became naturalism's dominant feature, shaping its fictional representation of sexuality in the nineteenth century. Furthermore, the rupture Foucault detects in the scientific shift from hereditary physiology to psychology at the turn of the century is, I will argue, reflected in naturalism's representation of sexuality from the turn of the century onward. Twentieth-century German, American and Canadian naturalist fiction increasingly highlights psychoanalytic determinants, thus reversing the earlier nineteenth-century Zolaesque displacement of psychology into physiology.

In my analysis of these shifts in naturalism's treatment of sexuality, I also propose to interweave Michel Foucault's theory with feminist theories. The relationship between contemporary feminists and the French discourse analyst is by no means unambiguous or without contradictions, but I contend that Foucault's theory intersects with naturalism and feminism at the following important points: the emphasis on the material body that is shaped in culture and history; the role of institutions as determining forces in the individual's life; and the role of sexuality as both a cultural construct and a determining force in human life. Although numerous critics have interpreted the naturalist emphasis on sexuality in terms of "liberation" and "frankness," a discourse that has been supported and encouraged by the authors themselves, Foucault and poststructuralist feminists (e.g., Chris Weedon and Kornelia Hauser) teach us that sexuality intersects with power and is thus far from constituting a "liberating" force.

This is not to dismiss the important work of earlier, pioneering theorists of American naturalism, including Donald Pizer, Eric Sundquist and, more recently, June Howard and Lee Mitchell, to name but a few. In contrast to these earlier writers, however, I will adopt a more specifically revisionary perspective that is prompted by a feminist, Foucauldian, and comparative approach. Exploring naturalism's intertextuality, its efforts at appropriating, recycling, and translating other genres and documentary texts, I will emphasize differences, multiplicity, and the subtle shifts that occurred from one time period to the next, from one culture to the next. Thus I will highlight some of the differences between Canadian and American naturalist forms.

Part 1 provides a theoretical frame by establishing a dialogue between naturalism, Foucault, and feminism; Part 2 applies this theory to Dreiser's early and middle fiction, to *Sister Carrie* (1900) and a representative sketch from *A Gallery of Women* (1929). Recently, Dreiser scholars have become very interested in Dreiser's treatment of desire (Walter Benn Michaels), consumer culture (Rachel Bowlby), and the creation of subjectivity through role playing (Philip Fisher).[6] These concerns intersect in interesting ways to crystallize new questions on the techniques of modern power in the twentieth-century social network, questions that I propose to explore in Part 2. Other Dreiser scholars interpret desire as the protagonists' ultimate quest for a "higher," spiritual ideal (Larry Hussman; Arun Mukherjee), or distinguish between real and enacted desires (Ellen Moers). New historicist Walter Michaels has given Dreiser scholarship new impetus by discussing desire as a force that does not work against but for capitalism and consumerism (see also June Howard and Rachel Bowlby). Although much of my argument is stimulated by this second line of thought, it will be my task to explore the more specific question of how much the creation of a desirable subjectivity implies an apparently paradoxical "voluntary subjection" to the norms and power networks of society. How is sexuality put to work in the social machinery of power?

In *Sister Carrie*, Dreiser's focus is on a radical deployment of sexuality, a sexuality that is detached from any family alliance and widely dispersed outside the boundaries of family and marriage. Deeply sexualized as a living icon of her consumer culture, Carrie Meeber's docile body rises to the top of her social order, so that her sexualized body becomes an oxymoronic icon of female empowerment and simultaneous subjection. Conversely, the disintegrating male body (encapsulated in George Hurstwood's social decline and suicide) represents the threat to a male

---

6 For titles and full citations of the critics mentioned in this paragraph, see "Select Bibliography on Theodore Dreiser" and "Select Bibliography on Naturalism."

order that is culturally challenged by women's growing demands for new economic and social rights. Whereas in nineteenth-century naturalism the diseased, disintegrating male body symbolized a proletarianized working class, in American twentieth-century naturalism it represents the more general "crisis of masculinity" prompted by the spectre of the *fin-de-siècle* new woman. Moreover, the new woman confronts the male naturalist narrator with his own crisis (of authority and masculinity). Trying to define female sexuality in masculine terms in his sketch on "Emanuela," the narrator is confronted with the very contradictions that we find at the heart of naturalism. The male narrative voice of authority simultaneously assumes the role of "liberating" the new woman's sexuality and frames and contains her sexuality in new (pre)conceptions of female sexual "normality."

Part 3 turns to F. P. Grove's German and Canadian version of naturalism, which I will discuss as a poetics of (parodic) difference, hoping to avoid any easy conflations between the two authors. A detailed comparison on the intertextual relationship between Dreiser and Grove is needed because it has become a critical commonplace to juxtapose Grove's name with Dreiser's, especially in short introductions and afterwords in Grove's reprinted works.[7] Establishing himself as a Canadian writer of prairie fiction, Grove was quickly embraced by his readers as the "Canadian Dreiser." It was Robert Ayre who introduced this epithet in 1932, and Northrop Frye repeated it in the obituary for Grove in 1948.[8] No doubt, the critics have sought to place Grove within a "recognized tradition" in order to assist his canonization as a Canadian author, an author who during his life time had always bemoaned what he perceived as the lack of an appreciative readership. But just as Grove rejected the label of naturalism for his writing, so he rejected any association with Dreiser. Indeed, he claimed emphatically in a letter to Carleton Stanley: "I am glad you defend me against Dreiser. I can't stand the man. Nor Sinclair Lewis. The more I dislike them, the less I say about them."[9]

---

7   See Kristjana Gunnars, "Afterword," *Settlers of the Marsh* by Frederick Philip Grove , New Canadian Library (Toronto: McClelland & Stewart, 1989) 267–75; and R. E. Watters, "Introduction," *The Master of the Mill*, by Frederick Philip Grove, New Canadian Library (Toronto: McClelland & Stewart, 1961) vii–xiii.

8   Robert Ayre, "A Solitary Giant," *Canadian Forum* 12 (1932), 255-57, rpt. in *Frederick Philip Grove: Critical Views of Canadian Writers*, ed. Desmond Pacey (Toronto: Ryerson, 1970) 17; Northrop Frye, "Canadian Dreiser," rpt. in Pacey, 186.

9   Frederick Philip Grove, *The Letters of Frederick Philip Grove*, ed. Desmond Pacey (Toronto & Buffalo: U of Toronto P, 1976) 504.

Grove's emphatic tone reveals more of his own "anxiety of influence" than of his actual knowledge or ignorance of Dreiser's works. And since Grove has taken so much pleasure in deceiving his Canadian readership about his real identity as the German writer Felix Paul Greve, we are bound to be all the more suspicious of such vehement protestations.

Grove's biographical story of transculturation is a fascinating one of faked and fictionalized identities. In 1909, Grove fabricated his suicide in Germany to escape huge debt payments and to start a new life in Canada, an adventurous personal history that has been meticulously pieced together by Douglas Spettigue in *FPG: The European Years* (1973).[10] After Grove (FPG) left Germany, his two early novels – *Fanny Eßler* (1905) and *Maurermeister Ihles Haus* (1906), both published under the name Felix Paul Greve – were forgotten in Germany until Spettigue rediscovered them in the course of his search for the "real" FPG and had them translated into English. But the works have remained somewhat marginalized in scholarship on Grove's writing: "Strictly as a novel this book should have remained unknown in Canada as it had been forgotten in Germany," writes K. P. Stich in a condemning review of the translated *Master Mason's House*.[11]

It cannot be coincidence that Grove has become canonized as the creator of tragic prairie patriarchs (Desmond Pacey) and as a literary con-man (Douglas Spettigue) and that the only two novels of Grove's that present female protagonists should be dismissed so easily.[12] With my emphasis on relationships of power, it is precisely these two novels that will provide a rich textual resource for an analysis of gender relations of power and for an exploration of women's strategies of resistance. It is my intention to shift the critical focus in Grove scholarship from the patriarchal prairie pioneers, or the "tragic failure" of the producer artist, or the artist as "con-man," to the techniques Grove develops to deal with more marginalized issues and characters: women, the immigrant arriving in Canada, the social outsider.

Grove was a translator before turning to fiction; Part 3 illustrates that much of his fiction is indeed an effort at appropriating and "translat-

---

10 Douglas Spettigue, *FPG: The European Years* (Ottawa: Oberon, 1973)

11 K. P. Stich, "F.P.G.: Over German Trails," rev. of *The Master Mason's House*, by Frederick Philip Grove, *Essays on Canadian Writing* 6 (1977), 149.

12 See Robin Mathews's criticism of the critics' negative evaluation of Grove's fiction in "F. P. Grove: An Important Version of *The Master of the Mill* Discovered," *Studies in Canadian Literature* 7 (1982): 241.

ing" literary and documentary texts and at recontextualizing his German fiction in the new Canadian literary tradition. I will discuss these "translations" as a typical feature of his naturalism. As Grove based his early fiction on the life story of his German lover (now better known as Elsa von Freytag-Loringhoven), his fiction sheds light on the appropriation of the female voice into male naturalist fiction. Furthermore, his first protagonist, Fanny Essler, emerges as a fictional figure in his Canadian writing, whereby her sexual picaresque is recycled, "translated" and recontextualized in a new culture and in radically different settings. Grove's version of naturalism thus has to be seen as a creative and parodic spiral, where one text gives birth to the next, highlighting the deep intertextual potential of the naturalist genre.

Thus Grove's fiction also echoes Baguley's point about naturalism's multigeneric quality, which both feeds on and degrades other generic forms, particularly the expressions of "high" art forms such as myth and tragedy. Grove's early and Dreiser's middle works of fiction not only make use of this parodic vision but, more importantly, their twentieth-century naturalism frequently turns into self-parody. Nineteenth-century French naturalism is deeply ironic, satiric, and parodic; twentieth-century German, Canadian, and American naturalist fiction appears more overtly self-deconstructive, whereby naturalism's parodic vision frequently comes full circle, turning upon and feeding on its own genre. The male narrative voice of authority continues to insist on the truth value of its analysis, but is often baffled by the feminist voices erupting in the text and contradicting the dominating male (narrative) ideology, thus critiquing the genre from within.

Parts 2 and 3 examine naturalism's self-deconstructive potential; Parts 4 and 5 focus more strongly on the transformative limits of the naturalist genre. Interweaving male power with male versions of sexuality, the second half of this study highlights naturalism's ideological boundaries and its complicity with dominant power principles. Again, this emphasis on male sexualized power has to be seen as a recontextualization of the conventions of nineteenth-century European naturalism, as David Baguley has described them. Baguley has countered the tendency of critics "to interpret naturalist literature as a *passive* depiction of reality" (*NF* 7), arguing that although naturalism draws its readers into a "readable" text, it never lulls them into easy mimetic complacency. Rather, the naturalistic text is a snare that takes on its own generic-ness, undermining the realist "contract" with the reader's expectations and instigating a new (dis)order. The naturalist text tends to confront the reader with scandal, excess, or frustrating endings that have the effect of shocking the complacent bourgeois consumers of books out of their secure expectations. At the heart of naturalism, then, Baguley recognizes the genre's deeply entropic vision: "Heredity, illness, obsession, sexuality, are disruptive factors which break up the fragile balance of differences, of structures, of codes. The characteristic movement of the naturalist novel is in the direction of disintegration and confusion" (*NF* 208).

It is this very entropic vision at the heart of naturalism that twentieth-century naturalist fiction increasingly renders problematic, as Parts 4 and 5 will illustrate. Despite its continual rupture of secure expectations, Dreiser and Grove's naturalism often inscribes new normative constraints, by justifying male sexual prerogatives with biological laws of nature or with psychological concepts of "normality." Naturalist fiction often disrupts conventional assumptions about sexuality, but it also participates in the cultural creation of new norms. Indeed, one might argue that twentieth-century American and Canadian naturalism self-consciously highlights what is present as an undercurrent of nineteenth-century naturalism, showing how easily naturalism can be put in the service of a conventional social order. In the course of history, naturalists have proliferated particular models on sexuality, classifying between normal and abnormal, healthy and unhealthy sexual practices. In their repeated association of prostitution with disease, of sexual excess with punishment, of normal sexuality with heterosexuality, their literature has not always had the effect of disrupting middle-class norms, but has often had a "normalizing" function.

Part 4 illustrates this point by examining Dreiser's exploration of the eroticization of bourgeois power in the Cowperwood trilogy. Dreiser presents the American robber baron F. A. Cowperwood as an eroticized icon of power, who displaces his power in other (female and artistic) "bodies." Establishing a metaphorical analogy between the capitalist speculator and the naturalist artist, Dreiser exposes the potential complicity of his fiction with the capitalist power principle. If anything, Dreiser highlights that naturalist fiction does not automatically have a "resisting" function, but can very easily become a tool of the dominant power principle (whether it be patriarchal or capitalist). Just as Foucault emphasizes that any resisting discourse can easily be co-opted to serve the power it opposes, so Dreiser's twentieth-century naturalism shows an ironic self-awareness of the genre's occasional complicity with dominant structures of power.

Continuing Dreiser's exploration of bourgeois power, Part 5 highlights that Canadian naturalism is far from simply imitating American conventions. In contrast to Dreiser, whose characters are generally involved in a wild spiral of promiscuity, Grove's Canadian fiction situates sexuality back into the patriarchal family institution. Thus Grove's sexualization of power is located into the private Canadian prairie farm, recontextualized to reflect the Canadian agricultural tradition. Even Grove's Canadian business novel, *The Master of the Mill* (1944), foregrounds the sexual dynamics within a single family, which goes hand in hand with the "incestuous" holding on to power, as the son inherits the father's strategies of power and his economic control over the family business. If the sons affirm the secure (male) boundaries of the naturalist genre, the women, and especially the daughter figures in Grove's German and Canadian fiction, rebel against naturalism's generic boundaries for women, just as they rebel against the confinement imposed on them in the patriarchal family. Even as they challenge the father's law they are, however, continually in danger of being seduced into submission by the father's institutionalized power. Although an increasingly strong figure, the Grovian daughter figure generally remains caught in naturalism's gender boundaries, unable to effect any real change in her father's house.

In naturalist fiction, it is the principle of power itself that is sexualized, which accounts for naturalism's emphasis on sado-masochistic scenes in the nineteenth century and its emphasis on rape and rapist sexualities in the twentieth century. The nineteenth-century prostitute is tied into sado-masochistic relations of power; the twentieth-century hetaira-actress titillates and tortures the male consumer with imaginary pleasures that he cannot afford. Nineteenth-century naturalism is concerned with adultery and sexual contagion; Dreiser's attention turns to premarital sex and its dangers while Grove explores the problem of rape in marriage. Thus, the sexualized prototypes of European naturalism do not simply disappear, but undergo changes in representation and ideological content. The naturalism that emerges in the twentieth century is dynamic, changing, and increasingly self-deconstructive. And yet it is also a narrative form in which male forms of power continue to dominate. Although the female characters are strong forces of rebellion and enjoy increased social, economic, and legal powers, their oppositional élan is often recontained within naturalism's secure boundaries. Thus, in Dreiser and Grove's American and Canadian naturalism, sexuality continues to constitute the privileged field of (female) subjection and docility, with naturalist structures and conventions continuing to frame and control female (sexual) rebellion.

I. Naturalism and Foucault

1

Naturalism's History of Sexuality

Drawing on Foucault's *History of Sexuality*, this chapter traces the roots of naturalist conceptions of sexuality and power to the eighteenth century, to pre-Revolutionary French literature, philosophy, and science. While the birth of naturalism is most commonly associated with the nineteenth century, Foucault's version of the Western "history of sexuality" identifies the eighteenth century as a birthplace of modern conceptions of sexuality: "There was a steady proliferation of discourses concerned with sex – specific discourses, different from one another both by their form and by their object: a discursive ferment that gathered momentum from the eighteenth century onward."[1] Indeed, the examples of Marquis de Sade, Restif de la Bretonne, and Jean-Jacques Rousseau show that modern naturalism finds its roots in the very discursive ferment Foucault describes. Writing in a transitional period, the three authors

---

[1] Michel Foucault, *The History of Sexuality, Vol. 1: An Introduction*, trans. Robert Hurley (New York: Vintage, 1980), 18. Further references to this work will be abbreviated *HS* and will appear in the text.

interweave sexuality with conceptions of power that set the stage for the sexualization of power that is to become a characteristic feature of French naturalist fiction one century later.

According to Foucault, Marquis de Sade's eighteenth-century fiction of libertinage presents an extreme example of a sexualization of power in literature: "In Sade, sex is without any norm or intrinsic rule that might be formulated from its own nature; but it is subject to the unrestricted law of a power which itself knows no other law but its own" (*HS* 149). In the eighteenth century, however, Sade's role was a transitional one: Sade associated sexuality with the blood of the nobility, but sex was in the process of becoming the preoccupation of the newly emerging bourgeoisie, which saw sexuality as a field of pleasure that had to be regulated and kept healthy. Naturalism's predilection for excess, for associating sexuality with pain and death, then, can be said to have its roots in this Sadeian tradition, while naturalism's ideological concern with sexuality has developed in opposition to Sade. Naturalist fiction, I will argue, rejected Sade's anarchic vision of sexuality and power by inscribing normative standards in its conventions, regularly "punishing" and ritually exorcizing the sexual transgressors. Since naturalist fiction is committed to a "regulation" of sexuality, it finds its ideological roots and generic conventions less in Sade's sexual excesses than in the fictional and philosophical writings of his contemporaries, who were intent on classifying, regulating, and "normalizing" sexuality in socially responsible forms: in the sexual pedagogy of Rousseau, in the scientific approach to sexuality of the *encyclopédistes*, and in Restif de La Bretonne's focus on the life of French prostitutes.

Jean-Jacques Rousseau's *Émile, ou de l'éducation* (1762) introduces an orthopedics of sexuality (that exerted a deep influence on F. P. Grove).[2] Indeed, Rousseau's pedagogical theory anticipates the rules and laws of literary determinism: he puts his fictional character Émile through an experiment – the very method that Zola used a century later. Moreover, Rousseau's pedagogical discourse emphasizes the relationship of "forces" that determine the young pupil Émile's health and well-being at each stage of his life. Rousseau cuts the child's evolution into segments, classifying each stage as needing a particular set of pedagogical directives to protect him both from "the dangers without" (the corrupted social institutions) and from "the dangers within" (the awakening sexual

---

2 See Margaret Stobie, *Frederick Philip Grove* (New York: Twayne, 1973), especially the chapter "Rousseau as Educator," 36–41.

passions that upset the pupil's equilibrium and make him "weak"). (These principles can be seen as direct forerunners of Zola's external and internal determinism.) At each stage, Rousseau's pedagogy suggests techniques of counteracting these dangers by advocating a technology of self that involves the pupil's internalization of the pedagogue's authority.

Often called "le Rousseau du ruisseau," Restif de la Bretonne (1734–1806) translated many of Rousseau's insights on the corruptive influence of the city into social realism, and thus became a clear forerunner of nineteenth- and twentieth-century naturalism, shaping its conventions, themes, settings, and rhetorical devices in his mostly autobiographical fiction. Not only is the sheer volume of Restif's manuscripts (one is over two thousand pages long) indicative of the often-cited naturalistic emphasis on descriptive detail, but his fictional projects also have a characteristically naturalistic agenda, as the following title of his most famous work suggests: *Le Paysan perverti, ou les dangers de la ville, histoire récente, mise au jour d'après les véritables lettres des personnages* (1776).

Several typically naturalistic features can be identified in this novel. First, Restif's emphasis is on documentary, realistic authenticity, and readers from Rousseau to Friedrich Schiller have credited Restif with his invaluable documentary representation of the social reality on the eve of the French Revolution. Also, Restif's treatment of sexuality reflects the naturalistic predilection for male fetishism and the "galleries" of sexualized women that populate nineteenth- and twentieth-century naturalist fiction. Moreover, Restif presents the city as a seductive force that shapes (and corrupts) the youth arriving from the country, the favourite motif of social realism in Balzac, Flaubert, Zola, and Dreiser; but above all, the city allows Restif to introduce a broad range of characters, including the typically naturalistic marginal figures, such as prostitutes and servants. Restif's treatment of sexuality and desire shows some striking parallels with Dreiser's: like Dreiser, Restif not only demands the right to a realistic portrayal of sexual behaviour that is freed from the shackles of moral codes, but is also interested in maximizing desire, in multiplying moments of sexual titillation by inscribing desire and sexuality in a pornographic epistemology, in a utopian project that regulates and normalizes what many contemporaries rejected as a devious sexuality.

Thus Restif does more than just fictionalize the prostitute in a realistic context: he proposes a project of regulating prostitution as a social institution. In a work entitled "Le Pornographe ou idées d'un honnête homme sur un project de règlement pour les prostituées" (1769), the primary focus is not on graphic pornographic descriptions; on the contrary, Restif literally focuses on "règlement," discussing in a detached, matter of fact – bourgeois – tone the institutionalization, policing, and "normalization" of female prostitution. Restif's theoretical project details plans on how to administrate a state-run brothel, an institution not much different in organization from a nineteenth-century factory. Restif's *projet de règlement* for prostitutes is characterized by the highest degree of order, and includes the spatial and remunerative classification of women according to age and beauty; a timetabling of their "work," meals, and "toilette"; and an apparatus of practical rules detailing the daily management of this institution. The reason behind Restif's pornographic utopia is to reduce "les inconvénients de la prostitution," above all, venereal disease: "On aura la plus grande attention à préserver les filles de l'horrible maladie qui rend cet établissement si désirable."[3] The prostitute becomes the object of the medical gaze (very much like her male customer, who is also subjected to medical examinations and a payment of a fine when found infected), but is simultaneously kept invisible in society, no longer walking the streets but sequestered within the walls of an officially sanctioned and medically controlled municipal institution.[4]

Restif's pornographic utopia is not a freak fantasy, but is the logical extension of a larger discursive phenomenon that Foucault describes as follows: "Toward the beginning of the eighteenth century, there emerged a political, economic, and technical incitement to talk about sex." In fact, sex was taken charge of "in the form of analysis, stocktaking, classification, and specification," so that sexuality was not simply repressed or condemned by the emerging bourgeoisie, it was "inserted into systems of utility, regulated for the greater good of all, made to function according to an optimum" (*HS* 23–24). The modern "policing" of sex takes a particular form, namely: "not the rigor of a taboo, but the necessity of regulating sex through useful and public discourses" (*HS* 25). The desire for such a "policing" of sexuality is, I argue, the "other" side of a naturalism that focuses on sexual crises, excess, disease, and the breaking of boundaries. Sexuality in naturalism is shown to erupt in the social network as a destabilizing force, but it is as often contained in social institutions, such as the family, the department store in *Au Bonheur des*

---

3   "Le Pornographe," *Oeuvres*, vol. 3 (Genève: Slatkine Reprints, 1978) 27.

4   For a discussion of prostitution in Restif de la Bretonne, see also Charles Bernheimer, *Figures of Ill Repute: Representing Prostitution in Nineteenth-Century France* (Cambridge, MA: Harvard UP, 1989) 17–22.

Dames, or the theatre in *Sister Carrie*. Sexual excess is controlled through bodily punishment, whereby the Sadean pains are appropriated as a technique of containment: Restif's *paysan perverti* not only loses his arm but also one eye in the course of his sexual misadventures, very much like the sexually notorious Mme de Merteuil in Laclos' *Les Liaisons dangereuses* (1782), who, "affreusement défigurée," is left with only one eye as a result of her syphilitic pox. These endings anticipate the demise of Zola's Nana, who is first disfigured and then ritually destroyed, so that the texts exorcise the threat of sexual and venereal contagion that these sexualized figures carry with them. However precarious, (male) order is re-established through such textual acts of symbolic retribution.

According to Foucault's account of the Western history of sexuality, the transition from the eighteenth to the nineteenth century brought with it a significant rupture. The concept of "sexual instinct" made its appearance in nineteenth-century medical discourse, along with a "medico-psychological" interest in perversions (*HS* 118). With the isolation of the "sexual drive," sexuality assumed its place in the domain of biology and medicine. What the Middle Ages considered to be religious "sins of the flesh" now became medical problems to be located deep down in the anatomy of the physical body. From the domain of a spiritual morality, devious sexuality shifted to the realm of scientific perversions, a shift that is reflected, for example, in Heinrich Kaan's *Psychopathia Sexualis* (1846). Even more important for a study of naturalism, however, is the nineteenth-century emergence of heredity as a privileged object of knowledge (particularly in the study of sexual relationships and matrimonial alliances). "The medicine of perversions and the programs of eugenics were the two great innovations in the technology of sex of the second half of the nineteenth century," writes Foucault (*HS* 118), arguing that this emphasis on perversion, heredity, and degenerescence influenced the social practices and led to a "coherent form of a state-directed racism" (*HS* 119).

Émile Zola's fiction is deeply steeped in the nineteenth-century history of sexuality, as he appropriated and further disseminated in his best-selling naturalist fiction what Foucault calls the "heredity-degenerescence" theory of the contemporary social, medical, and biological sciences. Creating "l'histoire naturelle et sociale d'une famille sous le Second Empire," Zola chose to show the workings of heredity in a line of degeneration, exposing the "fatality" of sexual (and generational) reproduction: the Rougon family (respectable middle class) is joined with the Macquart (lower class), the latter endowed with negative genetic material (Macquart is an alcoholic). These negative genetic traces resurface according to the logic of deterministic laws in later generations, whenever a character finds him- or herself in a negative environment that triggers the emergence of a genetic "weakness" and thus provokes his or her fall.

This dominant degenerescence model also explains the strong sense of (negative) teleology in Zola's writing: "J'ai un but auquel je vais," he writes in the preface to *L'Assommoir*. "J'ai voulu peindre la déchéance fatale d'une famille ouvrière, dans le milieu empesté de nos faubourgs."[5] The author's note of social criticism with its implicit demand for social change is thus in uneasy contradiction with his genetic determinism and the eugenic implications of the heredity-degenerescence theory. Indeed, the social criticism is somewhat undermined in the novel by the fact that Gervaise Macquart and her husband Coupeau have a genetic disposition to sensual weakness and alcoholism respectively, and these inevitably cause their downfall as soon as their good fortune leaves them. In the Rougon-Macquart cycle, the original "contamination" is sexually transmitted from generation to generation through the blood line. As a result, the sexual act is a site of danger that conjures up fears and the need for control and effective policing, generally represented in Zola's fiction in its "exorcising" of the lower-class brute (and best encapsulated in Coupeau's *delirium tremens* and subsequent death). Despite Zola's vehement social engagement and his spectacular anti-racist "J'accuse" in the Dreyfus affair, Foucault's point on the racist implications of the degenerescence theory applies to Zola's writing: it exudes a paranoia of proletarianization and sexual contagion, conjured up in powerful images of a diseased social body.

Dissociating his naturalism from the religious and moralistic notions of sexuality and anchoring his characterization firmly in a genetically predetermined body, Zola deliberately renounced his characters' "libre arbitre." In the preface to *Thérèse Raquin* (1867), he describes his protagonists as "[des personnages] dépourvus de libre arbitre, entraînés à chaque acte de leur vie par les fatalités de leur chair."[6] This theory, however, creates an unresolved contradiction: there is a tension in Zola's writing between a genetic determinism (with its eugenic implications) and his social determinism (with its implicit demand for social change). While Zola's theory glosses over this contradiction by categorically privileging a physiological-biological determinism, this antinomy developed into a crisis point in twentieth-century American naturalism.

---

5   Émile Zola, préface, *L'Assommoir*, Livre de Poche 97 (Paris: Fasquelle, 1983) 7.

6   "Préface de la deuxième édition," *Thérèse Raquin*, Livre de Poche 34 (Paris: Fasquelle, n.d.) 8.

American naturalism defies Zola's renunciation of "libre arbitre," reinscribing moments of choice and acts of free will within its textual conventions. In fact, many North American critics have complained of modern naturalism's "inconsistency," its oscillation between determinism and free will, without ever privileging one or the other. More recently, however, June Howard has theorized this inconsistency as the typical American version of naturalism, arguing that the antinomies between determinism and free will, between beast and human, are its constitutive element. Similarly, John Conder has discovered an oxymoron – a "free will determinism" – at the heart of American naturalism.[7]

Apart from the cultural differences, this growing emphasis on "free will" in twentieth-century American naturalism was prompted by another rupture in the historical deployment of sexuality: the advent of psychoanalysis. According to Foucault, psychoanalysis displaced the biological degenerescence theory as the dominant discourse at the turn of the century:

> And the strange position of psychiatry at the end of the nineteenth century would be hard to comprehend if one did not see the rupture it brought about in the great system of degenerescence: it resumed the project of a medical technology appropriate for dealing with the sexual instinct; but it sought to free it from its ties with heredity, and hence from eugenics and the various racisms. (*HS* 119)

Sigmund Freud's emphasis on sexuality lent itself to an appropriation by naturalists, since Freud himself had appropriated the term determinism in his "Three Essays on Sexuality" (1905) for his explication of psychical processes. In fact, he warned his readers not to "ignore the realms of determinism in our mental life. Here, as in still other spheres, determinism reaches farther than we suppose."[8] This emphasis on determinism and logical causality in psychical reactions created a new anchorage point for naturalism and prompted its significant shift from hereditary to psychological causality, with the determining forces shifting from the genetic realm to the unconscious. Despite his strong critique of Freudian psycho-analysis, Foucault gives Sigmund Freud credit for opposing

---

7 For a detailed discussion of this issue, see June Howard's chapter "The Antinomies in American Naturalism," in her *Form and History in American Naturalism* (Chapel Hill & London: U of Carolina P, 1985); and John Conder, *Naturalism in American Fiction* (Lexington: UP of Kentucky, 1984).

8 Sigmund Freud, "Determinism – Chance – And Superstitious Beliefs," *The Basic Writings of Sigmund Freud*, trans. and ed. A. A. Brill (New York: Modern Library, 1938) 150.

the political and institutional effects of the perversion-heredity-degenerescence system and making it somewhat obsolete in the twentieth century.

Thus the rupture from Zola's naturalism to Dreiser and Grove's social realism is marked not only by a cultural shift from French to American or from German to Canadian naturalism, but also corresponds to the rupture in the scientific formations by the end of the nineteenth century. With the exception of Frank Norris, the major North American naturalists – and particularly Dreiser and Grove – did not see themselves as following Zola's tradition. When Grove turned his creative attention to prose fiction between 1903 and 1904, naturalism *à la* Zola was firmly established and institutionalized in the European literary tradition, presenting a challenge for a new generation of social realists to move beyond; and it was above all Zola's scientific emphasis on the degenerescence theory that was increasingly rejected.

These ideological changes were reflected and debated, for example, in the widely publicized "Naturalismusdebatte" during the convention of the Social Democratic Party in Siebleben, Germany, in October 1896 (an event that was bound to influence Grove's social realism barely ten years later). Here, the majority of the social democratic delegates openly protested against the tendency in naturalism to emphasize the biological, instinctive, and pathological as their version of a truthful representation of human nature.[9] As a result of such widely publicized debates, traditional German naturalism that had followed the degenerescence model in the 1880s was to be replaced by the psychological novel at the turn of the century. Indeed, those who equated naturalism exclusively with Zola's biological determinism marked the nineties as the death of German naturalism, as Hermann Bahr did with the telling title *Die Überwindung des Naturalismus* (1891).[10] When in 1929 the Canadian Grove polemically disqualified Zola's naturalistic theories as "pseudo-science" based on the "current aberrations of the day," he articulated this rupture by situating himself in a tradition with Flaubert's social realism. Indeed, as a translator of Flaubert's letters, Grove appropriated in his theory Flaubert's earlier ideological opposition to Zola.[11]

---

9 See Ursula Münchow, *Deutscher Naturalismus* (Berlin: Akademie Verlag, 1968) 159.

10 Rpt. in Hermann Bahr, *Zur Überwindung des Naturalismus, Theoretische Schriften 1887–1904*, ed. Gotthart Wunberg (Stuttgart: W. Kohlhammer Verlag, 1968) 33–102.

11 Frederick Philip Grove, *It Needs to Be Said ...* (Toronto: Macmillan, 1929), 58, 64. For a discussion of Flaubert's opposition to Zola, see Baguley, *NF* 22. Although Flaubert was a "figure tutélaire" for Zola and the contemporary French naturalist circle, he did not hide his disdain for Zola's scientific emphasis.

Thus naturalism was not "dead" at the turn of the century, but rather assumed a new shape within the scientific deployment of sexuality. The rupture, then, from the nineteenth-century Zolaesque naturalism to the twentieth-century expression of naturalism shifted radically from an interest in heredity and degenerescence to psychology; from physical (animal) need to (human) desire; from genetic bloodlines to parental authority; from venereal diseases to psychological problems; from a genetic body to a psychologized body; from an instinctive body to a body constructed through clothing and social practices. As a result, the boundaries between naturalism, the psychological novel, and decadent writing became rather fluid, especially in their presentation of characters: "Determiniert und präformiert, zerrissen und oft leidenschaftlich egoistisch bildet [der naturalistische Charakter] die Vorstufe zum Nervenmenschen der décadence, zum Hypersensiblen des fin de siècle."[12] Determinism continued to be a characteristic element of twentieth-century naturalistic discourse, as Lee Clark Mitchell has pointed out in her study on American naturalism,[13] but the determining factors have clearly shifted to psychological influences and social practices (what Hippolyte Taine had introduced as "le milieu").

In his discussion of the new psychoanalysis at the *fin-de-siècle*, Peter Heller has argued that Sigmund Freud, Wilhelm Fliess, and Otto Weininger opened up a new inner domain "as symbolic territory for the enactment of social themes of domination/subjection," translating power relations between men and women into a psychical *Innenwelt*.[14] External – social – relationships of power were interiorized, relegated to a microscopic, personal psychical structure, just as in the nineteenth century they had been relegated into individualized genetic structures. What is more, with its spectacular claim of a fundamental bisexuality, psychoanalysis revived the gender issue of "incubus-succubus" in new terms: "the quarrel is about who is to be on top, that is, (in the parlance of a pervasive myth equating active superiority with the male, passive inferiority with the female), who is to be the man, who the woman."[15]

---

12 Günther Mahal, *Naturalismus* (München: Wilhelm Fink Verlag, 1975) 93. "Determined and pre-formed, ripped-apart and often passionately egotistical, [the naturalistic character] is the forerunner of the decadent neurotic and the hypersensitive character of the *fin de siècle*" (my translation).

13 *Determined Fictions: American Literary Naturalism* (New York: Columbia UP, 1989).

14 Peter Heller, "A Quarrel Over Bisexuality," *The Turn of the Century: German Literature and Art, 1890–1915*, ed. Gerald Chapple and Hans Schulte (Bonn: Bouvier Verlag, 1981) 111.

15 Heller 98.

Thus psychoanalysis formulated the question of engendered power in new terms, by raising the question of who would play the role of "man" or "woman," and it is in these terms that it re-enters twentieth-century naturalistic fiction.

At the same time, however, it also has to be remembered that these naturalist changes from physiological-biological to psychological determinism did not occur in a sudden shift, but as a gradual movement with significant overlappings. Thus Dreiser's and Grove's twentieth-century naturalism has more in common with Flaubert's emphasis on desire in *Madame Bovary* (1857) than with Zola's genetic determinism in *L'Assommoir*; more with Zola's exploration of consumer pleasures in *Au Bonheur des Dames* than with his emphasis on fundamental "needs" in *Germinal* (1885). Conversely, Zola, Guy de Maupassant, and others have to be credited with anticipating in French naturalist fiction many of the psychological findings of Freud: their novels provide significant examples of the psychiatrization of perversions, reflected especially in their predilection for fetishism, "which, from at least as early as 1877, served as the guiding thread for analyzing all the other deviations."[16] Examples of psychologized perversions abound in nineteenth-century naturalism, ranging from the female kleptomaniac in Zola's *Au Bonheur des Dames*, through the female fetishistic obsession with sentimental keepsakes in Maupassant's *Une Vie* (1883), to scopophilia and sado-masochism in *Nana*. Also, the figure of the *femme fatale*, so typical of *fin-de-siècle* literature, is anticipated by nineteenth-century naturalistic characters, most notably by Zola's Nana. Zola clearly displaces the psychological onto the physiological, but the reverse transition is not difficult to make, as the psychological interest in Zola's *Thérèse Raquin* and *La Bête humaine* (1890) suggests.

The transition from physiology to psychology in French fiction is probably best illustrated by Huysmans's *A Rebours* (1884), and in Germany by Thomas Mann's first novel *Buddenbrooks: Verfall einer Familie* (1900). With its radical challenge of the heredity-degenerescence theory within *fin-de-siècle* naturalism, this novel occupies a pivotal position in the development of European naturalism, and strongly influenced F. P. Greve. Although Mann labelled his novel "für Deutschland der vielleicht erste

---

16 Foucault, *HS* 154. For a detailed discussion of fetishism in nineteenth-century French realism, see Emily Apter's *Feminizing the Fetish: Psychoanalysis and Narrative Obsession in Turn-of-the-Century France* (Ithaca: Cornell UP, 1991).

und einzige naturalistische Roman,"[17] critics have been reluctant to follow the author's categorization because the novel differs radically from the nineteenth-century naturalist tradition. "While an implicit belief in heredity forms the backbone of *Buddenbrooks*," as Lilian Furst has observed,[18] the novel's juxtaposition of hereditary degenerescence with the "emergence of artistic sensibility" thoroughly subverts the very notion of hereditary degeneration that usually involves the sinking of humanity to the level of brutish existence. Tracing the Buddenbrooks family through three generations, Mann's novel is characterized by Zola's structural teleology towards generational disintegration. The family, however, is doomed because of the features that elevate them above the common middle class: the hypersensibilities and hypochondria of the young family members are connected with their penchant for art. Endowed with superior sensitivities, they cannot survive in the real world. The novel's emphasis on the Buddenbrooks' physical diseases – Tony's stomach troubles, Thomas' bad teeth, Hanno's death by typhus – are bodily symptoms of, and symbols for, the characters' deeper mental and emotional states that are out of sync with the demands of a competitive world. While the money-grabbing bourgeois world establishes itself in a robust body, the "spiritual aristocracy" in *Buddenbrooks* is doomed to die.

Exploring the nature of naturalism in an essay of the same name, David Baguley has pointed out that nineteenth-century European naturalism is characterized by two different kinds of plots: the Goncourtian type with its tragic fall inspired by biological fate, and the Flaubertian type with its "plots of resignation that take the character steadily nowhere."[19] Twentieth-century naturalism clearly tends towards the second, Flaubertian type, one that reveals constant disillusionment and the insufficiency of life itself. Thus, despite the growing rejection of the heredity-degenerescence model in the twentieth century, the plot of decline remains prominent in twentieth-century social realism. The reason for this may be found in the turn-of-the-century philosophical emergence and popularity of Friedrich Nietzsche, whose philosophy deeply

---

17 "Perhaps Germany's first and only naturalist novel" (my translation). Thomas Mann, *Betrachtungen eines Unpolitischen, Gesammelte Werke in Einzelbänden* (Frankfurt: Fischer, 1983) 88.

18 Lilian R. Furst, "Thomas Mann's *Buddenbrooks*: 'The First and Only Naturalist Novel in Germany,'" *Naturalism in the European Novel: New Critical Perspectives*, ed. Brian Nelson (New York & Oxford: Berg Publishers, 1992) 232.

19 Baguley, "The Nature of Naturalism," Nelson 22.

influenced Dreiser and Grove's version of naturalism.[20] The plot of decline in twentieth-century naturalism is, however, less an expression of biological decay than naturalism's way of echoing what Gustav Mahler at the time called the *fin-de-siècle* experience of "panic terror," the loss of objectivity, of certainty and of value (that simultaneously gave birth to modernist art forms and more radical formalist experimentations).[21] Thus, in the world of naturalism, biological pessimism was replaced with twentieth-century skepticism, while enthusiasm about new sexual freedoms was followed by the realization that the new forms of sexuality created new forms of domination and subjection.

---

20 For Nietzsche's influence on Grove, see Axel Knönagel, *Nietzschean Philosophy in the Works of Frederick Philip Grove* (Frankfurt: Peter Lang, 1990).

21 Quoted in William Brazill, "Art and 'The Panic Terror,'" Chapple and Schulte 533.

2

"Liberating" Sexuality

Naturalists, who claimed for themselves the right to articulate the "truth" about sexuality, were often accused of producing pornography and found themselves battling against anti-pornography forces. During the Victorian era, explicit sexuality was silently tolerated only in the realm of pornography, which flourished as literature's social "other." Similarly, nineteenth-century American writing about prostitution was tolerated only in the sub-literary Gothic thriller. Turn-of-the-century social reformers, to be sure, produced a growing documentary literature on the prostitute, debating her in terms of "the great social evil," but the prostitute entered "serious" American literature only slowly and in sanitized forms, as "a seduction victim," as "a saintly sufferer," or as "a triumphantly manly heroine."[1] In his recent study on *Foucault and Literature*, Simon During writes that literary discourse has also been "slow to appropriate

---

1 Laura Hapke, *Girls Who Went Wrong: Prostitutes in American Fiction, 1885–1917* (Bowling Green: Bowling Green State U Popular P, 1989) 1–3.

27

sexuality or to create sexual desire."[2] Although literature has been an extremely rich field of sexualization, the sex act itself has often been relegated to the margins of the literary discourse, and thus has often been silenced.

Such silences and sanitizations can be partly attributed to anti-pornography legislations, such as the 1873 Comstock Act, the first federal anti-obscenity law in the United States, named after the founder of the New York Society for the Suppression of Vice, Anthony Comstock. This law made it a crime to make, sell, or import books and pictures deemed obscene. The Comstock Act can be seen as directly related to the emergence of a mass market press that thrived on sensationalism, but also had a clearly repressive social function in that it was used to ban "contraceptive and abortifacient drugs and devices"[3] as well as to censor the emerging realist-naturalist literature. As Laura Hapke's study on the prostitute in American fiction shows, any turn-of-the-century literary writing about prostitution risked being criminalized and censored as pornography, a fact Hapke attributes to the tenacious survival of Victorian concepts of "feminine purity," reflected even in medical treatises emphasizing the "feebleness" of female sexual desire.[4]

In both the United States and Canada the spectre of the new woman was accompanied by the negative image of the prostitute, vividly debated in terms of "white slavery." The working-class woman and her leisure time became the focus of a debate that was motivated by what social historians have termed a "moral panic," namely, the fear of spreading promiscuity and the spectre of the "fallen woman" in the city. In North America and Europe alike, this moral panic created a legal and normative apparatus of control that centred on the body of the working woman. In 1886, Canada's legal system even criminalized "seduction," whereupon the yearly rate of convictions increased from nine to almost thirty-five per cent between 1911 and 1917.[5] In the United States, this

2 Simon During, *Foucault and Literature: Toward a Genealogy of Writing* (London & New York: Routledge, 1992) 172.

3 Gayle Rubin, "Thinking Sex: Notes for a Radical Theory of the Politics of Sexuality," *Pleasure and Danger: Exploring Female Sexuality*, ed. Carole S. Vance, ed. (Boston: Routledge & Kegan Paul, 1984), 268. For a critical discussion of Comstock's repressive influence on *fin-de-siècle* America, see also H. L. Mencken's "Puritanism as a Literary Force," *A Book of Prefaces* (New York: Knopf, 1917) 195–283.

4 Hapke 1–20.

5 Karen Dubinsky, "'Maidenly Girls' or 'Designing Women'? The Crime of Seduction in Turn-of-the-Century Ontario," *Gender Conflicts: New Essays in Women's History*, ed. Franca Iacovetta and Mariana Valverde (Toronto: U of Toronto P, 1992) 50.

adherence to a concept of femininity as the Victorian angel in the house had its effect on those who were opposed to images of female sexual impropriety: "Thus when writers like Crane, Frederic, and Phillips decided to place the prostitute center stage, their work called up fears, evoking the horror of censor and genteel author alike. Even had there not been the official censorship of Comstock's Society for the Suppression of Vice, American writers worked within a context in which it was difficult to find a non-moralistic description, even if the focus was sociological, economic, or medical."[6] There was a fear that writings about female impropriety could somehow "infect" the social body, as Lyn Pykett has observed in her discussion of the British reception of sexualized literature: "Much of the hostility to naturalism's representation of sexuality is based on fears of the dangers posed to the nation's health by a failure to control and regulate reading habits (and ultimately the actions) of an emerging mass audience."[7]

The fact that any form of writing about the prostitute was censored as "pornography" may explain why realistic-naturalist authors distanced themselves so vehemently from the pornographic label. Restif did blithely entitle his project on a state-run brothel "Le pornographe," but Emile Zola, significantly, dissociated his writing on the French prostitute from its etymological label. Claiming a new, powerful position as a social agency with the right and obligation to speak truthfully about sexual matters, naturalism's ideological battle-cry became "the truth." This, in turn, created a dilemma for twentieth-century writers interested in representing sexuality, as Simon During observes:

> Thus, in the first decades of this century, avant-garde writers like D. H. Lawrence, James Joyce, Henry Miller and Theodore Dreiser found themselves writing about sexuality in terms which could neither produce readerly desire nor accept the cultural values attached to official "obscenity" rulings. For them sex could be used against the apparatus of normalization and productivity; it could be turned against domesticity. Here sex has a different use: both the aesthetic value of avant-garde writings and their "truth" was directly appealed to in the courts which tried to prosecute them as pornography. Their status as art is officially sanctioned in their fight with censorship aimed at pornography and the protection of family life.[8]

---

6 Hapke 16.

7 Lyn Pykett, "Representing the Real: The English Debate about Naturalism, 1884–1900," Nelson 172.

8 During 172.

Accused of producing pornography, naturalists from the nineteenth century on reacted with two complementary strategies. The first is a radical dissemination of sexuality into literature by displacing it into social relations, economic relations, inscribing sexuality as a marker between social classes. The second strategy involves sanitizing the sex act itself with an increased focus on sexual desire rather than on sexual pleasure. These strategies go hand in hand with the aggressive discourse of liberating literature from puritanical forms of sexual repression and the simultaneous defensive demarcation of a clear boundary between a serious, naturalistic literature (which articulates the "truth" on sexuality) and pornography (which arouses sexual desire through explicit images).

The social struggle around this specific question of who is entitled to speak the truth on sexuality illustrates Foucault's point that "truth isn't outside power, or lacking in power."[9] For the Foucauldian archaeologist, then, the task at hand is not to discriminate between true or false discourses, but to examine through what rules and what apparatuses discourses establish themselves as true in a society. Thus the archaeologist examines "systematically changing discursive practices, such as who has the right to make statements, from what site these statements emanate, and what position the subject of discourse occupies."[10] Applying this principle to the history of naturalism, the Foucauldian archaeologist is interested in how naturalism has institutionalized itself as an agency with the right (and duty) to produce sexual truths.

Naturalism established itself, in part, through its rivalry with the judicial institutions, a rivalry that was often masked by a discourse of opposition, adopted by naturalists and juridical institutions alike. Indeed, the history of naturalism has become associated with its "obscenity" trials: in 1857 the spectacular trial against Flaubert's *Madame Bovary*; in 1888 and 1889 the trials against Henry Vizetelly, the British publisher of Zola's translated works; in 1890 the equally spectacular trial in Leipzig against three German naturalists, Alberti, Conradi, and Walloth, for violating sexual taboos and spreading obscenities. Also, in 1916 the New York Society for the Suppression of Vice successfully blocked the distribution of Dreiser's *The "Genius"* by making the publisher yield to public pressure, forcing him to withdraw the book from the market. Although

---

9 Michel Foucault, *Power/Knowledge: Selected Interviews and Other Writings, 1972–1977*, ed. Colin Gordon (New York: Pantheon, 1980) 131. Further references to this work will be abbreviated *PK* in the text.

10 Hubert L. Dreyfus and Paul Rabinow, *Michel Foucault: Beyond Structuralism and Hermeneutics* (Chicago: U of Chicago P, 1983) 67–68.

Flaubert won his trial, basing his defence on the author's right to artistic creativity and freedom of expression, the *Leipziger Naturalistenprozeß* ended with a defeat for the naturalist authors: their books were disqualified as popular literature (*Unterhaltungsliteratur*) and the authors were denied the legal privilege of artistic and creative freedom granted to serious art.[11] Similarly, Dreiser lost his court case against the John Lane Company in 1918.

It is this history of opposition to judicial apparatuses and forces of public morality that eventually ensured the canonization of naturalism as a liberating force in literary histories. In *The Sexual Revolution in Modern American Literature*, Charles Glicksberg writes that daring to write "the truth, however maligned and unacknowledged, about sex, Dreiser led the revolt against the hypocritical moral conventions that were crippling the intellectual and spiritual development of America."[12] Glicksberg's argument suggests that sex itself brings with it change, exploding old conventions and revolutionizing life. "Dreiser came to be, for his restless contemporaries, the representative writer of the age, a liberating force of great importance for the times," writes Thomas Riggio in the introduction to Dreiser's *Diaries*.[13] And to give some legitimacy to the new, "unexpurgated" Pennsylvania edition of *Sister Carrie* (1981), a work that is sexually more explicit than the original Doubleday edition, Alfred Kazin observes in the introduction: "To the always alienated and radical Dreiser, Carrie represents the necessity of transformation, sex as revolution."[14]

It was this idea of Dreiser as the "liberator" of American literature from "puritanism" that the critics had in mind when they labelled Grove

---

11 See Jutta Kolkenbrock-Netz, *Fabrikation, Experiment, Schöpfung: Strategien ästhetischer Legitimation im Naturalismus* (Heidelberg: Carl Winter, 1981), particularly her chapter entitled "Naturalismus und der Staat: Zur Funktionsweise des ästhetischen Diskurses im Strafprozeß," 140–73.

12 Charles Glicksberg, *The Sexual Revolution in Modern American Literature* (The Hague: Martinus Nijhoff, 1971) 46.

13 Thomas P. Riggio, Introduction, *American Diaries: 1902-1926*, by Theodore Dreiser (Philadelphia: U of Pennsylvania P, 1982) 27.

14 Alfred Kazin, Introduction, *Sister Carrie*, by Theodore Dreiser (New York: Penguin, 1983) ix. This view of Dreiser as a sexual liberator has originated very early on. See H. L. Mencken, "Theodore Dreiser" and "Puritanism as a Literary Force," *A Book of Prefaces* (New York: Knopf, 1917); John Cowper Powys, "Modern Fiction," *Sex in the Arts: A Symposium*, ed. John Francis McDermott and Kendall B. Taft (New York: Harper & Brothers, 1932) 54; and Richard Poirier, *A World Elsewhere: The Place of Style in American Literature* (London: Chatto & Windus, 1967) 245.

a naturalistic "Canadian Dreiser." In the introduction to the New Canadian Library edition of Grove's *Settlers of the Marsh*, Thomas Saunder
uses very telling language to describe Grove's achievement in literature: "On the subject of sex, [*Settlers*] is the frankest of all of Grove's
novels and, in a puritanical Canada, it was condemned as obscene,"[15] an
opinion that has been adopted by many readers. Saunder's discourse
implies that Grove's writing has a sexually liberating effect in a morally
backward or misguided country. Grove himself would probably have
shared this opinion, as he explained the bad sales of the book with its
sexual honesty, comparing it to the realism of Flaubert's *Madame Bovary*.

In fact, even the most recent naturalist theories emphasize naturalism's "liberating" force to the point of mythologizing it in critical discourse: "Like a Trojan horse of fiction, the naturalist text was a dangerous
intruder, penetrating into the protected domains of bourgeois proprie-
ties," writes David Baguley in his theory on European naturalism, emphasizing that the naturalist text "admitted more explicit sexual matter
into its range of reference and attacked the modes of representation of
bourgeois culture, especially its reassuring, edifying literature" (*NF* 173).
It is, however, naturalism's very liberationist mythology (appropriately
expressed by Baguley in a language of male penetration) that needs to
be problematized in the context of feminism and Foucault's history of
sexuality. Foucault's theory forces us to examine naturalism not so much
as an ultimate force of liberation but rather as a discourse rivalling the
prerogatives of social purity forces. After all, naturalism demanded for
itself the right to speak truthfully about sexual matters and suggested
new ways of regulating sexuality in literature.

While naturalism promoted itself in a discourse of opposition to the
repressive juridical powers, the "real" problems of twentieth-century
realist-naturalist authors often went much deeper and were more complex than the simple juridical-moralistic repression theory suggests. Thus,
the "censorship" involved in Dreiser's *Sister Carrie* was not a juridical
one, but consisted in Dreiser's voluntary submission to the dynamics of
the market place: "Dreiser was submissive to every suggestion that might
assure publication,"[16] and easily acquiesced to enormous changes and
cuts suggested by his friend Arthur Henry, as well as to stylistic changes
suggested by his wife, Jug Dreiser. In many cases these changes improved
the novel's flow and style, but they also had the effect of sanitizing the

---

15 Thomas Saunders, Introduction, *Settlers of the Marsh*, by Frederick Philip Grove
    (Toronto: New Canadian Library, 1966) viii.

16 Kazin xiii.

novel's depiction of sexuality. The "censorship" involved, however, was one that had Dreiser's approval.

Once on the market, *Sister Carrie*'s problem was not that it was openly censored but that it was quietly ignored by a mass audience (and reviewers) who refused to buy and read his literature: "Few New York dailies noticed *Carrie*, and many of the most important literary magazines ... were conspicuous by their silence," writes Dreiser biographer Richard Lingeman.[17] When Stuart Sherman openly dismissed Dreiser's naturalism as "barbaric" in his review in 1917,[18] his negative evaluation did not so much "suppress" Dreiser's work, as finally stimulate a debate that would continue for decades to come, initiating Dreiser's subsequent canonization as *the* American naturalist.

While the eventual canonization of Dreiser's literature went hand in hand with the more general social rejection of "puritanism" and "Victorianism" in American society, naturalist authors quickly learned to exploit the advertisement potential of "suppression" stories. The censorship of a book and the ensuing debates were cleverly appropriated as a marketing strategy by a new generation of naturalists. Dreiser's *The "Genius"* is a case in point. The publisher's suppression of the novel motivated many American and British authors to declare their solidarity, thus promoting the book itself to the point that Hamlin Garland, a very respected American realist writer, accused the whole anti-censorship movement that gathered around Dreiser's novel of being "a piece of very shrewd advertising."[19] What is more, as naturalist authors both Dreiser and Grove shared the strategy of creating and perpetuating "legends" of suppression around their works. Dreiser's story of Mrs. Doubleday's suppression of *Sister Carrie* has been revealed to be a gross exaggeration kept alive over the years by the author himself.

Likewise, Grove encouraged a censorship tale around *Settlers of the Marsh* (1925), claiming that he had been forced to cut the novel until it

---

17 Richard Lingeman, *Theodore Dreiser: At the Gates of the City 1871–1907* (New York: G. P. Putnam's Sons, 1986) 298. Also, Harper & Row's reader turned down the novel by pointing to its lack of interest for female readers: "I cannot conceive of the book arousing the interest or inviting the attention, after the opening chapters, of the feminine readers who control the destinies of so many novels," quoted in Kazin x.

18 Stuart P. Sherman, "The Barbaric Naturalism of Mr. Dreiser," *The Nation* 101 (1915): 648, rpt. in *Dreiser: A Collection of Critical Essays*, ed. John Lydenberg (Englewood Cliffs: Prentice-Hall, 1971) 63.

19 Quoted in Philip Gerber, *Theodore Dreiser* (New Haven: College and UP, 1964) 125. For the Comstock Society's activities against Dreiser, see also Mencken 108, 138–43.

was only a "garbled extract" that was bound to fail on the market. Margaret Stobie and Henry Makow have pointed out that this tale is largely a legend of the author's own making.[20] Grove further blamed the bad sales of *Settlers* on the novel's sexual explicitness, as he does in a letter to Lorne Pierce in 1925: "[I]t was the old story of Flaubert's *Madame Bovary* over again. A serious work of art was classed as pornography; but with this difference that the error in Flaubert's case, increased the sales; he lived in France. In my case, in Canada, it killed them."[21] While the public controversy surrounding the book's explicit treatment of sexuality was indeed lively, the novel was not banned from Canadian libraries, as Grove claimed it was. Indeed, Grove was aware of the advertisement potential of a ban, as illustrated by an early letter to André Gide (14 August 1905) in which he comments on the expected success of his first novel, *Fanny Essler*: "In all this I'm relying heavily on my novel, which will certainly be charged by the public prosecutor. That is the best advertisement I could hope for."[22]

Thus, in a clever gesture of self-promotion, the authors openly situated themselves in a discursive struggle against a repressive juridical power, emphasizing naturalism's success in overcoming these sexual repressions in literature by creating their own liberationist mythologies. Such mythologies are, however, problematic, and not just because of the authors' duplicity. In *The History of Sexuality*, Michel Foucault demonstrates in great detail that discourses of sexual liberation should not be taken at face value since, while promising an illusory freedom, they are often part of a larger apparatus of power. Foucault by no means denies the very real sexual repressions in Western society and history; his philosophical critique is anchored in his conviction that "real power" escapes "the rules of jurisprudence" (*HS* 88). Underlying this argument is Foucault's thesis that modern power has developed much more sophisticated strategies than the repressive apparatus of the law, and to understand Foucault's logic, it is important to remember that he distinguishes between two significantly different conceptions of power. The first, the juridico-discursive model of power, is the "old" type of power, a monarchical power whose main arm is the law. This power is negative and

---

20 See Stobie 111–13 and Henry Makow, "Grove's 'Garbled Extract': The Bibliographical Origins of *Settlers of the Marsh*," *Modern Times: The Canadian Novel*, vol. 3, ed. John Moss (Toronto: NC Press, 1982) 38–54.

21 Quoted in Makow 40–41.

22 Quoted in Douglas Spettigue, "Felix, Elsa, André Gide and Others: Some Unpublished Letters of F. P. Greve," *Canadian Literature* 134 (1991): 31.

repressive in that it limits the individual by laying down the law, by saying "no" to individual freedom, and by imposing restrictions. Foucault acknowledges that this type of power still exists in modern society, but he emphasizes that it has been virtually displaced in its importance by a new type of power that is much more flexible, productive, and efficient. The new "bio-power" takes sex as its target, attaching itself to the individual body and concerning itself with its health and welfare. Thus the proliferation of discourses on sexuality in the course of the last three centuries has gone hand in hand with the proliferation of sites of power and control over the body. But despite these changes, our thinking about power has not yet changed: "At bottom, despite the differences in epochs and objectives, the representation of power has remained under the spell of monarchy. In political thought and analysis, we still have not cut off the head of the king" (*HS* 88–89). Western thinking about power is still dominated by concepts such as repression, the law, and by manipulating ideologies that mask the truth. According to the old juridico-discursive model of power, speaking the "truth" is automatically equated with "liberation" and freedom: truth implies a stepping out of a repressive power regime. It is this very juridico-discursive model that naturalism invoked in its struggle to establish itself as a major form of literature, and it is this model that Foucault critiques.

Without glossing over the reality of sexual repressions, Foucault has argued against "the repressive hypothesis," by emphasizing the sophisticated workings of modern bio-power: "[Power] masks itself by producing a discourse, seemingly opposed to it but really part of the larger deployment of modern power."[23] In other words, naturalism's liberationist discourse only appears to be in opposition to the dominant social power structures; it is really part of the larger deployment of power. By constituting itself as a rebelling discourse, naturalism adopts the mask of opposition, while in fact contributing to the larger deployment of a sophisticated form of bourgeois bio-power. In order to explore this point fully, it is necessary to trace Foucault's historical account of the new bio-power and its use of sexuality.

Foucault has argued that "sexuality is originally, historically bourgeois" and "induces certain class effects" (*HS* 127). Thus at the end of the eighteenth century when the bourgeoisie asserted its political and juridical dominance over the aristocracy in the French Revolution, it set sex – its body, its health – against the blood of the nobles. Also, it was in

---

23 Dreyfus and Rabinow 130.

the bourgeois family that "the sexuality of children and adolescents was first problematized, and feminine sexuality medicalized": continually alerted to the pathology of sex, the bourgeoisie followed an urgent need to keep the body under "close watch and to devise a rational technology of correction" (*HS* 120). In the nineteenth century the deployment of sexuality spread from the bourgeoisie through the entire social body, which was "provided with a 'sexual body'" (*HS* 127). Human bodies became saturated with sexuality and tied into networks of power through the following processes: the hysterization of women's bodies, involving the construction of women's identities on the basis of their reproductive function; the pedagogization of children's sex; the socialization of pro-creative behaviour; and the psychiatrization of perverse pleasures (*HS* 104–5). This sexualization of the whole society went hand in hand with the deployment of administrative control mechanisms that cen-tred on sexuality. Thus, the spread of bio-power entailed administrative measures to eradicate perversions among the working class and to con-trol social dangers such as racial degeneracy, bad public hygiene, and prostitution.[24] It is these very motifs that nineteenth-century literary natu-ralism appropriated as its thematic concerns.

Once sexuality infiltrated the lower classes, however, the sexualized body lost its function as a social marker, so that the bourgeoisie needed to give itself a new – class-specific – sexuality to demarcate its social boundaries. According to Foucault, it was the advent of psychoanalysis that allowed the bourgeoisie to claim for its own class a "repressed" sexuality, using repression as a mark of social difference that separated the bourgeoisie from the "sexually uninhibited" lower class. Psycho-analysis not only made a connection between sexuality and the law of repression, it also granted the bourgeoisie a new privilege: the ability to talk about sexuality and to challenge sexual taboos in discourse. The increasing popularity of the confession in psychoanalysis meant a new "command to talk about that which power forbade one to do."[25] At a time when psychoanalysis allowed higher class individuals to express their incestuous desire in discourse, "the regime of sexuality applied to the lower social classes ... involved the exclusion of incestuous prac-tices" (*HS* 129). For the French bourgeoisie, the father figure was elevated into an object of compulsory love through psychoanalysis's discovery of the Oedipal complex, while the French laws of 1889 and 1898 entailed a loss of parental authority, especially for the lower classes.

---

24 See Dreyfus and Rabinow 141.

25 Dreyfus and Rabinow 141.

Thus the bourgeoisie gave itself a sexuality that could only be "liberated" through speech and that stimulated an unmitigated desire to reveal the truth about itself. The bourgeoisie even attached a cash value to sexual authenticity. At the turn of the century, the "truth" sold well in newspapers, magazines, and photography. With the emergence of mass market journalism, "truth" circulated in many different forms, creating the success of tabloids such as *True Stories* and *True Confessions* in the United States and the magazine *Truth* in Britain which thrived on publicizing political and social scandals. As well, authentic women's stories were a hot commodity at the turn of the century. Margarete Böhme's best-selling novel about a prostitute, *Tagebuch einer Verlorenen* (1905), was so popular in Germany that it was turned into a movie in 1929, starring American actress Louise Brooks in the role of the protagonist-prostitute. Böhme's novel, deliberately presented in the form of a woman's sexual confession, was followed by a wave of imitations. The fictional confession thus stimulated other women to articulate their sexualities in similar terms, creating a proliferation of documentary truths on women's personal experiences.[26]

Dreiser and Grove's naturalism was born into this particular notion of truth as discursive freedom from sexual repression. Incorporating the highly marketable sexual confession (and with it the "authentic voice" of the female body) into their naturalism, they managed to carve out for themselves a niche in the literary canon at a time when avant garde writers were starting to attract attention with exciting new forms of narration. As Simon During puts it: "It was because truth as exposé, as confession, as demystification and as contact with social suffering and sexuality was so highly valued and saleable, that Dreiser could uphold the novel's traditional claims to verisimilitude and creativity by processing and transforming reportage."[27] It may be true that, in comparison with documentary reportage, "in Dreiser's time, novels ... focus more directly and in more detail on sexual desire and acts to explain their characters,"[28] but the process of transforming reportage and confession into fiction is more complex than During suggests. In many cases, the

---

26 See Hanne Kulessa, "Nachwort," *Tagebuch einer Verlorenen*, ed. Margarete Böhme (Frankfurt: Suhrkamp, 1989) 259. For a discussion of the proliferation of British confessional novels, see also Lyn Pykett, *The "Improper" Feminine, The Women's Sensation Novel and the New Woman Writing* (London & New York: Routledge, 1992).

27 During 228–29.

28 During 229.

fictional transformation involved a sanitizing of the confessional stories that formed the basis of Dreiser's novels.

A case in point is Dreiser's transformation of the life stories of his sisters, which entailed a "process of heightening and cleansing," as Donald Pizer has pointed out.[29] Dreiser's sister Emma, for instance, had considerable sex experiences and was rather indiscriminate in her sexual alliances before she eloped with a well-to-do man named Hopkins; her fictional counterpart Carrie Meeber, in contrast, is presented in her youthful innocence, and is more or less abducted by Hurstwood. The model for *Jennie Gerhardt* (1911), Mame Dreiser, "was in her youth as much pursuer as pursued, and she was also frequently domineering and vain," in contrast to Jennie's passivity and spirit of generosity.[30] We find a similar sanitizing of female promiscuity in *Fanny Essler*, where Grove glossed over some of the affairs of the promiscuous real-life model Elsa. Indeed, Baroness Elsa's autobiographical confession (written 1923–26 and sent to Djuna Barnes) is much more irreverent and explicit in its treatment of sexuality than *Fanny Essler*.

This sanitizing of women's confessional voices through appropriation into (male) naturalism illustrates Foucault's emphasis on the power effects inherent in confessional discourses. Foucault has conceptualized the "confession" of truth as a widespread cultural phenomenon that goes far beyond the religious domain. The confession plays a significant role as a modern strategy of knowledge and power: "In any case, next to the testing rituals, next to the testimony of witnesses, and the learned methods of observation and demonstration, the confession became one of the West's most highly valued techniques for producing truth. We have since become a singularly confessing society" (*HS* 59). Involving a ritual of interrogation and inquest, the production of truth through confession is inevitably tied into networks of power that can easily turn into a prison for the confessing person. The production of a confession occurs in a relationship of power, with the persons extracting "the truth" occupying the dominant position of authority, since this position allows them to interpret and recodify (and ultimately co-opt) a personal confession for their own purposes. Dreiser, who was a journalist before turning to

---

29   Donald Pizer, *The Novels of Theodore Dreiser: A Critical Study* (Minneapolis: U of Minnesota P, 1976) 34.

30   Pizer 100. For an examination of the complexity involved in Dreiser's transformation of real-life stories into fiction, see also Shelley Fisher Fishkin's "From Fact to Fiction: *An American Tragedy,*" *Theodore Dreiser's "An American Tragedy,"* ed. Harold Bloom (New York: Chelsea House, 1988) 103–26.

novel writing, was a master at extracting truthful confessions in the question-answer ritual of the interview, and it is these voices that he selects or silences, heightens or tones down, for the purposes of his fiction. In this light, the naturalist emphasis on the new female sexuality has to be seen as a deeply ambiguous gesture: it gives a voice to formerly silenced groups at the same time as it appropriates, shapes, and often contains these voices within the boundaries of male naturalist conventions.

Thus writing "openly" and "frankly" about sexuality by drawing on real-life stories does not necessarily entail a sexual liberation, but can lead to its very opposite, as Patrick Hutton notes with Foucault: "The sexual revolution of the twentieth century, Foucault believes, has less to do with permissive behavior than it does with a widening discussion of sexuality. The discussion professes to demystify sex in the name of its liberation, yet it is subtly coercive in its classification of techniques of sexual behavior."[31] An active agent in the demystification of traditional sexuality, naturalism has indeed inscribed new ways of "[policing] sexuality by publicly defining codes of legitimate and illegitimate sexual behavior,"[32] and by presenting a new textual field for the production of regulated, "authorized" discourses on sexual matters. This makes naturalism both a literary reflection of and an active agent in the social proliferation of sexuality as a *scientia sexualis*.

Dreiser and Grove participate in a "normalization" process by inscribing sexuality in "codified" and "clean" discourses. According to Grove, the only way to deal with sexuality is "realistically": "I advocate frankness in matters of sex; clean, searching, unimpassioned, and unprejudiced discussions of their bearings and their importance. Sex is real; as real as mountain tops and barren sea."[33] This position echoes Zola's description of the naturalist as an unimpassioned observer. Foucault, however, points to an ironic duplicity in the realm of such sexualizations, asking "whether, since the nineteenth century, the *scientia sexualis* – under the guise of its decent positivism – has not functioned, at least to a certain extent, as an *ars erotica*. Perhaps this production of truth, intimidated though it was by the scientific model, multiplied, intensified, and even created its own intrinsic pleasures" (*HS* 70–71). Foucault's criti-

---

31 Patrick Hutton, "Foucault, Freud, and the Technologies of the Self," *Technologies of the Self: A Seminar with Michel Foucault*, ed. Luther H. Martin et al. (Amherst: U of Massachusetts P, 1988) 130.

32 Hutton 130.

33 Grove, *It Needs to Be Said* ..., 52–53.

cism is well taken. It appears that under the guise of cleanliness and truthfulness, the naturalists inscribe in their text a sublimated and sanitized pleasure that indirectly reinscribes the very sexual repression from which they propose to "free" the literary discourse.

Another way of reinscribing sexuality in socially acceptable forms can be found in naturalism's emphasis on the force of sexual desire. Foucault has argued somewhat polemically that in Western culture it is desire that has taken centre stage and the sexual act itself and pleasure have been marginalized: "Acts are not very important, and pleasure – nobody knows what it is!"[34] Similarly, Roger Seamon has observed that the world of American naturalist fiction is characterized by "a deep, endemic and pervasive joylessness," a world in which the Freudian reality principle reigns, so that the usual sources of delight "*do not yield real pleasure.*"[35] If the pleasurelessness of the naturalistic writing style functions to deny the audience pleasure in order to rouse "guilt in the complacent bourgeois reader," it also corresponds to a larger bourgeois deployment of a discursively contained sexuality that reinscribes a link between sexuality and guilt, fear, and repression. Thus naturalism established itself as an agency for both sexual liberation and sexual control.

---

34 Michel Foucault, "On the Genealogy of Ethics: An Overview of Work in Progress," interview conducted by Dreyfus and Rabinow at Berkeley in 1983, Dreyfus and Rabinow 243.

35 Roger Seamon, "Naturalist Narratives and Their Ideational Context: A Theory of American Naturalist Fiction," *The Canadian Review of American Studies* 19 (1988): 51.

3

Power and the Docile Body

The last chapter was concerned with Foucault's critique of some of the ideological underpinnings of naturalism's treatment of sexuality; this chapter focuses on the areas in which naturalism intersects with Foucauldian conceptions of power and sexuality. Dreyfus and Rabinow have observed that Foucault "obviously rejects the naturalistic view that the body has a fixed structure and fixed needs."[1] At the same time, however, they also emphasize Foucault's invaluable insights into body-moulding techniques, a traditionally naturalist preoccupation: Foucault "is asking how the body can be divided up, reconstituted, and manipulated by society." Foucault's theory, of course, changed in the course of his life. In *The History of Sexuality* and *Discipline and Punish: The Birth of the Prison* (1975), Foucault's theory intersects in fascinating ways with many of the classical concerns of naturalism, but the "later" Foucault revised many of his earlier statements to emphasize more strongly the

---

1 Dreyfus and Rabinow 111; following citation 112.

41

possibility of personal freedom available to individuals in the social network of power: "All my analyses are against the idea of universal necessities in human existence. They show the arbitrariness of institutions and show which space of freedom we can still enjoy and how many changes can still be made."[2] The role of the intellectual, then, is "to show people that they are much freer than they feel, that people accept as truth, as evidence, some themes which have been built up at a certain moment during history, and that this so-called evidence can be criticized and destroyed."

Foucault's early work shares with naturalist fiction a deep interest in the extent to which the human body and mind are shaped through social practices and institutions and how far human beings are free to change the constraints of their lives. As Regina Benjowski has observed in her reading of Foucault: "Diese Konstitution des Menschen als Subjekt ist im Hinblick auf den wechselnden Anteil und die unterschiedliche Effizienz von Eigen- und Fremdbestimmung für Foucault ein Schlüsselproblem."[3] Indeed, like most naturalist writers, Foucault is interested in the power effects and body-moulding techniques operating in social hierarchies and institutions (such as the prison or the hospital), and in the role of architecture and spaces as body-shaping forces. Foucault shares with naturalist fiction a critical focus on marginalized figures (the madman, the hysteric, the prisoner, the criminal), but since he is interested in showing "how we have indirectly constituted ourselves through the exclusion of some others: criminals, mad people, and so on,"[4] his theory can be applied as a critical tool to examine the use naturalism makes of marginalized characters.

Foucault's theory also intersects with naturalist fiction in his radical rejection of the self-reflective subject as the driving force of history. According to Foucault, subjectivity is deeply divided and has a life only on the basis of the external practices and discourses it internalizes. As Lee Clark Mitchell has observed in *Determined Fictions: American Literary Naturalism* (1989), naturalism anticipated these poststructuralist "attacks on the 'subject' that have become an integral part of the philosophical

---

2 Michel Foucault, "Technologies of the Self," Martin et al. 11; following citation 10.

3 "This constitution of the human being as subject is a key problem for Foucault with respect to the varying degrees and different efficiencies in its self-determination and its determination through others" (my translation); "Philosophie als Werkzeug," *Denken und Existenz bei Michel Foucault*, ed. Wilhelm Schmidt (Frankfurt: Suhrkamp, 1991) 176.

4 Michel Foucault, "The Political Technology of Individuals," Martin et al. 146.

tradition in this century." In fact, naturalism's most interesting innovation is precisely what has generally led the critics to dismiss it as bad writing: "its disruptive narratives and estranging styles" through which "naturalists challenged us to reconceive certain long-standing premises about the 'self.'" Naturalism's narrative form and language – its repetitions, its doubling of characters, its awkward styles – draw attention to the fact that "the closer one attends to the self, the less it tends to cohere – as if the very process of depiction somehow dismantled subjectivity, breaking the self apart piece-by-piece and absorbing it into an indifferent world."[5]

Highlighting the "death" of the transcendental subject, Foucault's project has been to theorize what naturalism fictionalizes: that the subject's constitution through social practices implies its simultaneous subjection in the social network of power. This undercurrent of social determinism in Foucault's conceptualization of the body and subjectivity has perhaps been best summarized by Patrick Hutton, who contrasts Foucault's "deterministic" approach with that of Sigmund Freud (who figures prominently in Foucault's critical writing, albeit as a negative touchstone). Whereas Freud insists on the determining power of experiences that "have etched the surfaces of our psyches," Foucault examines "the formal rules that we have designed to discipline life's experiences."[6] According to Foucault, the whole social order is based on a principle of self-management that both affirms and challenges the notion of personal freedom. Subjectivity is constructed through "technologies of self," which are generally not created by the individual but are always already present in the social order: "The subject constitutes himself [sic] in an active fashion, by the practices of self, [but] these practices are nevertheless not something that the individual invents by himself. They are patterns that he finds in his culture and which are proposed, suggested and imposed on him by his culture, his society and his social group."[7] Foucault is interested in the determinism that results from the various ways individuals examine and classify themselves and each other in society, a technique of disciplinary power whose historical emergence he discusses in detail in *Discipline and Punish*.

---

5 Lee Mitchell, *Determined Fictions: American Literary Naturalism* (New York: Columbia UP, 1989) 123, 17.

6 Hutton 136, 137.

7 Michel Foucault, "The Ethic of Care for the Self as a Practice of Freedom," interview January 20, 1984, *The Final Foucault*, ed. James Bernauer and David Rasmussen (Cambridge, MA: MIT Press, 1988) 11.

Disciplinary power is a technique of exercising power without the use of violence. Its target is the body, which is rendered docile and productive through a host of disciplinary techniques that include spatial arrangements, whereby every body is assigned a "proper" place; timetabling, whereby the body's activities are divided according to time; isolation and recombination of different body forces in an assembly-line system; and instruction, whereby different levels of bodily expertise are demarcated from one stage to the next on the basis of examinations and testing. These disciplinary techniques hierarchize individuals on the basis of their abilities, their level, their "nature," assigning each individual a place in the scheme of order by endowing him or her with a "personal" identity. Thus, the social order is based on a continual method of comparison, of reward and punishment: "The perpetual penality that traverses all points and supervises every instant in the disciplinary institutions compares, differentiates, hierarchizes, homogenizes, excludes. In short it *normalizes*."[8]

Given this conception of disciplinary techniques, it is no coincidence that Foucault's paradigmatic model for the workings of modern power is an eighteenth-century prison model: Jeremy Bentham's Panopticon, in which the prisoners' cells surround a tower. A particular window arrangement makes it possible for the supervisor in the tower to see the prisoners, while the prisoners cannot see the supervisor in the tower and therefore continually suspect that the supervisor's gaze is on them. Feeling themselves continually under a supervising gaze, the prisoners will inevitably interiorize this supervising gaze, and as a result also internalize the prison rules. Thus the prisoners end up disciplining themselves: "There is no need for arms, physical violence, material constraints. Just a gaze. An inspecting gaze, a gaze which each individual under its weight will end by interiorising to the point that he is his own overseer, each individual thus exercising this surveillance over, and against, himself" (*PK* 155).

As Bentham's Panopticon is built on a clever usage of visibility, so modern power relies on the visibility of every individual and a whole apparatus of mutual surveillance, a power principle that Foucault terms "panopticism." From the eighteenth century on, this panoptic modality infiltrated social institutions (army, schools, and medical field), serving "to reform prisoners, but also to treat patients, to instruct schoolchildren,

---

8 Michel Foucault, *Discipline and Punish: The Birth of the Prison*, trans. Alan Sheridan (New York: Vintage Books, 1979) 183. Further references will appear in the text, abbreviated *DP*.

to confine the insane, to supervise workers, to put beggars and idlers to work" (*DP* 205). The principle of panopticism is ingenious in its simplicity: social institutions entice individuals into policing themselves, into becoming "normalized," with each individual confirming "the behavioral norms of the society at large."[9] With individuals monitoring themselves and developing "techniques of self-management," the locus of power is no longer a huge, external apparatus at the top of the hierarchy but rather is distributed in a multiplicity of different loci – in the interpersonal relationships at all levels of the hierarchy.

In its desire to create a sense of reality, naturalist fiction not only mimics these disciplinary techniques, but, more importantly, also interweaves them with the construction of individual identity. In his discussion of French naturalism, Philippe Hamon has observed that the realist-naturalist text "sometimes seems fascinated by this constructed dimension of the real that fragments not only an inhabitable space ..., but also fragments the gestures and strategies of the characters into timetables, technical directives."[10] Indeed, examples of spatial fragmentations abound in naturalist fiction: in the different floors in the building of Zola's *Pot-Bouille* (1882), in the factory of *An American Tragedy*, and in the different sections of the department store in *Au Bonheur des Dames*. In these works, spatial differences correspond to differences in the characters' activities, remunerations, and status. Spatial divisions are thus directly linked to naturalism's deterministic ideology, with architecture functioning as "a structure manipulating the characters whom it constrains to travel a particular distance" or "to carry out a particular action."[11] The compartmentalization, classification, and ordering of life are the very determinants – or technologies – that shape the emergence of various types of individuals.

Composed of "the very notion of distinction" inherent in such spatial fragmentations and categorizations, the naturalist world draws attention to Foucault's concept of disciplinary power, which constructs individuals through the very technologies that subject them, by regulating their bodies and minds. Relying on such scalar divisions, modern power does not work so much from the top of the hierarchy but is omnipresent in the social network, working at every level of the social hierarchy while regenerating the hierarchy each moment anew through the principle of

---

9   Hutton 127.

10   Philippe Hamon, "The Naturalist Text and the Problem of Reference," Nelson 32–33.

11   Hamon 33.

inclusion and exclusion. By emphasizing the "reality" of these disciplinary powers, naturalist fiction – like Foucault – insists on making the
body visible by showing how the biological and the historical are interwoven with each other in accordance with the development of modern
technologies of power.

As a site through which docility is accomplished and subjectivity constituted, the body has also been of central concern to poststructuralist
feminists. Acknowledging Foucault's invaluable insights into the
sexualization of the body throughout history, Lois McNay writes in her
recent work *Foucault and Feminism*: "One of the most important contributions that Foucault's theory of the body had made to feminist thought
is a way of conceiving of the body as a concrete phenomenon without
eliding its materiality with a fixed biological or prediscursive essence."[12]
Since Foucault's theory generally glosses over the gender configuration
of power, however, it was left mainly to feminists to identify women's
bodies as the locus of male power.[13] Drawing on Foucault's theory of
panopticism and disciplinary power, poststructuralist feminists have
elaborated on the specific ways in which the female body is constructed
and rendered docile in society. This is how German feminist Kornelia
Hauser has "translated" Foucault's conception of power into feminist
theory: "There is a mode of individualization specific to women; it operates above all through the field of sexuality. (Whole sectors of industry devote themselves to offers of individualization: a perfume which is
one woman's own, the exclusive scent of a certain soap, that 'certain
something' of a cigarette made for women only.)"[14] Created on the basis
of norms that ask for a particular female body language, advertisement
often invites women to realize their particular, individual "type" by
buying a particular product.

Zola illustrates this principle of power by exploring the modern consumer economy in the emerging department stores in *Au Bonheur des
Dames*. Octave Mouret's new displays of varieties of colours and mate-
rials appeal to different types of women: to the aristocratic shopper, the

12 Lois McNay, *Foucault and Feminism: Power, Gender and the Self* (Cambridge: Polity Press, 1992) 17. Further references will appear in the text abbreviated *FF*.

13 See Irene Diamond and Lee Quinby, introduction, *Feminism and Foucault: Reflections on Resistance*, ed. Irene Diamond and Lee Quinby (Boston: Northeastern UP, 1988) ix–xx.

14 Kornelia Hauser, "Sexuality and Power," *Female Sexualization: A Collective Work of Memory*, ed. Frigga Haug et al., trans. Erica Carter (London: Verso, 1987) 202; 200 for quotation below.

fashion-conscious sales clerk, and the economically minded bourgeois woman. At the same time, Mouret's Parisian "Paradise for Women" is a "normalizing machine" since, for an outside observer, the heterogeneous personalities melt into a homogeneous mass, into a "masse épaisse de chapeaux," as soon as the women enter the store. The very product that promises to make a woman "different" from the next person also draws her into the "normalizing" machinery, into predictable buying patterns.[15] This example illustrates that normalizing, panoptic power does not *force* women into submission: "In mediating to the masses a set of values, norms, attitudes, beliefs and so on, ideology cajoles them into 'voluntary' submission," is how Hauser describes the implications of Foucault's normalizing power for women. In *Au Bonheur des Dames*, the women are seduced by a new consumer economy that cajoles them into submission: "elles se sentaient pénétrées et possédées par ce sens délicat qu'il avait de leur être secret, et elles s'abandonnaient, séduites."[16]

Sister Carrie carries this point even further. None of her lovers forces Carrie Meeber to look, speak, or act as she does, and yet in everything she does we have to question her "freedom," because she always acts in imitation of a pregiven model; she is in "voluntary" submission to the often unspoken behavioural norms of her society, when she constructs herself according to the all-powerful American beauty myth. Thus norms and normalization go side by side with their apparent opposite, the construction of the individual and individualization. As social practices and rules are assimilated by individuals in the process of socialization, these rules "take on a semblance of 'naturalness', and constitute what is known as individual 'character.'"[17] Thus by highlighting the construction of the female body while simultaneously questioning the female protagonist's freedom, naturalism exposes the cultural constraints involved in the practices and technologies of self that the social order uses to subjugate women.

At the same time, however, feminist approaches force us to raise the question whether the emphasis on the docile female body in naturalism (as well as in Foucault's theory) does not perpetuate the stereotype of the passive female victim, whose submission to a male seducer is al-

---

15 For a detailed discussion of the concept of the "machine" in naturalism, see Mark Seltzer, *Bodies and Machines* (New York & London: Routledge, 1992).

16 Émile Zola, *Au Bonheur des Dames* (Paris: Unide, 1971) 74. Further references will appear in the text, abbreviated *AB*.

17 Hauser 198.

ways already predetermined. Lois McNay has summarized this feminist critique as follows: "Yet despite Foucault's assertions about the nature of resistance, on the whole, this idea remains theoretically
undeveloped and, in practice, Foucault's historical studies give the impression that the body presents no material resistance to the operations
of power. In *The History of Sexuality*, bodies are 'saturated' with disciplinary techniques, sex is 'administered' by a controlling power that
'wrapped the sexual body in its embrace'" (*FF* 40). Just as naturalist fiction emphasizes what Baguley calls *la chair molle*, inscribing a sexualized,
subjected female body, so in Foucault's theory the language of power
itself is sexualized, with a masculine seductive power "wrapping itself"
around a feminized body, "penetrating" it, and putting it to work.
Sexualized power presents itself in a seductive male guise, against which
the feminized body knows virtually no resistance: its voluntary submission is guaranteed. Just as naturalism is characterized by a sense of inevitability, there is a sense in Foucault's theory that the seductive appeal
of power cannot be escaped. The docility of the body is logical, predictable, always already assured.

Foucault's theory is characterized by certain blind spots in the domain of gender; poststructuralist feminist theory helps put in critical
perspective the naturalist emphasis on a femininity that is automatically entrapped in the network of power relationships. At the same time,
however, feminist theory will also be helpful in identifying those sites
in naturalist fiction in which the female body rejects the docility that
Foucault sees as its inevitable fate. McNay's feminist emphasis on resistance and social change challenges Foucault's theory of the omnipresence of power: "What Foucault's account of power does not explain is
how, even within the intensified process of the hysterization of female
bodies, women did not slip easily and passively into socially prescribed
feminine roles" (*FF* 41). This feminist perspective also helps to illumi-
nate one of the contradictions of twentieth-century naturalist fiction:
naturalism emphasizes women's entrapment in gender roles but also
shows these women as challenging the very roles that confine them.

Furthermore, feminist theory is invaluable for an examination of the
intersection of sexuality and power in the construction of the male body
in naturalism. Rosalind Coward has argued that the male body is virtually absent in literature: "Men's bodies and sexuality are taken for
granted, exempted from scrutiny, whereas women's bodies are exten-
sively defined and overexposed. Sexual and social meanings are imposed

on *women's* bodies, not men's."[18] This feminist analysis of the male body is important for a discussion of naturalism, a literature that often presents the reader with the spectre of the disintegrating, suffering, and metaphorically castrated male body, in figures ranging from Zola's Coupeau in *L'Assommoir* to Dreiser's Hurstwood in *Sister Carrie*. The very representation of the male body seems to imply a loss of male power, signalling a process of victimization as well as feminization.

Moreover, realist-naturalist fiction is obsessed with seeing, observing, analyzing, and dissecting the physical body in microscopic detail, to make visible what seems to be invisible, to foreground the taboo, the private realm, the hidden pleasures and pains. While Foucault's concept of panopticism is important for a discussion of the all-seeing narrative "eye of power" in naturalist fiction, feminist theory draws attention to the consistent masculinizing of this panoptic eye. Naturalism offers a whole catalogue of male characters who appear to be in a position to see all (e.g., Mouret overlooking the complex operations of the *grand magazin* in *Au Bonheur des Dames*, or Cowperwood monitoring the financial shiftings in New York and Chicago), but women are seldom allowed to share this specular privilege. (One of the few female exceptions, Mme de Mertueil in *Les Liaisons dangereuses*, is a master spy, and her eventual exposure in public and the loss of one eye constitute a clear symbolic retributive punishment for overstepping social and textual boundaries.) Above all, it is the male narrators in naturalist fiction who enjoy panoptic privileges. Since the narrators are seldom dramatized (in other words, they do not appear as physical bodies in the works), they are placed in the privileged position of "seeing without being seen."[19] Endowed with an extremely powerful – panoptic – eye, they are in a position to gaze at, objectify, and desire the female characters and to comment on, rival with, or be complicitous with the male characters in the novels. Some phenomenological philosophers – above all Jean-Paul Sartre – have equated such a privileged specular position with the eye of God, or the "absolute Subject"; Foucault, in contrast, warns of a phenomenological

---

18 Rosalind Coward, *Female Desire* (London: Granada Publishing, 1984) 229.

19 See also June Howard's *Form and History in American Literary Naturalism*, particularly chapter 4, entitled "Naturalism and the Spectator." Howard emphasizes that the spectator's privileged position has its limits too: "The barrier that separates the privileged spectator from the unfree actor, the free from the helpless, seems to imprison both, because the spectator rarely becomes involved in the action and when he does, his privilege seems alarmingly precarious" (126).

approach "which gives absolute priority to the observing subject."[20] And this has important implications for a Foucauldian evaluation of the narrator's position of power in naturalism.

Discussing the techniques through which naturalism makes the reader believe that the constructed world "refers to the real," Philippe Hamon has legitimized the male narrator's powerful position, arguing that this is naturalism's technique of convincing the reader of the reality and truth of what is represented: "I, the reader, need as mediator a certain image of the giver of the statements, an image of an authorized, knowing, serious narrator-author; I need to believe in him, in the competence or frankness of his telling."[21] Thus, this reliable author-narrator creates a "reality effect" through the powerful support of ideologies, academies, encyclopedias, and scientific discourses, in short through the very discourses that have been sanctified as truthful by the author's contemporary society. Hamon's theory of the narrator's credibility sounds plausible enough as long as the reader's and the narrator-author's ideologies broadly overlap; or as long as the scientific knowledges the narrator-author disseminates are deemed correct and valid according to the latest research findings. But the situation becomes much more complex when a late-twentieth-century reader is confronted with a nineteenth-century narrator whose pet ideology happens to be social Darwinism, a theory probably considered outdated and even dangerous by the majority of today's readers; or when a contemporary female reader is asked to accept as a credible truth what she might perceive as the author-narrator's sexist perspective on women.

Thus, instead of accepting the omniscient or semi-omniscient commenting male voices in naturalist texts as expressing a reliable standard whereby to judge the characters and events, Foucault and feminists ask us to see such a privileged male voice as just one voice amongst many. In his theory on panopticism, Foucault reminds us that even the supervisor in the Panopticon does not have absolute power or insight into what happens. The supervisor is only part of a larger network and by no means in a god-like position of holding all the strings. This, I would suggest, is also the position of the narrator-author in most naturalist works. Rather than submitting to the narrator's judgement, as many

---

20 Michel Foucault, *The Order of Things: An Archaeology of the Human Sciences* (New York: Vintage, 1973) xiv. See also Sartre's chapter entitled "The Look," in his *Being and Nothingness: A Phenomenological Essay on Ontology*, trans. Hazel Barnes (New York: Washington Square Press, 1966) 340–400.

21 Hamon 41.

critics have done, the Foucauldian reader is forced to raise questions such as: What is the bias or the underlying ideology of this narrating voice? How is this narrating voice contradicted by other voices in the text or how does it contradict itself? How successful is the author in undermining the legitimacy of such "master discourses"? Rather than submit to the tyranny of what is to be "seen" on the texts' surface level, the reader is forced to examine what is relegated to the margins of the texts, into its gaps, into the not-to-be-seen. In other words, one of the intellectual reading pleasures of a naturalistic novel is to plunge into the network of power relationships in order to detect the narrator's ideological bias and to unravel the sexual/textual web through which the narrative voice tries to seduce the reader into complicity with a particular version of the truth. Thus the reader has to analyze how the narrator's position of power is implicated in the economy of pleasure and desire that the novel constructs.

Just as the narrative relationships in naturalist fiction are saturated with power, so its thematics and characterization are obsessed with power relations. It is this very focus on power that creates another anchorage point with Foucault's theories. Recognizing a Nietzschean will to power in human relationships, Foucault has analyzed power in terms of force relations, suggesting that rather than discuss power in terms of "contract or alienation," we should analyze it "primarily in terms of *struggle, conflict* and *war*" (*PK* 90). Indeed, the role of political power "is perpetually to re-inscribe this relation through a form of unspoken warfare; to re-inscribe it in social institutions, in economic inequalities, in language, in the bodies themselves of each and everyone of us" (*PK* 90). And this is the very conception of power adopted in naturalistic works: naturalism foregrounds power as struggle (in the paradigmatic battle between the lobster and the squid in Dreiser's *The Financier*), as conflict (between the different rivalling social factions; between male and female), erupting occasionally in physical battles (in the sexual rivalries between Gervaise and Virginie in *L'Assommoir* or between Aileen and Rita in *The Titan*), or in the very metaphors of war so prominent in Dreiser's fiction. The Nietzschean will to power is translated in twentieth-century naturalism into a "will to succeed" in a socioeconomic context and to dominate in individual relationships. In all of these battles, wars, and struggles, power manifests itself as a relation of forces.

According to Foucault, power is not something that is acquired, seized, or shared, but is exercised from innumerable points in the social hierarchy; it lives only in relationships and should thus not be equated with – or reduced to – a concrete capacity or property. Foucault shares naturalism's vision of a human world that is saturated with power: "It seems to me that power *is* 'always already there', that one is never outside it" (*PK* 141). Thus the world is a place of perpetual struggle that should not be reduced to the binary struggle between two big subjects – the bourgeoisie versus the proletariat, for example – but instead is a place in which "[w]e all fight each other" (*PK* 208). Emphasizing the omnipresence of power, Foucault radically opposes a traditional view that links power to prohibition, to the big "No," a power that is seen as essentially repressive and negative.

This refusal to attach power to an "absolute Subject," such as "the Sovereignty of the Father, the Monarch, or the general will" (*PK* 140), leads Foucault to reject the importance of the legal apparatus in modern society. Instead, he argues, the importance of the law has been virtually displaced by a modern power that makes use of desire, pleasure, and the body, a power that works through pleasurable seduction rather than through repressive control. And yet, although naturalist fiction frequently emphasizes the predominance of the norm as an agency of power, many other naturalist works explore the power of juridical apparatuses (e.g., the power of laws denying a woman an abortion, or the law's power of taking a person's life, dramatized in Dreiser's *An American Tragedy*). Given these contradictions, it should come as no surprise that McNay has challenged the Foucauldian thesis that "[w]e have entered a phase of juridical regression" (*HS* 144). From a feminist perspective, McNay has emphasized the importance of the legal framework for women's emancipation in the struggle for equal rights: "Whilst not underestimating the discrepancy that often exists between formal and substantive rights, many freedoms have often derived from changes within the law, the most obvious example being the granting of female suffrage. Other legally established rights, such as the possibility for a woman to have an abortion, cannot be dismissed simply as another example of control over the body; rather, it has given women significantly more freedom in the control of their lives" (*FF* 45).

In twentieth-century naturalist fiction, the question of legal rights is addressed in a characteristic form. Many women are shown to claim for themselves the rights that males enjoy, so that in numerous ways their emancipatory strategies consist in appropriating the dominant masculine discourse in an effort to change social reality. Such discursive appropriations imply new freedoms for women but at the same time often reflect the fact that the women remain entrapped in the larger network of power. From a Foucauldian perspective, it could be argued that granting women particular rights at a time when juridical powers become less important constitutes modern power's clever strategy of glossing over the fact that women's bodies are controlled by a much more sophisticated forms of power. After all, Foucault is clearly opposed to an equation of power with enslavement: "Where the determining factors saturate the whole there is no relationship of power; slavery is not a power relationship when man [*sic*] is in chains."[22] Thus by its very definition, power always includes spaces of freedom: "It would not be possible for power relations to exist without points of insubordination, which, by definition, are means of escape."

Foucault, furthermore, distinguishes between different levels of power relationships within the social network, whereby the space for freedom differs in various types of relationships. The type of power relationship that guarantees a maximum of freedom for the partners involved consists in "strategic games" between partners, with each individual trying to "control, to delimit the liberty of others." The opposite type of relationship is characterized by "domination," or "what we ordinarily call power," since the space of freedom is greatly reduced, or can be said to exist only unilaterally. The third type, what Foucault calls the techniques of government, is somewhere in between "the games of power and the states of domination," allowing for more freedom, play, and reversal than a relationship of domination.[23]

Contradicting Jean-Paul Sartre's notion that "power is evil," Foucault describes power in terms of strategic games, manoeuvrings, and tactical shiftings. Since power is exercised from numerous points, there is no real binary division or opposition between rulers and ruled; indeed, as earlier noted, power relations could not exist without points of insubordination: "Every power relationship implies, at least *in potentia*, a strategy of struggle, in which the two forces are not superimposed, do not lose their specific nature, or do not finally become confused. Each constitutes for the other a kind of permanent limit, a point of possible reversal."[24] Although points of resistance are present everywhere in the power network, resistance will not automatically change the nature of the power relationship, but is really intrinsic to that same power relationship. Thus patriarchy can shift into matriarchy, but this is only a reversal of power relationships that can easily be reversed again: the power principle itself does not necessarily change.

---

22 Michel Foucault, "Afterword: The Subject and Power," Dreyfus and Rabinow 221; following citation 225.

23 Foucault, "The Ethic of Care for the Self," 19–20.

24 Foucault, "The Subject and Power," 225.

Naturalism is full of such reversals of power that do not challenge the principle of the power relation itself: the *femme fatale* destroys males only to be destroyed herself; the male victimizer becomes victimized himself. Thus the discourses of resistance in naturalist fiction have to be examined in the larger framework of power. Also, naturalism has often presented itself in oppositional, even revolutionary, terms: as a leftist literature in a bourgeois culture, as a literature of social engagement in a period of *laissez faire* capitalism, and as an aesthetic *enfant terrible* in a culture of gentility. Foucault and feminism – with their different (even conflicting) emphases – force us to examine both naturalism's function as an oppositional force and the limitations of this opposition. With this in mind, let us return to David Baguley's emphasis on the vision of "entropy" in European naturalist fiction: "At the heart of this entropic vision of naturalist literature is the real crisis of human values, a recurrent thematics of disintegration, of spent energies, of crumbling moral and social structures."[25] This entropic vision should not mislead the reader into defining naturalist fiction too quickly as a destabilizing force. With the help of Foucauldian and feminist theories, this study will emphasize that naturalist fiction is defined by its ideological contradictions: its resisting impulses and its opposite function as the arm of power; its inscription of desire as a driving force of consumer culture and as a force that often moves beyond the boundaries of the systems of order that wish to contain it.

The ideological contradictions at the heart of naturalism are mirrored in its aesthetic and generic form, best exemplified in Grove's fiction. E. D. Blodgett has observed that Grove's works follow a comic structure, in which the female characters rebel against institutional constraints, challenging a rigid patriarchal "law," represented by comic blocking characters. Despite this comic set-up, however, the women's rebellion is always aborted: "the disruption never leads to the advent of a new order, but is at best frustrated comedy," whereby "all value-systems hang in suspense."[26] David Baguley's generic insights into naturalism's privileged endings illustrate a similar point: the deprivation ending, the banal ending, and the sententious ending all emphasize the denial of any positive "liberating" (or truly comic) solution to the problems presented. These frustrating endings reflect naturalism's frequent grounding in two contradictory ideological impulses: the oppositional, resisting impulse generally articulated in the challenging of class and gender boundaries;

25　Baguley, "The Nature of Naturalism," 26.

26　E. D. Blodgett, *Configuration: Essays on Canadian Literatures* (Toronto: Essays on Canadian Writing Press, 1982) 147.

and the opposite impulse, articulated in a desire for order and regulation that places the new woman or the rebelling daughter back into the straitjacket of confining norms.

By claiming for themselves the right to write about sexuality, many naturalists challenged middle-class norms at the same time as they paradoxically consolidated their position as bourgeois, middle-class writers. Dreiser and Grove worked hard to overcome their *petit-bourgeois* background, reflecting in their autobiographical writing a fear, if not a paranoia, of sinking into a proletarianized lower class that they had fought so hard to escape. Naturalism's entropic vision with its challenging of systems of order also has an underside of paranoid fear: fear of women's sexual anarchy and dominance, of sexual disease, of proletarianization. These fears in turn give birth to an apparently insatiable desire for order inscribed in naturalism in a variety of forms: Zola's deterministic laws, Arno Holz's mathematical formula for naturalism, as well as the inscription of systems, categories, hierarchies, and taxonomies within naturalism's texual boundaries. These aesthetic, structural, and formal aspects underscore naturalism's desire for order. This "schizophrenic" oscillation between disorder and order causes Restif to introduce the anarchic prostitute in his fiction but also to write a treatise on how to regulate and control prostitution by turning it into a "normalized" social institution. Similarly, Dreiser's Carrie Meeber is not punished for her sexual transgressions but controlled in a much more effective way: she is seduced into voluntary submission to society's norms.

Just as Foucault denies that an ultimate liberation is possible, naturalism illustrates a very similar point. While naturalistic works have a "propensity to break through the constraints of frameworks,"[27] they seldom advocate a complete revolutionary reversal of power relations and even less the removal of forces of order. Insisting on the quiet triumph of the reality principle, naturalism demonstrates that the notion of an existential (Sartrian) freedom is an illusion, emphasizing with Foucault that there is no "ultimate" liberation: human beings can only resist in the power network in which they are placed, but this resistance will eventually be appropriated by the dominant power principle. Conversely, naturalist fiction rarely plunges into extreme irony – or the "unincremental repetition" of absurdity. Naturalism always presents a touch of social criticism and encourages a resisting position by keeping up a "realistic" hope for possibilities of social change.

---

27 Yves Chevrel, *Le Naturalisme* (Paris: Presses Universitaires de France, 1982) 93.

II. Dreiser, Naturalism and the New Woman

4

Sister Carrie:
Sexualizing the Docile Body

As a prolific producer of sexualized body-images, Carrie Meeber marks in American naturalist fiction the economic and cultural dawn of the twentieth century. Turning its back on the nineteenth-century agricultural economy, Dreiser's first novel does more than just reflect the spirit of a transitional age: it explores the deployment of sexualized power in the modern consumer and popular culture. The cosmopolitan world of *Sister Carrie* (1900) is one of casual sexuality that never leads to any permanent alliance in such forms as marriage and family. Indeed, Carrie's family truly vanishes from the textual web. The novel opens with the protagonist's train ride into Chicago, through which "the threads which bound her so lightly to girlhood and home were irretrievably broken."[1] Travelling from Chicago to New York and, as an actress, from stage to stage, Carrie Meeber remains in transit for the rest of the novel; in her

---

1 Theodore Dreiser, *Sister Carrie* (New York: Modern Library, 1961) 1. Further references will appear in the text abbreviated *SC*.

rocking chair, she is in motion even when she sits. This association with perpetual movement is appropriate because Carrie's body is an icon of change. When she steps out of the chorus to become a glamorous stage actress, she also emerges as the female equivalent of the American self-made man: she breaks through class boundaries, moving from her working class background to the top of the social hierarchy. Continually in movement, without any true attachments, Carrie's body is the perfect icon for the twentieth-century consumer culture.

Dreiser's radical questioning of traditional forms of alliance, to be sure, has its roots in French naturalism. As early as the eighteenth century, *Le Paysan perverti* shows a brother-sister couple undergoing their misadventures in the city; they are separated from their parents who are left to mourn the follies of their children. Zola's Nana is genetically linked to her parents, especially to her mother Gervaise's propensity for sensual "weakness," but she is really a metaphorical orphan, growing up as a neglected street urchin. In *Au Bonheur des Dames*, Denise, another orphan, arrives in Paris in charge of her younger brother. The family alliance is frequently threatened in nineteenth-century naturalism; Dreiser, however, goes a step further and initiates the twentieth century with a radical erasure of typical forms of kinship in his protagonist's life. The novel's title, then, is highly ironic, suggesting a family alliance that is virtually absent in the novel. Although Carrie's first lover, Charles Drouet, introduces himself at one point playfully as her brother, this role is the ironic mask of a womanizer who knows no loyalties.

Indeed, marriage, kinship, and a permanent name are foreign concepts to Dreiser's new woman. Carrie Meeber's two "marriages" are fakes – the one to Drouet is a mere facade, the second one to George Hurstwood is formally contracted, but is a mock wedding since Hurstwood has not even been legally divorced from his first wife. Moreover, Carrie's continual changing of names – from Caroline Meeber to Carrie, Mrs. Drouet, Mrs. Wheeler, and Carrie Madenda – reveal her lack of, or disregard for, any permanent kinship alliance. Just as she changes her names, so she changes her homes, moving from Minnie Hanson's home in Chicago to Drouet's, then to Hurstwood's in New York, only to leave Hurstwood and move into a tenement apartment with her friend Lola, and finally to settle in the Waldorf Astoria hotel, a home that subverts the very idea of a home. Carrie is truly alone, even when she is with other people. If attached, she only feels this attachment through its absence, as when she says good-bye to Drouet after having just met him on her train ride into Chicago: "She felt something lost to her when he moved away. When he disappeared she felt his absence thoroughly. With her sister she was much alone, a lone figure in a tossing, thoughtless sea" (*SC* 11).

In the light of Foucault's conception of power, this erasure of family alliances is no coincidence in a novel concerned with the sexualization of power in a modern consumer culture. In *The History of Sexuality*, Michel Foucault opposes the deployment of alliances – defined as "a system of marriage, of fixation and development of kinship ties, of transmission of names and possessions" (*HS* 106) – to Western society's deployment of sexuality, "a new apparatus which was superimposed on the previous one, and which, without completely supplanting the latter, helped to reduce its importance" (*HS* 106). Although the system of alliance and the deployment of sexuality have in common that they connect up with a circuit of partners, Foucault contrasts the two systems term by term: "The deployment of alliance is built around a system of rules defining the permitted and the forbidden, the licit and the illicit, whereas the deployment of sexuality operates according to mobile, polymorphous, and contingent techniques of power" (*HS* 106). Whereas the deployment of alliance is attached to the law and statutes, the deployment of sexuality engenders a continual extension of areas and forms of control and is concerned with the body's sensations and pleasures. Foucault summarizes the difference between the two systems as follows: "Lastly, if the deployment of alliance is firmly tied to the economy due to the role it can play in the transmission or circulation of wealth, the deployment of sexuality is linked to the economy through numerous and subtle relays, the main one of which, however, is the body – the body that produces and consumes" (*HS* 106–7).

It is Carrie's visible body (as both product of the consumer economy and specularized object of consumption) that becomes a field on which the city inscribes its network of desire and power. Disrupting forms of alliance between parents and children, brother and sister, husband and wife, Dreiser's city is a deeply sexualized space that takes hold of the individual's material body, seducing him or her into pleasurable submission in an expanding economy of consumer goods, so that "the characters in the novel are caught within the circumference of [the city's] materiality."[2]

The womanizer, with his "insatiable love of variable pleasure" (*SC* 4) and with his lack of deep loyalties, allegorizes both the erasure of forms

_____

2 Richard Lehan, "The City, the Self, and Narrative Discourse," *New Essays on "Sister Carrie,"* ed. Donald Pizer (Cambridge: Cambridge UP, 1991) 67.

of alliance and the deployment of seductive controls that take hold of Carrie as soon as she enters the city. When Carrie meets Charles Drouet, the narrator establishes a metonymical connection between his role as a "masher" and the city as a seductive magnet: "The city has its cunning wiles, no less than the infinitely smaller and more human tempter" (*SC* 2). Insisting that the "gleam of a thousand lights is often as effective as the persuasive light in a wooing and fascinating eye" (*SC* 2), the narrator simultaneously embeds Carrie's seduction by Drouet in a language of power: "Now she felt that she had yielded something – he, that he had gained a victory" (*SC* 8). And yet, while Carrie is seduced even on her way into Chicago, her allegorical "fall" also initiates her eventual triumph in the city. Just as Carrie is willing to "yield" to Charles Drouet's seduction, in order to triumph over him in the end, so her economic and social success is based on her willingness to "yield" her body to the city's seductive embrace.

If, for Dreiser, the womanizer represents the city's seductive "penetration" of the human body, the actress cum prostitute represents this material body as a specularized object of desire. In a newspaper article titled "The City," written in 1896, Dreiser evokes the big city in female terms, presenting it as the illusory fulfillment of all dreams, as a fictional cornucopia of pleasure, beauty, and sex in a framework of moral laxity. He represents the city in the figure of the naturalist prostitute, a figure who appeals to the pleasures of the eye and titillates the scopophilic voyeur: "Like a sinful Magdalen the city decks herself gayly [*sic*], fascinating all by her garments of scarlet and silk, awing by her jewels and perfumes, when in truth there lies hid beneath these a torn and miserable heart, and a soiled and unhappy conscience."[3] Mary Magdalene, to be sure, is the traditional icon of the "virtuous prostitute" with the compassionate heart, who "holds up a comforting mirror to those who sin and sin again, and promises joy to human frailty."[4] Dreiser's analogy between the city and Mary Magdalene fits the title heroine of *Sister Carrie*, who innocently (and almost unknowingly) leaves victims in her wake.

"Yet amid all, men starve," Dreiser continues in "The City," deliberately disrupting the initial image of peace and compassion by cataloguing the "misery," the "hunger," the "isolation and loneliness," and "the

---

3   Theodore Dreiser, "The City," *Theodore Dreiser: A Selection of Uncollected Prose,* ed. Donald Pizer (Detroit: Wayne State UP, 1977) 97.

4   Marina Warner, *Alone of All Her Sex: The Myth and the Cult of the Virgin Mary* (New York: Vintage, 1983) 235.

rummaging in garbage cans" of the "wild-eyed shrunken outcast," who lives in the midst of the city glamour. Like George Hurstwood in *Sister Carrie*, who ends as a Bowery bum, the suffering outcast in this earlier article is a "wretched, dwarfed specimen of masculine humanity," and thus Dreiser evokes the image of the male as metaphorically "castrated" by the female city. Here, the earlier image of the city-prostitute inevitably slips from the compassionate Magdalene to the Whore of Babylon, who carries death already in her body.[5] The city turns into a naturalistic female threat, an aggressive freak, a destructive monster; she is the man-destroyer, a paralyzing Medusa figure, whose seductive and destructive aspects are unified in the image of the city-prostitute, a figure who may turn around to hunt and haunt the unsuspecting newcomer. Given the female city's potential for destruction, it is a space where "man" can survive only by entering into it like a conqueror or like the ancient dragon slayer Perseus. For this city-dragon slayer, "looking" is one of the weapons to slay the dragon, or, as Peter Conrad puts it in his discussion of Dreiser's own experience of New York, "seeing the city is for Dreiser an acquisition of power over it, a visual annexation of terrain."[6]

Indeed, if Dreiser's naturalist universe is ruled by the forces of desire and pleasure that inscribe themselves on Carrie's body as soon as she arrives, it is also ruled by a Foucauldian "eye of power" that "penetrates" her body and ensures her "yielding" to the city's economy. Just as Mark Seltzer reminds us that realist fiction is "preeminently concerned with seeing,"[7] so in Dreiser's big cities gazes are not only omnipresent but are explored as a sophisticated technique of sexualized power. Inscribed in the city's architecture, the emphasis on seeing, the eye, and the visual permeates the novel. Dreiser's Chicago and New York use daylight to increase visibility by incorporating glass in the city's architecture. These windows give the appearance of social transparency, of breaking down walls and barriers, but, in fact, they increase the invisible barriers between inside and outside, multiplying and intensifying the points of

---

5 Dreiser, "The City," 98.

6 Peter Conrad, *The Art of the City: Views and Versions of New York* (New York: Oxford UP, 1984) 179. Conrad points to the female quality of Dreiser's city, albeit in a different sense from the one outlined above: "Dreiser's city is ruled over by a Darwinian matriarch, an indiscriminately fecund 'Mother Nature,' who spawns (as Eugene in *The 'Genius'* marvels) 'such seething masses of people; such whirlpools of life!'" (183).

7 Mark Seltzer, "*The Princess Casamassima*: Realism and the Fantasy of Surveillance," *American Realism: New Essays*, ed. Eric J. Sundquist (Baltimore & London: Johns Hopkins UP, 1982) 111.

power in the city by creating new hierarchies, intensifying the possibilities for disciplinary power. For example, Carrie, looking for work in Chicago, is daunted by these big windows and the gazes she suspects behind, gazes that magnify her own sense of insignificance. As a newcomer to the city, she enters a store only when she feels she is unobserved, and she is eager to disappear in the crowd, into the anonymity of the "not-to-be-seen," when she exits. Like the prisoner in Bentham's Panopticon, who cannot see the supervisor's eye but feels its omnipresence, so Carrie does not understand the working of the city's power. For her, the city is "the mysterious city"; its streets are "wall-lined mysteries to her," whose power networks escape her understanding.

Foucault describes this panoptic modality in *Discipline and Punish*. Applied to the whole social framework, the principle of Bentham's prison model implies an utopian dream of absolute visibility, absolute legibility, and the power of the collective and anonymous gaze on each individual: "Because, without any physical instrument other than architecture and geometry, [the panoptic schema] acts directly on individuals; it gives 'power of mind over mind'" (*DP* 206). In the social framework, the ultimate effect of panopticism is self-policing; everyone becomes a self-supervisor. Dreiser illustrates this (Foucauldian) rupture between the inflexible eye that watches the dungeon, on the one hand, and the ingenuity of the panoptic city, on the other. Anticipating Foucault's theory, Dreiser opposes the panoptic city with repressive, archaic dungeon spaces that fill Carrie with nausea and boredom.

Indeed, Carrie is the first in a long line of Dreiserian characters who are forced to descend into metaphorical dungeons. Like Clyde Griffiths's humiliating descent into the "shrinking room" of his uncle's collar factory in *An American Tragedy*, Carrie's entrance into the world of economy marks a "descent" into the nineteenth-century naturalist world of a dimly lit shoe factory. Here, not only is her enjoyment of bodily pleasure suspended, but her body is "tortured" in monotonous and menial work: "Her hands began to ache at the wrists and then in the fingers, and towards the last she seemed one mass of dull, complaining muscles, fixed in an eternal position and performing a single mechanical movement which became more and more distasteful, until at last it was absolutely nauseating" (*SC* 42–43). Yet Dreiser also locates the repressive power of the "dungeon" in the private domestic space, as when Carrie lives with her sister Minnie Hanson in Chicago or with Hurstwood in her New York apartment. Satisfying the most basic needs, these domestic dungeons give a sense of security to Carrie, but they are also dark, closed, claustrophobic spaces that evoke stagnation, depression, and a sense of being buried alive, so that the body oscillates between two extremes, lethargy and rebellion. Unlike the naturalist fiction of the nineteenth century (e.g., Zola's *L'Assommoir*), *Sister Carrie* quickly "liberates" its female protagonist from this metaphorical inferno. The "eye" of the "dungeon ward" in *Sister Carrie* is not very effective, revealing such repressive relations to be archaic. Carrie has no trouble leaving the Hanson and the Hurstwood dungeons in Chicago and New York: she simply leaves little notes behind.

The factory, then, is only a backdrop that allows Dreiser to highlight the contrasting reality of the panoptic city, that is, the public city-spaces: the stores, the streets, the saloons, the theatres, and the hotels, spaces where the private becomes public and where life is imbued with pleasure and desire, not repression. Chicago and New York – Dreiser's celebrated New World cities – not only energize the movement of author, narrator, and characters with their raw, sensualized drive; they also imbue the newcomer to the city with a sense that it is right, and even necessary, to base one's life on a principle that can be summarized in just two words: "I want." *Sister Carrie* represents the city as a space of desire, in which the darkness of the dungeon is swept away by a flood of everlasting light, a space that conquers the blackness of the night with lamps, lanterns, and electricity. Thus, Dreiser's fiction follows the tradition of Zola's *Au Bonheur des Dames*, which contrasts the dimly lit, old-fashioned boutiques with the "foyer d'ardente lumière" of Mouret's newly emerging Parisian department store, which not only exploits but creates new desires. Mouret's *Au Bonheur des Dames* is based on the principle of Foucault's Panopticon, bathing the merchandise in light through new architectural designs: "Partout on avait gagné de l'espace, l'air et la lumière entraient librement, le public circulait à l'aise" (*AB* 193–94). Similarly, Dreiser highlights the architectural and spatial transformations that create the Chicagoan Panopticon, in which power relationships are multiplied and invested with pleasure, not repression. The panoptic city is like the mythical Argus, endowed with hundreds of eyes, which never sleep and never tire.

Illustrating the mechanisms of sexualized power, Chicago's best saloon, Fitzgerald and Moy's, is presented as such a panoptic microcosm, shining out "with a blaze of incandescent lights, held in handsome chandeliers" and refracted in the polished surfaces of the bar and the glassware (*SC* 48). The appeal of this "lighted place" is such that the narrator muses: "It must be that a strange bundle of passions and vague desires give rise to such a curious social institution or it would not be" (*SC* 52). Indeed, the club's magnetic attraction relies on creating and perpetuating social hierarchies in moments saturated with sensualized power: "Drouet, for one, was lured as much by his longing for pleasure as by his desire to shine amongst his betters" (*SC* 52). Amidst the sparks of Fitzgerald and Moy's, every customer receives a finely tuned and graded greeting from its manager, Hurstwood, a gesture that assigns a social hierarchy even to the socially prominent. In this panoptic universe, the "eye of power" wraps itself around the individual body in a seductive embrace. Indeed, the narrator's language describing this power principle is intertwined with overt sexual tropes, as when he likens the club to "a strange, glittering night-flower, odour-yielding, insect-drawing, insect-infested rose of pleasure" (*SC* 53). In this club "for men only," the sensual attraction consists in recognizing in each other's body one's personal social status; here, the male gaze, inspecting the body of another male, is deeply eroticized. Hurstwood, "dressed in excellent tailored suits of imported goods, a solitaire ring, a fine blue diamond in his tie, a striking vest of some new pattern, and a watch-chain of solid gold," attracts Drouet's attention: "Drouet immediately conceived a notion of him as being some one worth knowing" (*SC* 49). What is sexualized in this homoerotic specular encounter is the principle of power that connects the two males; the "lure" is sparked by Drouet's recognition of Hurstwood as a socially superior person, whose acquaintance might be useful, while Hurstwood enjoys an eroticized pleasure of confirming his superior status in Drouet's presence.

Chicago's panoptic universe takes hold of Carrie's body in a similar fashion, by absorbing her into the social hierarchy in such moments of specular scrutiny. According to Foucault, the panoptic modality of power relies on "hierarchical surveillance, continuous registration, perpetual assessment and classification" (*DP* 220), which is guaranteed through the anonymous, social gaze on the individual. When entering a Chicagoan department store for the first time, Carrie recognizes in the dismissive gaze of the female sales clerk "a keen analysis of her own position" (*SC* 25) and becomes immediately aware of her shortcomings and lacks, a recognition that, in turn, stirs up the desire to be in this shopgirl's "higher" position. In Dreiser's world the "fixing" of a person's social identity takes place through such acts of mutual inspection, which are imbued with both masochistic and sadistic pleasures. In this naturalist universe, identity is based on a system of difference, not on an innate, unchangeable identity. "The heart understands when it is confronted with contrasts" (*SC* 360), the narrator formulates, thus confirming that the construction and perpetuation of the social hierarchy of power relies on such moments of social interaction, not on innate physiology. Deeply rooted in desire, such moments are imbued with pleasure and pain.

Moving beyond the conventions of nineteenth-century hereditary determinism, Dreiser's naturalism gives birth to a humanity that finds

itself on the uneasy borderline between desire and free will: "Our civili-
sation is still in a middle stage, scarcely beast, in that it is no longer
guided by instinct; scarcely human, in that it is not yet wholly guided
by reason" (*SC* 83). Although in some instances the narrator conflates
instincts with desire, *Sister Carrie* reveals how much the force and direction of desire are subject to cultural influences. Indeed, the treatment of
desire in *Sister Carrie* in many ways confirms the neo-Freudian theory of
Jacques Lacan. According to the French psychoanalyst, desire is not innate as instinctual needs are, but is a cultural phenomenon that has its
ultimate roots in a fantasy, and therefore distinguishes itself from need
by its "paradoxical, deviant, erratic, eccentric, even scandalous character."[8] Desire is by nature insatiable and self-perpetuating, unlike the instinctual needs, such as hunger and thirst, which can be easily satisfied
once the proper object is found. Laplanche and Pontalis have succinctly
summarized Lacan's position by making the following distinctions:

> Need is directed toward a specific object and is satisfied by it. Demands
> are formulated and addressed to others; where they are still aimed at an
> object, this is not essential to them, since the articulated demand is essen-
> tially a demand for love. Desire appears in the rift which separates need
> and demand; it cannot be reduced to need since, by definition, it is not a
> relation to a real object independent of the subject but a relation to a
> phantasy.[9]

In the cultural framework, then, desire is transformed into innumerable demands without ever exhausting itself, a phenomenon that has
become the basis of the success of modern consumer capitalism. Creating continually new, desirable objects for its customers, this economy
will never be able to "fulfill" the customer completely and thus in fact
perpetuates the desire for buying, perpetuates the chase for the next
object that gives the illusion of being the ultimate key to satisfaction.

Émile Zola, to be sure, was the first to expose the power principle
behind the sexualized appeal of consumer goods in the modern mass
market economy. His characterization of Octave Mouret appropriately
interweaves the language of power with the language of pleasure: the
personification of Mephistophelian seduction ("Il était la séduction"
[*AB* 304]), "Mouret enveloppait tout le sexe de la même caresse" (*AB* 34).
Describing modern power's use of sexuality, Foucault uses very similar

---

8 *Écrits: A Selection*, trans. Alan Sheridan (New York & London: Norton, 1977) 286.

9 Jean Laplanche and J. B. Pontalis, *The Language of Psycho-Analysis*, trans. Donald
   Nicholson-Smith (New York: Norton, 1973) 483.

terms: "The power which thus took charge of sexuality set about con-
tacting bodies, caressing them with its eyes, intensifying areas, electri-
fying surfaces, dramatizing troubled moments" (*HS* 44). With his
"passion de vaincre la femme" (*AB* 194), Mouret conquers women by
examining and inspecting their bodies and by touching and caressing
them with new merchandise, designed not to satisfy but to awaken and
inscribe on their bodies continually new "feminine" desires and pleasures, which simultaneously engender new sites of power.

Similarly, it is the Chicagoan department store – in 1884 "in its earli-
est form of successful operation" (*SC* 23) – that appeals, caresses and
awakens Carrie's desire and takes control in shaping her body. Just as
the newly installed display windows increase the desire of those outside to be inside, by confronting them with their lack, their not having,
their being less, so the city's power takes hold of Carrie by tempting her
with merchandise behind glass. Once Carrie has entered the department
store, her body is "penetrated" by new seductive voices (that echo
Drouet's voice from the novel's opening): "'My dear,' said the lace collar she secured from Partridge's, 'I fit you beautifully; don't give me
up.' 'Ah, such little feet,' said the leather of the soft new shoes; 'how
effectively I cover them. What a pity they should ever want my aid'"
(*SC* 111). This animation of the clothes with cajoling voices is a clever
technique to emphasize how much they are invested with an interiorized
desire. To describe Carrie's voluntary submission to these forces, Dreiser
uses an appropriate double discourse. Evoking a naturalist sense of inevitability to emphasize the merchandise's irresistible power, his language also underscores a reality of free will, suggesting that there is a
space of freedom in this pleasurable submission. For example, after becoming Drouet's mistress, Carrie "could possibly have conquered the
fear of hunger and gone back" to a life of hard work, "but spoil her
appearance? – be old-clothed and poor-appearing? – never!" (*SC* 111–
12). This space of freedom, in turn, confirms the Foucauldian idea that
power includes and even produces forms of resistance. In Dreiser's naturalist universe, power never implies slavery but always entails the subject's complicitous submission to the promise of pleasure and desire.

While Dreiser's treatment of consumer seduction echoes Zola's (and
anticipates Grove's) emphasis on compulsive female shopping, Dreiser's
refuses to attach this desire to a psychological dysfunction. Zola, for
example, explores kleptomania as a logical extension of the new consumer economy that produces new types of "voleuses," among them
"les voleuses de profession," "les femmes enceintes dont les vols se
spécialisaient," and thirdly, "les voleuses par manie, une perversion du

désir, une névrose nouvelle qu'un aliéniste avait classée, en y constatant le résultat aigu de la tentation exercée par les grands magasins" (*AB* 209). Grove makes a similar association between shopping and psychological disease when, for Fanny Essler, the desire for clothes becomes more important than eating. In one scene, she impulsively buys a pair of gloves and then realizes not only that she has spent her last money but also that the desired object, once it has become a possession, ceases to be desirable. For Zola's and Grove's female shoppers, compulsive shopping is rooted in a repressed or frustrated sensual desire, which leaves the customers as unsatisfied as the sexual act itself. For Zola and Grove, then, compulsive shopping is an act of *Ersatzbefriedigung*, whereas for Dreiser the pleasures of shopping are not *ersatz*, not secondary, but equal in importance to other sexual activities. If anything, Dreiser makes an effort to "normalize" the sartorial drive that stimulates Carrie into action.

The difference between Zola's conception of sexualized power and Dreiser's is even more significant in light of Foucault's theory on panopticism and power. Zola, significantly, describes Octave Mouret as "le roi absolu" in his Parisian consumer kingdom, as a figure who holds all the strings from above and whose eye sees all: "Mouret se planta, seul et debout, au bord de la rampe du hall. De là, il dominait le magasin, ayant autour de lui les rayons de l'entresol, plongeant sur les rayons du rez-de-chaussée" (*AB* 83–84). Placed in the store's strategic centre, Mouret appears like an eroticized centre of power: he is the originator of the store, the head behind its architectural design, and the head of a hierarchy of control that consists of a number of *chefs*, *sous-chefs*, and *inspecteurs* who all report back to Mouret. He is a man endowed with "le génie de la mécanique administrative" (*AB* 37). Zola does not even shrink from evoking the language of religion, whereby the department store itself becomes a modern "cathedral," with Mouret dominating over the different *rayons* as an all-seeing eye of god.

In contrast, Dreiser's conception of power is more "Foucauldian." There is no "monarchical" centre of power in *Sister Carrie*, nor do any of the characters possess Mouret's *génie* or omniscient eye. Whereas Mouret's position of power evokes the supervisor's position in the Panopticon, Foucault and Dreiser refuse to present a form of power with a capital *P*. In an interview reprinted in *Foucault Live*, Foucault highlights this point, revising his earlier position as put forward in *Discipline and Punish*: "In reference to the reduction of my analyses to that simplistic figure which is the metaphor of the Panopticon, ... it is easy to show that the analyses of power which I have made cannot at all be reduced to this figure."[10] Dreiser's naturalist fiction illustrates the same point. There is no supervisor nor a single "eye of god" in *Sister Carrie*, suggesting that there is no undivided or ultimate locus of power. Just as Dreiser distanced himself in his naturalist fiction from his religious childhood beliefs in an all-powerful god, so he distanced himself from the idea of a unified figure of power.

Indeed, power in *Sister Carrie* does not emanate from one fixed locus but is omnipresent and widely dispersed in the social body, attaching itself to many different processes and appearing in continually new forms. "Power is not omnipotent or omniscient," but it is often "blind," writes Foucault, arguing that because of this "blindness" power is forced to devise continually new, heterogeneous strategies of control: "If it is true that so many power relationships have been developed, so many systems of control, so many forms of surveillance, it is precisely because power was always impotent."[11] In contrast to Zola's emphasis on Octave Mouret's powerful personal control, Dreiser makes his readers repeatedly aware of the limitations of those in a position of power. These limits are exemplified by Charles Drouet, who is, significantly, set up as a mediocre, banal character, just as Carrie's second seducer, Hurstwood, is confronted with his inevitable downfall after becoming caught in the city's intricate network. Likewise, Carrie herself, who eventually triumphs over the two men, is often described as blind, while her body is suggestive of sexualized docility. In contrast to Zola's personification of power in Octave Mouret, Dreiser uses Carrie's continually changing body to represent the mobile forces of power, to describe how the docile body becomes an anchor and a tool for power relations.

Much of *Sister Carrie* is devoted to the birth-giving of Carrie's body in power relationships, whereby the absence of any form of permanent kinship in Carrie's life allows Dreiser to highlight the construction of this character through norms and social practices. Carrie is not genetically determined, as Nana is, nor is she psychologized, as Grove's Fanny Essler or some of Dreiser's later characters are; instead, the technologies of her self-construction have a Foucauldian ring. Foucault has suggested that human bodies are inevitably constructed in the social network: "it is not that the beautiful totality of the individual is amputated, repressed, altered by our social order, it is rather that the individual is carefully *fabricated* in it, according to a whole technique of forces and bodies" (*DP* 217; emphasis added). Adopting these social technologies, Carrie creates her

---

10 Michel Foucault, "Clarifications on the Question of Power," *Foucault Live* (Interviews, 1966-84), ed. Sylvère Lotringer (New York: Semiotext[e], 1989) 183.

11 Foucault, "Clarifications on the Question of Power," 183, 184.

body systematically through daily exercises, not so much by internalizing but by inscribing on her body the signs of what society recognizes as feminine "grace." Imitating the "graceful carriage" of the railroad treasurer's daughter, Carrie learns to use "her feet less heavily" (*SC* 116); she purses her lips and gives her head a little toss and thus gains the first distinctions as an apprentice in the *école des femmes* of American society. In her poststructuralist feminist theory, Kornelia Hauser has demonstrated how much such body- and self-constructions entail the subject's "normalization "and "docility." Hauser explains that, in a consumer culture, women orient "themselves toward the same standard" at the same time that they "individualize" themselves as "different" from each other on the basis of the same norm. Thus, at the same time that women buy into these individualizing norms, they become also thoroughly sexualized and "normalized."[12] Carrie Meeber is born through the very technologies that subject her in the social network, so that her body and subjectivity are produced in and through power. Power anchors itself in Carrie's body, penetrates it, and achieves its docility, and through this very docility also turns her sexualized body into a new tool of seduction. Constructed through the city's myriad of sartorial and behavioural discourses and practices, Carrie's body eventually becomes a living advertisement for the modern consumer culture.

It is this bodily complicity with her consumer culture that has led Walter Benn Michaels to identify Carrie's "insatiable" body as "the body of desire in capitalism."[13] It is her desire that makes Carrie survive in her society, Michaels argues, while Hurstwood, who has stopped desiring and lives only to fulfill his basic needs, finally dies. Yet Dreiser's narrative does not unequivocally support the desire that gives birth to Carrie's body, as Michaels's argument suggests. After all, desire is also what subjugates the female body, as Dreiser demonstrates through the microcosmic power play that regulates the economy of desire in *Sister Carrie*. In *Deceit, Desire, and the Novel* (1965) René Girard has suggested the model of "triangular desire" to indicate that desire and the object of desire are never directly linked but are mediated by a third agent, a model or a rival.[14] It is this mediation of others in directing desire that

---

12 Hauser 198.

13 Walter Benn Michaels, "Fictitious Dealing: A Reply to Leo Bersani," *Critical Inquiry* 8 (August 1981): 169.

14 René Girard, *Deceit, Desire, and the Novel: Self and Other in Literary Structure*, trans. Yvonne Freccero (Baltimore & London: Johns Hopkins UP, 1976) 1–52.

creates relationships of power. Discussing the *nouveaux magazins* in Zola's *Au Bonheur des Dames,* David Bell has pointed out that in the realm of fashion the subject's needs and desires are determined by a "collective other": "the individual subject never buys a fashion commodity for its intrinsic concrete worth or usefulness, but only because that commodity has been designated as desirable by the other."[15]

Thus it should come as no surprise that underneath the narrator's overt eulogy of desire, Dreiser's *Sister Carrie* presents a second, more critical voice by emphasizing that Carrie's desire for clothes is not her "own" desire, but is always already mediated in her society's (male) power structures. In *Sister Carrie,* it is the male characters who play the role of mediators by initiating the protagonist into the realm of fashion. On the train into Chicago, Charles Drouet insinuates all the objects that will become desirable for Carrie: clothing, the theatre, the crowds. Drouet's cliché that Carrie reminds him of some popular actress not only becomes a desirable goal but also becomes Carrie's identity later in the novel. Insisting "upon her good looks," Drouet, like a true Pygmalion lover, quickly becomes "a good judge" and "a teacher" for Carrie the female novice: "He went on educating and wounding her, a thing rather foolish in one whose admiration for his pupil and victim was apt to grow" (*SC* 113). Drouet holds up models that indicate that Carrie is "lacking," and as a result of a newly born desire "to improve," she imitates those women that Drouet points out to her as models and thus inscribes Drouet's model of judging on her body.

But voyeurism is not really an end in itself for Drouet (nor is the model of promiscuity that Dreiser valued necessarily "feminine," as Michaels argues).[16] Drouet accompanies Carrie to the department store to fit her into new clothing, savouring one piece after the other, "feeling the set of it at the waist and eying it from a few paces with real pleasure" (*SC* 85). Drouet's pleasurable dressing of Carrie's body acts as a kind of foreplay to the sexual act itself. As the examples of Drouet, Hurstwood, Lester Cane, and Clyde Griffiths show, in Dreiser's naturalist fiction such moments of male specular pleasure are a synecdoche for masculine sexual pleasure; the male gaze is the first step in a sexual ritual that culminates

---

15 David F. Bell, *Models of Power: Politics and Economics in Zola's "Rougon Macquart"* (Lincoln: U of Nebraska P, 1988) 112–13.

16 Michaels 169.

in phallic penetration and "possession." As a promiscuous womanizer, Drouet represents himself (and his male desire) in the long series of those women he seduces, and looking is only the first step of this male form of self-representation by sexual appropriation and accumulation. Thus, the archetypal capitalist activity is linked less to the female body and female desire, than to male desire and the Don Juan masculinity in the novel. This also explains the strong, very genuine interest Drouet has in seeing Carrie "improve": every time she develops a "new" face and a "new" body, she continues to constitute a new object of seduction for Drouet, and thus allows him to reconstitute himself as an eternal seducer-appropriator through her. Dreiser's main narrative voice does not criticize this male form of "self-representation," but celebrates it: Drouet, we are told, "would remain thus young in spirit until he was dead" (*SC* 137).

The narrator, to be sure, is complicitous with his male character, even while criticizing Drouet for his crudeness and tactlessness. "Drouet was not shrewd enough to see that this was not tactful. He could not see that it would be better to make her feel that she was competing with herself, not others better than herself" (*SC* 113), the narrator argues, implicitly advocating a principle of manipulation (and normalization) that has become common practice in modern advertisement, which tells women to "improve" their own personal type and to reach their own potential by buying and using a particular product. Although most of the time the narrator sympathetically approves of what Carrie does, he is really Drouet's better double, sharing his male character's feminized, sartorial desire by helping him "dress" Carrie.

At the same time, the author also doubles himself in Carrie: she is born in the same year as Dreiser, she shares his desire for the big city, and she moves up the social ladder like Dreiser himself. Given Dreiser's Flaubertian identification with his female protagonist, the narrative-authorial participation in dressing Carrie can be seen as the author's own, safely displaced and sublimated desire for cross-dressing. Since J. C. Flugel speaks of the social curtailing of male sartorial display as "The Great Masculine Renunciation,"[17] it should come as no surprise that Dreiser simultaneously conceals and exposes his *Verkleidungstrieb* in his writing. While the authorial voice insists that a "woman should some day write the complete philosophy of clothes" (*SC* 5), Dreiser himself was a contributor to fashion magazines (like Flaubert). Overtly

---

17 Quoted in Apter 80, 82.

reinscribing the conventional naturalist boundaries between male and female (sartorial) desire, he covertly dresses himself in women's clothing in his naturalist fiction.

This *mise-en-abîme* of specular gazes and sensualized power penetrating the female body is carried even further when Carrie's body is on stage. Like Zola's Nana, Carrie Meeber triumphs in her society as an actress who lacks any real acting talent but successfully compensates her audience with "autre chose." And yet, Nana and Carrie are radically different characters, reflecting the cultural differences and shifts in the expressions of naturalist fiction in the twentieth century. To conceptualize these differences, recall how Nana appears on stage in the novel's opening chapter, dangerous in her nakedness: "Tout d'un coup, dans la bonne enfant, la femme se dressait, inquiétante, apportant le coup de folie de son sexe, ouvrant l'inconnu du désir. Nana souriait toujours, mais d'un sourire aigu de mangeuse d'hommes."[18] Nana's female sexuality is mythologized as she appears in her role of Venus, while she is simultaneously degraded as *La Mouche d'Or*. As a sexual icon she represents the danger of eros with its implicit threats of social contamination and corruption. The power relationships in *Nana* involve the sado-masochistic pattern so typical of naturalist fiction, whereby Nana is alternatively victim and victimizer, continually reversing positions of power without escaping the entrapment in power itself.

If Nana's prostitution on and off stage represents the late-nineteenth-century commercialization of life, Carrie's body as a sexualized beauty icon represents the increasingly subliminal seductiveness of Chicago's and New York's urbanite consumer economy. Dreiser aligns the new, financially independent woman with the naturalist prostitute, by emphasizing that Carrie's spectacular success on stage is built on a very subliminal fantasy of power and pleasure for the male audience. When Carrie is on stage, men project different fantasies into her body; for each she becomes something different, like the prostitute who is called on to become any feminine type her customer requires. Like a pornography-artist, she is detached from the desires she arouses in the male audience. In ironic reversal of Nana's power, Carrie gives the male spectators the illusion that she is "in need of protection," which immediately stirs up the desire to "ease her out of her misery by adding to his own delight" (*SC* 205–6). Angela Carter reminds us that this projection of female vulnerability was also Marilyn Monroe's ambivalent key to

---

18 *Nana*, in *Les Rougon-Macquart*, vol. 2, ed. Henri Mitterand (Paris: Gallimard, 1961) 1118.

success on screen; she projected "the enigmatic image of irresistibility and powerlessness, forever trapped in impotence."[19] Like America's Monroe-like Hollywood actress, Carrie the Broadway actress becomes, as Philip Gerber has put it, a "celebrity, modern style."[20]

With her moodiness and melancholia, Carrie is a convenient popular representation in a time of economic depression, labour turmoil, and unemployment. Like Madonna in our own *fin de siècle*, Carrie offers her audience a "material" body as an object of desire, for men to be desired as a sexual object, for women to be desired as an object of imitation, and thus she survives in a competitive market economy by becoming an icon for the consumer culture herself. In her exploration of the American beauty myth, Lois Banner has pointed out that in the 1890s a new type of show girl became popular on the American stage: she neither sang nor danced but was included to show the latest in fashion and beauty. She did not participate in the physical fitness or feminist emancipation movement, but represented a conservative plump, sensual, and passive type of beauty.[21] This modern hetaira-actress, as Simone de Beauvoir has argued, "does not repudiate that passive femininity which dedicates her to man";[22] so Carrie's acting talents, according to the narrator, are based on a "passivity of soul," a soul that is "the mirror of the active world." Although Carrie rises to fame as a Broadway actress whose picture and name are multiplied seemingly *ad infinitum* over the big city, she is really a showgirl who shares with Nana the lack of any real acting talent. This aligns her more with the entrapment of the naturalist prostitute than with the new woman who "writes" her own life as an artist.

This alignment of Carrie's body with passivity and docility is deliberate, as Dreiser's journalistic writing shows, particularly his interview and article on American singer Lillian Nordica, published in January 1900 (the year of *Sister Carrie*'s publication). In her interview with Dreiser, Nordica emphasized the importance of "strength of character, determination, and the will to work" as determining factors of her successful career on stage: "I discovered that real fame, – permanent recognition, which cannot be taken away from you, – is acquired only by a lifetime

---

19 Carter 71.

20 Philip Gerber, "A Star is Born: 'Celebrity' in *Sister Carrie*," *Dreiser Studies* 19 (1988): 15.

21 Lois W. Banner, *American Beauty* (New York: Knopf, 1983) 152.

22 Simone de Beauvoir, *The Second Sex*, ed. and trans H. M. Parshley (New York: Vintage, 1974) 632.

of most earnest labor."[23] Writing *Sister Carrie*, Dreiser decided to silence this female success story, and instead to interweave Carrie's artistic and professional career with the American beauty myth, a myth deeply ingrained in American popular culture with all its constraining and misogynistic implications. Dreiser, to be sure, invests the female beauty myth with a new meaning, using it as a subtext to inscribe in naturalism women's newly acquired powers: her ability to have her own income and to become independent of male support, and her ability to make it like a self-made man. Thus, by recontextualizing the old myth, Dreiser also gives it a somewhat new ideological twist.

When Theodore Dreiser published *Sister Carrie*, his language promoting the novel suggested a clear-cut ideological agenda: to portray life and human nature "as it is," to free his characters from the shackles of Victorian morality and to provide some kind of documentary truth on the rapidly changing social life in the city. Dreiser's representation of *fin-de-siècle* femininity, however, is by no means as clear-cut as his promotional discourse suggests: the gender ideology inscribed in his naturalism reveals deep contradictions and unresolved tensions. Although *Sister Carrie* celebrates the New Woman as an American success story, Carrie "makes it" by mimicking traditional femininity. If there is a "feminist" quality in *Sister Carrie*, it is expressed in the motif of a woman claiming a new power and role for herself while making clever use of her traditional femininity. Granted, Carrie does not speak the language of the new woman, nor is she connected with the contemporary women's movement. But at the same time as she presents herself as a "docile body" on stage, she manages to manipulate and parody the traditional text of female submission and sentimental melodrama she enacts as an actress. "[L]ove is all a woman has to give" (*SC* 208), Carrie says in her role as Laura in her first amateur performance, thus articulating a cliché that seduces both Hurstwood and Drouet, but that is exposed for what it is to the reader, who knows that Carrie is deliberately playing at what she is not. (After all, she has just proved in her relationship with Drouet that it is not traditional "love" that she gives him.) Playing a harem girl later in New York, Carrie draws attention to herself when she steps out of the chorus to tell the vizier: "I am yours truly" (*SC* 474). By ironically acknowledging an illusory power relationship while using words that

---

23 "The Story of a Song-Queen's Triumph," *Selected Magazine Articles of Theodore Dreiser: Life and Art in the American 1890s*, vol. 2, ed. Yoshinobu Hakutani (Rutherford: Fairleigh Dickinson UP, 1987) 38, 49.

clearly digress from the original script, Carrie gives her language a satirical effect. She even manages to steal the audience's laughter from the powerful vizier, which signifies that for the first time Carrie has become a "somebody" in front of the audience. She has gained an identity different from the rest of the chorus by challenging the conventions of speaking and also by challenging the vizier under the guise of exaggerated feminine humbleness.

At the same time, Dreiser also articulates the deep crisis of masculinity produced by the spectre of a powerful women's movement. It is, above all, the novel's subtext that inscribes in Dreiser's naturalism a deeply felt "crisis of masculinity." George Hurstwood's tragedy and deep befuddlement are related, both structurally and thematically, to Carrie's social success and triumph. Indeed, Hurstwood's male powers are supplanted by female powers, and Carrie's role comes to double that of Hurstwood's first wife, Jessica. Representing the shift in women's growing social and judicial powers in American society, Mrs. Hurstwood makes her husband realize the end of his male prerogatives in the first third of the novel, just as Carrie confronts him with his limitations in the second half.

Thus, it is no coincidence that Hurstwood's confusion and downfall should be initiated by Mrs. Hurstwood's categorical demand for a divorce, an event that corresponds to the changes in marital conventions in the late 1890s. Turn-of-the-century America witnessed a rising divorce rate caused mainly by middle-class women who no longer tolerated unsatisfactory relationships with unfaithful husbands. The more specific historical model for Mrs. Hurstwood's action was probably Alva Vanderbilt's spectacular divorce from her husband in 1898 on the grounds of adultery, a divorce that signalled to males an end of their sexual prerogatives (many married men had until then enjoyed extramarital affairs as their "natural" right).[24] Similarly, Hurstwood's final quarrel with Jessica is prompted by his infatuation with Carrie and by his angry insistence on his (male) rights: "As long as I'm in this house I'm master of it, and you or any one else won't dictate to me – do you hear?" (*SC* 239), he tells his wife, only to find out that his patriarchal language of authority has lost its power. The discursive power appears to have shifted to Mrs. Hurstwood, who interrogates her husband like a prosecutor and speaks a new language of judicial empowerment: "'I'll find out what my rights are. Perhaps you'll talk to a lawyer, if you won't to me"

---

24 For a discussion of Alva Vanderbilt's influential social role, see Banner 191, 194.

(*SC* 239), she tells Hurstwood, who is "on the defensive at a wink and puzzled for a word to reply" (*SC* 237). Metaphorically stripped of his legal and financial powers (all his assets are in his wife's name), Hurstwood quickly moves beyond the realm of legality, eloping with Carrie after taking money from his employer, Fitzgerald and Moy's.

Although it is prompted by such shifts in legal powers, Hurstwood's downfall is mainly attributed to normative practices, illustrating Foucault's point that the juridical powers have become secondary in importance to normative powers (represented in the novel by Carrie). With Hurstwood's demise juxtaposed to Carrie's social rise, his "worn-out masculinity" is metaphorically supplanted by a new "femininity." This shift is represented in the changing sensualized body-images. It is precisely Hurstwood's body-image, carefully fabricated in Fitzgerald and Moy's club "for men only," that gives him his powerful identity. He has a stout constitution, which in his society signifies the well-to-do, solid businessman, and he adorns and caresses this body with the best clothing and most careful attention. Comparing himself with others, he confirms the sense of his own importance. In the "female" city, however, Hurstwood's formerly powerful body-image undergoes a negative metamorphosis that is spectacular in its visual impact. Once in New York, in the big (social Darwinistic) pond, Hurstwood does not plunge into absolute anonymity, as Ellen Moers (and the narrator) argues. On the contrary, his problem is that his identity has changed to that of thief and fugitive, a fact he cannot escape in a panoptic society. Hurstwood's problem is that at every turn he meets people from his past in whose gaze he reads what he has become. Entering a hotel lobby, he is immediately recognized as a tramp and asked to leave. It is only logical that Hurstwood should become depressed about his new identity and, as a result of the depression, lose further interest in his body, which marks the beginning of his end. Dreiser stresses how quickly this body changes, how it becomes thinner, how Hurstwood starts looking sinister and how he finally becomes physically sick, only to recognize this bodily deterioration in every gaze he encounters. While caring for the body is invested with desire, pleasure, and a *joie de vivre*, this process of bodily disintegration is accompanied by masochistic depression and leads to Hurstwood's suicide.

Dreiser dresses this crisis of masculinity in the typically naturalist (i.e., Spencerian and physiological) language of determinism, in which Hurstwood's bodily decline is conceptualized as a law of nature:

> A man's fortune or material progress is very much the same as his bodily growth. Either he is growing stronger, healthier, wiser, as the youth ap-

proaching manhood, or he is growing weaker, older, less incisive mentally, as the man approaching old age. (360–61)

Constant comparison between [Hurstwood's] old state and his new showed a balance for the worse, which produced a constant state of gloom or, at least, depression. Now, it has been shown experimentally that a constantly subdued frame of mind produces certain poisons in the blood, called katastates.... The poisons ... inveigh against the system, and eventually produce marked physical deterioration. To these Hurstwood was subject. (*SC* 362)

If one ignores the contextual framework of this quotation, it might seem that Hurstwood's bodily deterioration takes place independently from other bodies in society. However, Dreiser's narrative as a whole emphasizes that the recognition of changes within oneself takes place exclusively in intersubjective – psychological – relationships. Self-recognition in *Sister Carrie* is possible only through comparison with others; even the mirror in one's own private room is only a replacement for the other's gaze, for the power relationship that cannot be escaped.

Through Hurstwood, Dreiser presents the spectre of the male body disintegrating, displaying its limitations in its physical materiality – its bodily pain and weakness. As the powerful male body-image thus turns into a vulnerable physical body, Carrie's physical body undergoes the reverse metamorphosis into a larger-than-life, abstract body-image of Carrie Madenda – the image of her fame and the fetish image of herself that she shares with her audience. Dreiser draws on all the registers of pathos to show that this picture finally dwarfs the male spectator, Hurstwood:

At Broadway and Thirty-ninth Street was blazing, in incandescent fire, Carrie's name. "Carrie Madenda," it read, "and the Casino Company." All the wet, snowy sidewalk was bright with this radiated fire. It was so bright that it attracted Hurstwood's gaze. He looked up, and then at a large, gilt-framed posterboard, on which was a fine lithograph of Carrie, life-size.

Hurstwood gazed at it a moment, snuffling and hunching one shoulder, as if something were scratching him. He was so run down, however, that his mind was not exactly clear.

"That's you," he said at last, addressing her. "Wasn't good enough for you, was I? Huh!" (*SC* 546)

As one of the "midwives" of Carrie's career, helping with a "subtle hand" to create her first success as an actress, Hurstwood is now invited to consume the finished product. Yet in his despondent state, Hurstwood can no longer afford this titillating image of consumption, which confronts him with his own impotence. It is these reversals that encode

Dreiser's perception of the shifts in power between men and women in the late 1890s. The male has been "stripped" of his juridical powers but, more importantly, he is also presented as a victim of normative practices. It is the two women who emerge as female icons of power, and both display a cruel, naturalistic, indifference to Hurstwood's fate. Just as Jessica quickly forgets about Hurstwood once he elopes with Carrie, Carrie herself conveniently forgets about him once she leaves him in New York. Neither of the women is even aware of his suicide.

No longer able either to produce or to consume, Hurstwood is seduced by the panoptic city into removing himself, relieving society of the burden he has become. No longer productive in the city's consumer economy, Hurstwood becomes, as Philip Fisher has observed, "obsolete like a pair of shoes rather than aged like a man. He is a left-over and a scrap. The Bowery of New York is a collective heap of discarded men."[25] Hurstwood is not destroyed by a retributive law – as Clyde Griffiths is in *An American Tragedy* – but he is the victim of a norm that has the fiendish power of confronting him continually anew with his uselessness. Tortured by the gazes of the panoptic city, he, significantly, commits suicide while "hidden wholly in that kindness which is night" (*SC* 554). The darkness of the night and the forgetfulness of death are the last retreat from the torturing gaze of the panoptic city: "'What's the use?' he said, weakly, as he stretched himself to rest" (*SC* 554). Since the norm is not necessarily less vicious than the traditional judicial apparatus, Hurstwood's fate makes the reader question Foucault's binary division between an archaic retributive law and a modern norm that is committed to bio-power and the preservation of life. In *Sister Carrie*, the norm is almost demonic in its capacity to infiltrate and inhabit the human mind and body, and as a victim of normative practices, Hurstwood is co-opted not only into acquiescing to but into carrying out his own destruction. Dreiser suggests that modern bio-power's commitment to life may be a seductive mask, hiding how effectively and quickly this power principle disposes of those who have become "useless" in the consumer economy.

With none of his family members even aware of Hurstwood's death, Dreiser presents a world in which the deployment of alliance has been supplanted by the deployment of sexuality. The absence of family alliance by the end echoes the novel's opening. After the description of

---

25 Philip Fisher, *Hard Facts: Setting and Form in the American Novel* (New York: Oxford UP, 1985) 175.

Hurstwood's suicide, the narrative voice turns immediately to Carrie's desire: "And now Carrie had attained that which in the beginning seemed life's object, or, at least, such fraction of it as human beings ever attain of their original desires" (*SC* 554). Representative of the fleeting consumer culture itself, Carrie's desires know no loyalties, but attach themselves to new objects: "Every hour the kaleidoscope of human affairs threw a new lustre upon something, and therewith it became for her the desired – the all" (*SC* 159). Given this emphasis on female desire in Dreiser's conceptualization of Carrie's oxymoronic docile body of power, female sexuality itself deserves closer attention and will be the focus of the next chapter.

5

Female Sexuality
and the Naturalist Crisis:
"Emanuela"

Surrounded by an aura of what Dreiser often calls a "pagan" sensuality, many of his female characters paradoxically also exude a strange sense of sexual abstinence, almost chastity. Philip Fisher has commented on Carrie Meeber's absence of sexual desires and "the lack of erotic quality" in her love relationships, at the same time that she enacts desires and eros very successfully on the theater stage.[1] Leslie Fiedler, commenting on the chastity of the "unchurched nun," Carrie Meeber, and on Jennie Gerhardt's almost asexual mothering of her two lovers, irreverently draws the conclusion that Dreiser "could never portray, for all his own later hectic career as a lover, any woman except the traditional seduced working girl of sentimental melodrama."[2] Yet, despite this penchant for the gender-stereotypical seduction theme, Dreiser has gained

---

1 Fisher 165–66.
2 Leslie Fiedler, "Dreiser and the Sentimental Novel," rpt. in *Dreiser: A Collection of Critical Essays*, ed. John Lydenberg (Englewood Cliffs: Prentice-Hall, 1971) 47.

the stature of a literary French Marianne who, by waving the flag of sexual liberation in his battle against the bulwarks of American literary "puritanism," has firmly established sex as a discursive fact. In his works, Dreiser celebrates sexuality as the major driving force in life, holding it up as a force of progress endlessly engaged in battles against sexually repressive social conventions and institutions.

Elevated to the level of a canonized critical "fact," Dreiser's discourse of sexual frankness and liberation is, nonetheless, problematic not only because it may reinscribe old stereotypes in a new language, as Fiedler's critique implies, but also because it innocently assumes the existence of sexuality as an innate, bodily fact, a fact that is presumed to be recoverable like a *Ding an sich* underneath layers of psychological repressions and literary censorship. Dreiser's discursive scientificity, underlined by his characteristic usage of materialistic imagery such as "magnetism" and "chemism," especially in his evocation of sexuality, strengthens the impression of the body as an easily graspable, physical, or natural entity whose existence is presumed to have been hidden behind veils of conventions. The tacit assumption behind such language is that "lifting the veil" and transcending conventions with a discourse of "frankness" will make the "real thing" automatically appear "as it is" and grant it a place in literature in its own right.

Michel Foucault, to be sure, rejects, debunks, and caricatures discourses of sexual liberation, arguing that what we nowadays subsume under the term *sexuality* is by no means "innate" or "natural," but rather a complex historical construct created over the last two centuries in our discursive practices. Even more importantly, in this process of transforming sex into discourse sexuality has been policed, because talking about sexuality in regulated, "authorized" discourses helps control it. In the discursive evolution, as Foucault sees it, the female body was taken charge of through a process that Foucault calls a *"hysterization of women's bodies,"* that is, the social identification of women's bodies with their reproductive organs, or the womb. By acknowledging the force of repression and by putting sexuality in discourse through the psychoanalytic talking cure, new personages made their appearance, such as the repressed, frigid, or anesthetic woman, who became the privileged object of psychological and sexological interest in the first quarter of the twentieth century.

Just as Foucault has emphasized that discourses of truth carry with them power effects, so Luce Irigaray's theory intersects with Foucault's in her polemical feminist critique of the "truths" produced by psychoanalysis: "La psychanalyse tient sur la sexualité féminine le discours de la vérité."[3] She accuses Freud of having theorized sexuality in exclusively masculine parameters and thus of having created a masculine rather than a feminine "truth" of sexuality: "he takes masculinity as the yardstick against which all objects and actions are assessed, constructing women as deviations from the norm."[4] The result of this bias is that psychoanalysis erases the conception of a positively defined woman's sexuality: "Son lot serait celui du 'manque,' de l' 'atrophie' (du sexe), et de l' 'envie du pénis' comme seul sexe reconnu valeureux" (*CS* 23). According to Irigaray, the ready acceptance of Freud's discourse of truth in our culture has even led women to mimic male desires: "La femme ne vivrait son désir que comme attente de posséder enfin un équivalent du sexe masculin" (*CS* 23). Female desire thus is constructed along powerful discourses of authorized male knowledge.

At the time Dreiser wrote *Sister Carrie*, Freudian psychoanalysis was not yet known to him. As Ellen Moers has pointed out, Freud's theory probably reached Dreiser after 1910, after Abraham Brill – a friend of Dreiser's from 1918 on – had translated some of Freud's major writings into English. It was mainly Freud's *Theory of Sex* (1905) that influenced Dreiser, introducing him to the concept of sexual "chemism" (*Sexualchemismus*), which he uses so obsessively in *An American Tragedy* to describe the sexual drive.[5] In *A Gallery of Women* (1929), a collection of nonfictional and semifictionalized sketches on the author's female friends and acquaintances, Dreiser presents some Freudian case studies in "Lucia," "Rella," and "Emanuela." Even his chapter titles mimic Freud and Breuer's psychoanalytic publications on female hysteria, in which the woman's first name signifies the case study that is to follow. The collection's title, "A Gallery of Women," suggests the work of an artist.[6]

Presenting a true touchstone for evaluating Dreiser's treatment of female sexuality, "Emanuela" deserves closer critical attention than it

---

3 Luce Irigaray, *Ce sexe qui n'en est pas un* (Paris: Les Éditons de Minuit, 1977) 85. Further references will appear in the text abbreviated *CS*.

4 Kornelia Hauser paraphrasing Irigaray's theory, 188–89.

5 Ellen Moers, *Two Dreisers: The Man and the Novelist As Revealed in His Two Most Important Works, "Sister Carrie" and "An American Tragedy"* (New York: Viking, 1969) 262–63. See also Frederic E. Rusch, "Dreiser's Introduction to Freudianism," *Dreiser Studies* 18 (1987): 34–38.

6 In Dreiser's *Twelve Men* (New York: Boni & Liveright, 1919), the titles of twelve sketches devoted to men follow a different pattern, assigning each male a particular characteristic, such as "A Doer of the World," "My Brother Paul," "Culhane, the Solid Man," and "A True Patriarch."

has so far been granted in Dreiser scholarship. Exposing the underlying gender ideology of his naturalist fiction, "Emanuela" highlights how easily Dreiser's reading of Freudian psychoanalysis converges with his earlier emphasis on sexuality, particularly in *Sister Carrie*. While the narrative voice in *Sister Carrie* represents the author's thinly veiled editorial voice, the first-person narrator in "Emanuela" represents his autobiographical persona. "Emanuela" shows how much psychoanalytic knowledge displaces the author's earlier scientific (Spencerian, physiological) discourses of authority, so that the later sketch functions as a condensed *roman à clef* that helps to unravel the power effects inherent in Dreiser's presuppositions about the sexual nature of his earlier heroines. In more explicit ways than *Sister Carrie*, "Emanuela" exposes an awareness of the contradictions and misogynistic patterns that emerge when a naturalist narrator takes sexual and textual charge of the female body, thus controlling the female within the boundaries of a male genre. Whereas *Sister Carrie* presents a woman who mimics traditional femininity and docility, "Emanuela" presents a strong, intellectual woman, who refuses to accept male versions of truth. By pointing to his younger self's sexual crisis when dealing with Emanuela's "stubbornness," Dreiser, as the mature narrator-author who relates his own past, highlights his naturalist crisis of authority, when inscribing female sexuality in his (autobiographical) fiction.

"Emanuela" presents an account of a beautiful and gifted woman-artist, whom the thirty-year-old narrator-author meets in New York artist circles and who, according to Dreiser's first-person account, repeatedly initiates the contact with him only to retreat with an almost physical repulsion from his sexual advances. "'I don't like you this way!',"she tells him, also confessing candidly that the "muddy depths" of sex are not for her, that she in fact does not want any sex relationship.[7] The narrator, irritated at being led by the nose, excels at exposing Emanuela's duplicity, namely, the fact that she "pursues" him for years, in fact never tires of "luring" him into accepting tantalizing *tête à têtes*, but each time almost ritually thwarts what he longs for most – the sexual contact.

But as Emanuela oscillates between her attraction for Dreiser's younger self and her physical repulsion, so the narrator himself oscil-

---

7 Theodore Dreiser, "Emanuela," *A Gallery of Women*, vol. 2 (New York: Horace Liveright, 1929) 683. Further references will appear in the text abbreviated *GW*. Richard Lehan has identified Emanuela as Ann Watkins, a freelance writer and literary agent, in *Theodore Dreiser: His World and His Novels* (Carbondale & Edwardsville: Southern Illinois UP, 1969) 264, n. 12.

lates between irresistible attraction and angry, frustrated retreat, an interplay that is paralleled by the oscillating discourses he adopts to describe and evaluate Emanuela. Describing his younger self as a briskly advancing Don Juan, the narrator lovingly weaves the threads of his idealizing love-romance tapestry, evoking Emanuela in terms of Minerva, Diana, Venus, and mythologizing her "white," "seraph"-like, virginal body, only to intersperse in his romance a cooler, scientific-analytical thread when it comes to dealing with her "freezing recessions." This discursive oscillation, better than anything else, illustrates the narrator's duplicity in his relationship with the young woman, whose body strikes him as "beautiful and voluptuously formed," but who refuses to fulfill what he sees as the "natural" functions of such a "perfect" body, namely: to have intercourse with a man.

"Was she not a clear illustration of some of Freud's prime contentions?" (*GW* 693), the narrator asks, taking recourse to a psychoanalytic authority – sanctioned as truthful by himself and the intellectual forerunners of his contemporary society. It matters little that Emanuela rejects this model of analysis for herself: "Oh, yes, she had read Freud, and had been impressed in part, but could not accept him fully. No. His analysis was too coarse and too domineering, left no place for anything but itself. And there was nothing that was the whole truth about anything" (*GW* 695). Despite her protests – sex cannot possibly be "the base of *all* dreams" – Dreiser imposes the Freudian discourse as truthfully revealing the secrets about her character, namely, her sexual repression, her "sex inhibition" and "the obvious pathologic fact in her case, that she was frigid – and yet not so" (*GW* 686–87).

Drawing on Freud's theory, he reads and writes her as a case of pathological frigidity, of desiring sex but having built up a "wall of reserve" against it and therefore having crossed the boundary into "abnormal" sexual behaviour – stubborn sexual resistance. Like Freud's studies on hysteria, Dreiser's description of his "case" is followed by his own interpretation, in which the narrative voice assumes the powerful authority of the unimpassioned psychoanalyst-interpreter. The narrator's different roles as analyst and lover, though, overlap and conflict with each other, exposing his duplicity and limits particularly in his frequent emotional outbursts. After having established the "fact" of Emanuela's "frigidity," he does, for instance, not abandon the chase as useless; on the contrary, despite his better judgment he continues it sporadically over a period of more than a decade, as if his realization of the woman's "frigidity" made the chase all the more intense, the sexual object all the more desirable.

Dreiser's Freudian language implies that frigidity is partly rooted in the organic and partly in childhood repressions, and he provides the proof for his theory of Emanuela's frigidity in showing her parents to be strongly conventional and puritanical characters. Freud, to be sure, recognized the roots of frigidity in psychological repressions during both childhood and puberty (as well as in anatomical factors).[8] Simone de Beauvoir, in contrast, gives a very persuasive definition of frigidity that refrains from making any biological assumptions, as it refrains from speculating about a far-away childhood. Locating the roots of frigidity in gender relationships of power, de Beauvoir writes that "resentment is the most common source of feminine frigidity; in bed the woman punishes the male for all the wrongs she feels she has endured, by offering him an insulting coldness."[9]

Just as Freud was not able to provide any firm, or ultimate, answers on the roots of female frigidity, so the sketch of "Emanuela" culminates in an epistemological crisis for Dreiser. If anything, "Emanuela" emphasizes the narrator's painful efforts to prove the truth-value of his analysis: "For what was the real truth about her?" (*GW* 702), he asks not once but repeatedly, occasionally subjecting his own conclusions to a skeptical re-questioning: "Or am I misreading you, and are you really moved by something which I cannot feel?" (*GW* 703). "Emanuela" exposes that the authority assumed by the male narrative voice in naturalism is simultaneously challenged by the narrator's hermeneutical crisis, when trying to read Emanuela's symptoms. As his hypothetical language suggests, he can only raise questions about her feelings but has no firm answers. In "Emanuela," naturalist certainty and narrative authority thus give way to a skeptical questioning of whose version of the truth is the "real" one.

Even more importantly, the text turns around against its author-narrator-analyst to expose that it is his language of truth – his usage of sanctified Freudian theory – that not only aids but makes possible the narrator's dominant position in this relationship, which culminates in

---

8 "Die sexuelle Frigidität des Weibes ... ist ein erst ungenügend verstandenes Phänomen. Manchmal psychogen und dann der Beeinflussung zugänglich, legt sie in anderen Fällen die Annahme einer konstitutionellen Bedingtheit, selbst den Beitrag eines anatomischen Faktors, nahe." "Female sexual frigidity ... is an insufficiently understood phenomenon. Sometimes it is psychogenic and hence can be influenced, but in other cases it suggests a constitutional condition, even an anatomical factor" (my translation). Sigmund Freud, "Neue Folge der Vorlesungen zur Einführung in die Psychoanalyse," *Gesammelte Werke*, vol. 15 (Frankfurt: Fischer, 1966) 141.

9 Beauvoir 439.

several overtly rapist scenes. But as he slips into the role of a rapist, his theory helps him to shift the desire for rape from himself onto his victim: "Unquestionably, in some errant, repressed and nervous way, she was thinking that I would assail and overcome her, cave-man fashion, and so free her once and for all of her long and possibly, – how should I know – torturing self-restraint – slay the dragon of repression that shut the Sleeping Princess from the world of her fancy" (*GW* 698). Projecting the desire for rape onto his female victim, Dreiser's younger self enacts the male part in a Freudian sex drama. Indeed, the narrator's conquering sexuality appears as the logical extension of Freud's theory of (active) male and (passive) female libido, as Freud describes it in his "Theory of Sex":

> The reenforcements of the sexual inhibitions produced in the woman by the repression of puberty produces a stimulus in the libido of the man and forces him to increase his activities. With the height of the libido there occurs a rise in the overestimation of the sexual object, which attains its full force only in that woman who hesitates and denies her sexuality.[10]

According to Freud, female frigidity (if caused by childhood repressions) can be overcome through the experience of powerful male sexual potency, "durch mächtiges sexuelles Erleben,"[11] so that the overcoming of female frigidity indirectly becomes a measuring stick for male potency. This Freudian interweaving of "normal" (hetero)sexuality with power (*mächtig* < *Macht*) provides the gender-ideological subtext for Dreiser's narrative.

Criticizing this aspect of psychoanalytic theory, Luce Irigaray has argued that the Freudian emphasis on the phallus implies a binary division between masculine activity and feminine passivity – "l'opposition activité clitoridienne 'virile' / passivité vaginale 'féminine'" (*CS* 23). The Freudian text, furthermore, entails for women a wish to be possessed by the phallus, a wish to be acted upon. Through this inscription of phallic penetration (and the phallic gaze) as the "normal" form of sexual behaviour, women's sexual pleasure is always already in danger of becoming a vicariously passive, even a "masochistic pleasure" for women, a pleasure that is not really her own: "Ne sachant pas ce qu'elle veut, prête à n'importe quoi, en redemandant même, pourvu qu'il la 'prenne' comme 'object' d'exercice de son plaisir à lui" (*CS* 25). Irigaray draws the conclusion that through normalizing cultural practices, women are

---

10 Sigmund Freud, "Contributions to the Theory of Sex," Brill 613.

11 Freud, "Die kulturelle Sexualmoral und die moderne Nervosität," *Gesammelte Werke*, vol. 7, Werke aus den Jahren 1906–1909 (Frankfurt: Fischer Verlag, 1941) 164.

made to love that which really subjugates them (the phallus as an icon of power), which in turn ensures the perpetuation of the "normal," hierarchically structured, gender relations.

Struggling against this "normalization" of her sexuality, Emanuela resists the narrator's framing of her sexuality within the naturalist boundaries of his sketch. Just as her female resistance, in turn, confronts the male narrator's younger self with a sexual crisis (in his role as a Don Juan lover), so it confronts the older narrator with a crisis of narrative authority (in his role as a naturalist voice of truth and reliable knowledge). Dreiser cannot really trust his psychoanalytic readings, since Freud himself had shown how cleverly the hysterical female body can mimic false symptoms. But since his sexual/textual authority (as a lover and a naturalist) can only be maintained by proving the truth of her frigidity, he becomes obsessed with demonstrating "scientifically" that Emanuela's "mental opposition" and "muscular rejection" are indeed pathological, uncontrollable bodily reactions. Unable to prove the ultimate truth of his Freudian analysis, he turns to the empirical, observable "reality" of his and her body, and finally invokes the traditional, nineteenth-century discursive authority – biology – to prove that her sexual resistance is not "natural." Throughout the sketch, he is concerned with backing up his analysis with observable, biological facts, and he goes so far as to trace what seems to him nature's inscription of Emanuela's "abnormal" psychological history on her body: "in her face was a trace of something – could it be a shadow of grossness? – her repressed emotions or desires at last gaining headway?" (*GW* 718–19). Even her physical beauty becomes a "biological" signifier that allows him to "prove" both her sexual "pathology" and the "normality" of his conquering desire. Thus, it is not so much that the asexual friendship Emanuela offers throughout the sketch does not count for much but that, according to the narrator's conception of male sexuality, a "happy camaraderie" with a beautiful woman like Emanuela is *biologically* impossible for a male:

> What nonsense! What lunacy! And I told her so. Men were not like that. I was not. She would not like me that way if I were. She was indulging in some unnatural, hopeless, futile dream. In God's name, what was all her physical beauty for? (*GW* 687).

Repeatedly, he demonstrates (with himself as the only example) that discussions about art and literary styles in the presence of her physically "perfect" body are at best boring and pointless for a male, at worst a torture. Thus, biology and psychoanalysis not only serve the narrator-author to inscribe female sexuality in terms of a compulsory heterosexuality but also to pathologize in his male naturalism a behaviour that is not in tune with "normalized" sexual behavior. But the fact that he can only articulate his male truth in the form of questions and in deeply emotional exclamations simultaneously reveals the self-contradictions of his naturalist fiction. The very obsessiveness of his desire (both to conquer Emanuela sexually and to impose a "normalized" sexuality in his narrative) undermines the very notion of the naturalist observer's objectivity and impartiality, so praised by Emile Zola.

"Emanuela," then, exposes the hermeneutical and gender crisis as well as the crisis of narrative authority encountered by the authorial voice in twentieth-century naturalist fiction. Finding that there is no ultimate, or single, scientific authority, the narrator obsessively multiplies different systems of knowledge in order to prove to himself that there is a coherent naturalist truth. But in this Babel of knowledges (that includes psychoanalysis, biology, empirical knowledge, and "common sense"), the reader is forced to recognize the narrator's limitations as a naturalist voice of truth. Furthermore, the narrator's incongruous blending of different roles – from amateur psycho-analyst and naturalist writer to scorned lover, friend, and rival – continually exposes his bias and unreliability: "I think you must be mad [crazy]. In fact, I'm sure you are" (*GW* 709), he finally closes his "analysis," stomping off more like the rejected and disappointed lover than impassioned psychologist. Thus exposing the narrator's limited and skewed perspective, the sketch unravels the naturalist claim to an authorized truth from within the genre. By playing so many different roles and by drawing on so many different knowledges, the narrator cannot help but deconstruct the notion of naturalistic truth itself, exposing it as a (male) construction.

What is more, "Emanuela" draws attention to the problematics and power politics of the narrator's tacit assumptions about female sexual passivity – also a striking feature of *Sister Carrie, Jennie Gerhardt,* and *An American Tragedy*, as it draws attention to the intense power play of Dreiser's euphoric celebration of the inner "magnetism" of the beautiful female body, which the author thematizes in the Cowperwood-*Trilogy* and *The "Genius"* (1915). Thus, the sketch shows the power effects inherent in any claim that a specific sexuality is "normal" or "natural," claims that are made in almost all of Dreiser's major works, either through overt commentary or through clever manipulation of narrative form.

To conceptualize Dreiser's inscription of a "normalized" sexuality in *Sister Carrie*, briefly recall Foucault's *History of Sexuality*:

> Thus, in the process of hysterization of women, "sex" was defined in three ways: as that which belongs in common to men and women; as that which belongs *par excellence*, to men, and hence is lacking in women; but at the

same time, as that which by itself constitutes woman's body, ordering it wholly in terms of the functions of reproduction and keeping it in constant agitation through the effects of that very function. (*HS* 153)

Dreiser's fiction inscribes this sexualization of the female body in a variety of forms. *Jennie Gerhardt, An American Tragedy* and *The "Genius"* explore the problem of unwanted pregnancies, whereby women are shown to be deterministically entrapped within the biological logic of a reproductive womb. In other works, this hysterization appears in sublimated forms. Although apparently "undersexed," Emanuela's body is shown to be filled with sex, albeit with a "repressed" and thus hidden and concealed sexuality, surfacing, according to Dreiser's analysis, in her "mothering" of the author-narrator, her cooking for him, her tucking him in in his bed. Like Emanuela, all of Dreiser's major female characters are assumed to be endowed with bodies saturated with sex, so that they cannot escape a sexual destiny. But being saturated with sex does not necessarily imply sexual activity for the female but often means its contrary; the sex-filled Dreiserian heroine is a rather static target that prompts the opposite sex to move, attracting the males like a honey-pot the buzzing flies.

Not only is Carrie's sexual initiation with her first lover Charles Drouet described in terms of her "yielding" and his "victory," but so is Roberta Alden's with Clyde Griffiths in *An American Tragedy*, and so is almost every other sexual relationship in Dreiser's fiction. "She struggled, but in vain," is how the narrator describes Carrie's seduction by her second lover, George Hurstwood: "Instantly there flamed up in his body the all-compelling desire" (*SC* 307). The language surrounding the sexual act with Hurstwood is submerged in tropes of male power and dominance, at the same time that it is embedded in a discourse that supports the "normalcy" of this sexuality. Earlier in the novel, when Carrie is even more firmly resisting the middle-aged saloon manager's advances, her lack of passion for Hurstwood is explained by "a lack of power on his part, a lack of that majesty of passion that sweeps the mind from its seat" (*SC* 241). Just as Freud argued that frigidity can be overcome through "mächtiges sexuelles Erleben," so the narrator's language implies that in order to be sexually aroused, a woman has to be taken possession of completely, has to be usurped completely, has to be overwhelmed both in spirit and in body.[12] In Dreiser's works, beginning

---

12 Although the unexpurgated Pennsylvania edition of *Sister Carrie* is sexually more explicit and daring (Carrie and Hurstwood, for example, make love before they are married), the gender ideology inscribed in the sexual roles is not essentially different from that of the original edition.

with *Sister Carrie* but also in *An American Tragedy* and the *Trilogy of Desire*, sex relations almost automatically create relationships of power, with the male inevitably dominating over the female body by imposing a form of sexuality that anticipates the male's conquering sexuality, from which Emanuela retreats with so much horror in the later work.

As Emanuela's stubborn sexual resistance is interpreted as an indicator for her "abnormal" psychology that provokes the narrator's irritation, puzzlement, and impotent anger, so its flipside – Carrie's passive acceptance of sexuality – is sanctified by the narrative voice as having a biological basis, hence excusing her transgressions against society's prohibition of premarital sex. Readers have commented that in crucial moments Carrie displays a striking passivity that seems to excuse her from any responsibility for her actions, a passivity that ultimately protects her "virtue."[13] This is typically Dreiserian, we might argue, characteristic of both men and women in his fiction. After all, passively wavering, Hurstwood turns into a thief, Clyde Griffiths into a "murderer." Yet the important difference is that Carrie's passivity extends mainly into the sexual realm, a realm in which Hurstwood storms ahead with the passionate single-mindedness of the enamoured lover.

From the omniscient narrator's point of view, Carrie is never a subject of the sexual act. Rather, sexuality, apart from being innate and constituting her body, is something that happens to her, a point that the narrator easily accepts as a "normal" bodily reality, in tune with biology and nature, and ultimately sanctioned by the fact that it is presumed to be pleasurable for the male. When Drouet invites Hurstwood to his newly established "house," thus signalling to his friend his recent sexual success, Carrie, as Drouet's "kept woman," is only present in the gap of the male text. "I'll introduce you" (*SC* 91), is all Drouet tells Hurstwood about her, while the object of the introduction remains suspended in a linguistic silence, not even given a name but somehow magically attached as a sexual body to Drouet and his "house."

The effect of this gap is that, in this instance, Carrie's sexuality comes into being and gains a life not by itself but detached from her own body, activated not in the sex act but in the pleasurable discourse of two males. Moreover, this conversational gambit, in which Carrie connects the two men through her very absence, takes place in a club "for men only," Chicago's Fitzgerald and Moy's. This reinforces the impression that the

---

13 For a detailed discussion of Carrie's moral ambiguity, see, for example, Terence J. Matheson, "The Two Faces of Sister Carrie: The Characterization of Dreiser's First Heroine," *Ariel* 11 (1980): 71–85. Matheson emphasizes the contradictions between the strong-willed, ambitious and the innocently passive Carrie.

woman has no control over her sexuality; in this instance, female sexuality is part of a male network, easily conjured up as a gap, a hole to be filled by the male desire that it generates.

As the male narrator strongly manipulates the reader's responses, he cannot help but reveal his own gender bias in the process. Although the narrators in *Sister Carrie* and "Emanuela" profess to argue against the sexual "conventions" of their society, much of their narration, in fact, affirms the conventional – hierarchically structured – gender pattern in the realm of sexuality. Given the early heroine's involuntary slippage into sex and the notion that Emanuela's body needs not so much to act in order to be "freed," but to be acted upon by a male in order to connect with life, it should come as no surprise that most of Dreiser's women are described as sexually passive creatures. If, for Dreiser, (hetero)sexuality is an inevitable factor in the constitution of a healthy body and an inseparable part of a person's subjectivity, then his sexual economy is also ruled by a gender-based "equation inevitable," a calculation of gain and loss, of power and impotence, which shifts the credit-power balance between male and female to the male side through the fact of the sexual initiation.

Just as the autobiographical narrator is obsessed with Emanuela's virginal state, so the moment of sexual initiation (always ritually delayed and endowed with a titillating suspension in Dreiser's fiction) takes on a special significance all the more important as the sexual act itself is usually relegated into the gaps of the text and thus silenced. While the female has the power to hold the male in an awesome suspension before the sexual initiation – we need only recall the melancholic, masochistic yearnings of Clyde for Roberta, of Eugene for Angela, of Cowperwood for Berenice – the sexual initiation in Dreiser's fiction inevitably inverts the relationship of power between male and female. This pattern explains the autobiographical narrator's helpless and frustrated anger at Emanuela, who by successfully and eternally delaying the sexual contact never allows him to place her on the "debit" side of the equation. In Dreiser's naturalist world, women inevitably lose by "giving" themselves to a partner, while the man wins: "how delicious is my conquest," is Drouet's reaction, while Carrie reflects, "what is it I have lost?" (*SC* 101), after the first sexual contact has been established. Similarly, in *An American Tragedy*, Clyde Griffiths's sense of self grows as a result of his seduction of the factory worker Roberta Alden; from a "simpleton" he turns into a conquering Don Juan in his own (and her) eyes, and thus becomes capable of even grander tasks and ready for the sexual conquest of rich women, the Sondra Finchleys of this world. Roberta, in contrast, feels she has given him "everything" and as a result further belittles herself in his eyes and flatters him, since her future depends on "her ultimate rehabilitation via marriage."[14]

Thus, the first sexual contact inverts rather than introduces a gender-imbalance "always already" present in Dreiser's sexual world. Granted, the narrator in *Sister Carrie* is careful to link this phenomenon critically to society's "arbitrary" sexual conventions (*SC* 101), but the fact remains that the narrator privileges and celebrates precisely those sexual courtship patterns that grow out of society's prohibitions. In Dreiser's fiction, it is in the crucial moment of the woman's "surrender" that the man is born into "masculinity," and in which ideal "femininity" is constituted as passive, yielding, and sacrificial, based on a "biological" body that is presumed to be ruled by the "economy of the gift," the womb that accepts and nourishes. Conversely, nonsacrificial and nonyielding women are allocated negative subject positions. Such women appear in Dreiser's naturalism in the figure of the cold, status-oriented, castrating female, who is rejected by the narrative's "master" discourse as ultimately undesirable. Mrs. Hurstwood's struggle for independence, fought with superior strategy and cleverness, can hardly call forth the reader's admiration, since it is submerged in an imagery of coldness that turns her into a money-hungry "python," who devours her husband, spitting him out (metaphorically) castrated, a half-man.

And yet, like "Emanuela," Dreiser's *Sister Carrie* should not be completely identified with the ideology of its male narrator. The novel itself occasionally counters and subverts its omniscient voice, by presenting a second voice that implicitly contradicts the male narrator's comments. For example, the only passage in the novel in which Carrie is portrayed as being subject of the sexual act is, significantly, filtered through the mind of a woman, Minnie Hanson, who dreams in the night of Carrie's sexual initiation that her sister is descending into a black pit:

> There was a deep pit, into which they were looking; they could see the curious wet stones far down where the wall disappeared in vague shadows. An old basket, used for descending, was hanging there, fastened by a worn rope.
> "Let's get in," said Carrie.
> "Oh, no," said Minnie.
> "Yes, come on," said Carrie.
> She began to pull the basket over, and now, in spite of all protest, she had swung over and was going down. (*SC* 89-90)

---

14 Theodore Dreiser, *An American Tragedy* (1925; New York: New American Library, 1981) 344.

This dream takes the place of the description of the sexual act itself,[15] and in her sister's eyes Carrie is not only sexually active but even invites Minnie to join her. It is interesting that the male seducer is absent, and that the scene of Carrie's "fall" foregrounds two women, with Carrie herself acting as the seductive voice.

Simultaneously "undersexed" and "oversexed," Carrie, then, is presented as an oxymoronic Victorian Vamp, as Sheldon Grebstein has observed.[16] The narrator clearly wishes to absolve Carrie of responsibility, embedding her sexuality in a deliberate language of passivity and determinism. And so does the author, who is partly complicitous with his narrator. After all, Minnie's dream is filtered through the mind of a woman who has been set up as thoroughly "conventional," a clever authorial manipulation designed to disqualify Minnie as an "unreliable" narrative "consciousness" when it comes to judging Carrie's "unconventional" sexual actions. And yet, by presenting this "second" voice as subconscious – it is the voice of Minnie's dream – and by presenting it as female, Dreiser inevitably creates a classical discourse of the Other, a discourse that not only speaks of female sexual activity but that also erupts into and thoroughly disrupts the narrative's male voice.

If in Minnie's dreams, Carrie's "fall" takes place amid "unsubtle symbols of genitalia,"[17] it also carries auto- and homoerotic connotations. After all, Carrie goes down in her own "basket" and invites another woman to join her. Granted, these (homo)sexual suggestions are never fully explored in the novel, but they are reinforced by Carrie's autoerotic attention to her own body, as well as by her continued friendship with Lola (after she becomes disillusioned with male sexuality and company). Carrie's, like Emanuela's, sexual abstinence creates a fascinating gap, particularly in light of Freud's argument that (hetero)sexual abstinence is fraught with dangers: under the guise of abstinence, a person may indulge in very seductive, "abnormal" forms of sexuality, such as mas-

---

15 For a detailed discussion of Minnie's dream as a reflection of her "own frustrated desires," see Joseph Church, "Minnie's Dreams in *Sister Carrie*," *College Literature* 14 (1987): 184.

16 Sheldon N. Gerbstein, "Dreiser's Victorian Vamp," *Sister Carrie* by Theodore Dreiser (New York: Norton, 1970), 551. "Dreiser has created a Victorian Vamp: a woman who is precisely that mixture of strengths and weaknesses which the nineteenth century conceived her to be, but who is at the same time in her unrequited sexual sins the first modern heroine. Eve-like, she yields to the flesh, but in the strongest Victorian tradition she does so only out of the confusion and need engendered by woman's innate helplessness and man's predatory lustfulness."

17 Church 183.

turbation, sexual fantasies, and homosexuality. According to Freud's logic, (hetero)sexual abstinence is "unhealthy" because it can lead to frigidity in women and loss of potency in men.[18]

Though Dreiser's dominant voice confirms the Freudian notion of (hetero)sexual normality, *Sister Carrie* implicitly critiques the "normalized" standard of female sexual passivity via some of its female characters. The fact that Dreiser creates a female protagonist who moves from one sexual relationship to the next, apparently to "give up" (hetero)sexual contacts when she becomes rich, inevitably exposes the limits of those sexual practices that the narrator presents as "normal" or "natural." If anything, the narrative implicitly signals that these "normal" sexual practices are not satisfying for women, at the same time that they are claimed to be highly pleasurable for men. But the narrative's critique of "normalized" sexual practices is mainly inscribed in the gaps of the text, with a marginalized voice occasionally erupting to "poke holes" into the dominating male narrative voice.

Stretching from *Sister Carrie* to "Emanuela," Dreiser's fiction shows that the new female sexuality, which emerged in America's urban centres between the *fin de siècle* and the twenties, was simultaneously exciting and threatening for him. Elizabeth Wilson's analysis of the sexualized female city applies to Dreiser's naturalist fiction: "At the heart of the urban labyrinth lurked not the Minotaur, a bull-like male monster, but the female Sphinx, the 'strangling one', who was so called because she strangled all those who could not answer her riddle: female sexuality, womanhood out of control, lost nature, loss of identity."[19] Dreiser's naturalist fiction is a textual field in which this female, urbanite sphinx gives birth to new fantasies of male conquest, fantasies that simultaneously echo male fears (of castration, of loss of power and masculinity). While turn-of-the-century women fought for their reproductive rights and asserted a claim to women's sexual pleasures in and outside of marriage, Carrie Meeber participates in the twentieth-century dissemination of female sexuality mainly as a fetishized commodity picture: as an actress, she is the incarnation of commodified sex-at-a-distance. This concept of female power encapsulates the ideological chasm in Dreiser's naturalism: it reflects his (feminist) commitment to inscribing in naturalism women's new powers, but it also reveals his simultaneous

---

18 Freud, "Die kulturelle Sexualmoral," 162–64.

19 Elizabeth Wilson, *The Sphinx in the City: Urban Life, the Control of Disorder, and Women* (London: Virago, 1991) 7.

(antifeminist) attempt to contain these very powers within the boundaries of the genre.

Carrie's female powers are, significantly, embodied in her (hetero)sexual indifference, in arousing male desire without being aroused herself. Emanuela and Carrie Meeber are not attached to any man but are desired by all men and have the gift of "eternally" generating male desire. The mature Carrie, weary of men's advances, seems almost timelessly desirable in her lethargic and unreachable sexual aloofness as a famous Broadway actress. Similarly, even though the narrator-artist of "Emanuela" is no longer interested in his aging friend, her sexual elusiveness inscribes itself forever into his memory, as she continues to preoccupy him as a "temperament and a life that cannot be driven from one's mind" (*GW* 662). These sexualized fantasies fit neatly into the conventions of a predominantly male naturalist genre, reflecting the author's desire to tame and discipline the female's dangerous sexuality – and, even more importantly, her intellect and creative powers – within textual boundaries.

Grudgingly agreeing that Emanuela is a successful popular writer and, as an editor, even publishing her stories in his magazine, Dreiser uses his sketch to ridicule her writing as "conservative" and "conventional." Infuriated that she should have criticized his own naturalist novels, the mature narrator takes sadistic pleasure in convincing the reader of his aging friend's bodily disintegration, which is accompanied by her creative stagnation, again "proven" to be scientifically inevitable because she has "never functioned properly as a woman" (*GW* 719). He would like to see himself as the initiator of Emanuela into true art, but not by discussing art with her on an intellectual level: by initiating her into sexuality, thus establishing her contact with "real life" and giving birth to her capacity to reproduce life in literature. The fact that Emanuela refused to be sexually active with a man "castrates" her as an artist in his eyes. Only through the experience of sex with a man might Emanuela have "better understood life, acquired that grip on reality which would have vitalized the literary or narrative gift that she had" (*GW* 720), even though sex for her would have to involve a submission to a sexuality that she finds repulsive.

Through Emanuela, we also witness the tragic fact that it is "normalization" that triumphs by the end of Dreiser's naturalist sketch. As a mature woman, Emanuela confesses to the narrator: "I should have married or given myself to you" (*GW* 721), a confession that stands out like a sad reminder that she has "failed" to become sexually "normalized" and pays the price in human isolation, once her body has undergone its metamorphosis into mature womanhood. At the same time, however,

Dreiser's naturalist fiction unravels its own gender bias by showing that Carrie and Emanuela cannot be totally captured or defined by the naturalist narrator's sexualized fantasy of power. Not only are the reader's sympathies drawn to Emanuela, but we cannot help but admire her apparently Quixotic resistance against "normalization." It is appropriate that the narrator should end his sketch on a deliberately ambiguous note: "It may be that she is dead – although I doubt it" (*GW* 721). His hypothetical voice suggests that he does not dare close the door completely, and thus the sketch's open-endedness suggests a slim chance that Emanuela may have discovered a new life, a life that is, however, far beyond the narrator's naturalist realm and imagination, a life that he is not capable of writing and that is therefore relegated into the gaps of his text.

III. Deconstructing the Naturalist Prostitute

6

Fanny Essler:
A Sexual Picaresque

As Dreiser was planting the first deconstructive seeds in his naturalist fiction in 1900, F. P. Grove was still deeply immersed in reading and composing neoromantic poetry. It was only after 1903, after his incarceration in Bonn and after being cast aside by the elitist *Neuromantiker* that Grove started his career as a prose writer by creating a Carrie-like protagonist. Like Carrie Meeber, Grove's Fanny Essler is an actress who is identified with the modern metropolis and becomes a desirable object for the male gazer at the same time that, endowed with an apparently insatiable body, she is presented as the incarnation of desire. Like Dreiser, Grove also turned to a woman's "true story" to create his first novel. *Fanny Essler* (1905) is closely based on the life of Else Ploetz, now better known as the Baroness von Freytag-Loringhoven, whose own memoirs closely overlap Grove's novel. In Grove's career as an artist, his creative "collaboration" with Elsa meant a radical departure from the neoromanticism of his epigone Stefan George. From George's poetic demand for "a transmutation of passion into art," Grove inscribed his lover's sexual "reality" into his fiction. From George's ideological insistence on elitism, Grove was forced to sell his prose in the larger mar-

ket place, inscribing his new motto into the epigraph of *Fanny Essler*:
"Jede wahre Kunst wendet sich an die Massen."[1] Using his lover's
sexualized story to sell his work to a mass public, the young, ambitious
novelist was, however, quickly accused of "prostituting" Elsa by those
close to the prestigious George-*Kreis*.[2]

That Grove should have been dismissed as a pimp by contemporary
readers is particularly interesting, since *Fanny Essler* is concerned with
the politics of prostitution and the victimization of a specularized female in naturalism. Grove, to be sure, gave the motif of prostitution a
significantly new twist, since his protagonist subverts the sexual stereotype that her society wishes to impose: Fanny Essler defines herself as
a woman who is sexually free, even wildly promiscuous, but not a prostitute. However, in her struggle to create a new identity for herself, Fanny
falls back into conventional entrapments. She is often victimized because
she insists on being what Angela Carter has polemically called the "good
bad girl," who professes to take money only as a "gift," not as payment
for sexual pleasure – a duplicitous convention that leaves Fanny extremely vulnerable, since it allows her male lovers not only to exploit
her sexually but to humiliate her at the same time. For most of her lovers, Fanny is a prostitute, albeit a special one that they need not pay
because Fanny is reluctant to ask for money.

In many ways, Fanny Essler parodies the naturalist insistence on prostitution, and one key to Grove's naturalism lies in the novel's deeply
parodic vision. Parodic appropriation and play are, indeed, the trade-
mark of Grove's German and Canadian fiction,[3] but more generally,
David Baguley has identified irony and parody as a characteristic feature of naturalist fiction: "In a sense, everything in the naturalist world
tends in time towards degraded repetition, which is the essence of satire
and parody" (*NF* 143). Naturalist fiction parodically brings "down to
earth" idealized situations, characters, and genres. If Grove's obvious

---

1 "All true art is addressed to the masses," my translation, *Fanny Eßler* (Berlin: Juncker,
   1905) [iv]. Further references will appear in the text, abbreviated *FE*; unless otherwise
   indicated, translated quotations are drawn from *Fanny Essler*, 2 vols., trans. Christine
   Helmers, A.W. Riley, and D.O. Spettigue (Ottawa: Oberon Press, 1984).

2 See Marcus Behmer in a letter to Ernst Hardt (dated February 19, 1907), in Ernst
   Hardt, *Briefe an Ernst Hardt: Eine Auswahl aus den Jahren 1998–1947*, ed. Jochen Meyer
   (Marbach: Deutsches Literaturarchiv, 1975) 53.

3 For a brilliant discussion of *Fanny Essler* as a parody of German *Neuromantik*, see
   Blodgett 112–53; for FPG's parodic intent in his poetic writing, see Elsa von
   Freytag-Loringhoven, "Autobiography," Djuna Barnes Collection, University of
   Maryland Archives, 165–66.

talent for parody and his predilection for the Flaubertian plots of resignation show an affinity for naturalism's ironic vision, his outspoken rejection of Zolaesque naturalism[4] suggests the opposite. In many ways, Grove's contribution consists in giving the naturalist conventions themselves a parodic twist that reflects his simultaneous struggle against and adherence to this genre.

If Grove's relationship with the naturalist genre is characterized by a complex ambivalence, his attitude towards the new woman and her sexuality is fraught with even deeper contradictions. A reader of Ibsen's *Hedda Gabler* (1890), Fanny Essler frequently challenges naturalism's gender stereotypes. Not only does she refuse to be a *Schablone* (a type) but, unlike Carrie, Fanny is a true "ex-centric" in the sense that she never fully belongs to any social group into which she is initiated. Yet she often finds herself back in the straitjacket of the genre's limiting conventions, portrayed as naturalism's sexualized victim. On the one hand, then, the novel endorses the new woman's cause, defending her unconventionality and her claim to sexual and artistic freedom as well as her desire for a new language. On the other hand, the naturalist conventions also provide the author with a convenient strategy to frame and "discipline" his rebelling female protagonist, in order to impose some order on the threat of her explosive articulation of formerly "repressed" artistic and sexual desires. As a result of such contradictions, Grove's naturalism is even more overtly self-contradictory than Dreiser's.

The structure of *Fanny Essler* exemplifies this point. Echoing the dramatic division so typical of naturalist fiction, the novel's structure highlights five focal points: Introduction of the Heroine, Berlin, Theatre, Love, and Death. The early announcement of the protagonist's death in the table of contents places the heroine in a naturalist tradition that is obsessed with the sexualized woman's death in a plot of decline, aligning her with Flaubert's *Madame Bovary*, Zola's *Nana*, Hardy's *Tess* (1891), Crane's *Maggie* (1892), and Fontane's *Effi Briest* (1895). Also, the early announcement of Fanny's death, combined with the evocation of typically naturalistic settings (Berlin, the theatre) and the explicit situating of the novel in the contemporary reality ("the novel takes place between 1892 to 1903") combine to suggest to the reader that this is the story of a contemporary "lost woman," who pays the price for her unconventional sexuality. However, while Grove's association of femininity with death signals a (typically naturalist) sexualization of the female body, *Fanny Essler* simultaneously maintains a parodic distance from this tradition

---

4 See Grove, *It Needs to Be Said ...*, 53–59.

by refusing to present the protagonist's death as part of a causal chain. Fanny's death is not linked to her promiscuity, nor does it grow out of a sense of naturalist – or tragic – inevitability; it is as arbitrary as Don Quixote's in Cervantes' picaresque. After a series of adventures, Fanny's death simply enforces the closure of a narrative that otherwise has no end.[5]

Fanny Essler's promiscuity places the novel into Germany's turn-of-the-century tradition of sexualized literature. Published in the same year as *Fanny Essler*, Margarete Böhme's bestseller on a prostitute, *Tagebuch einer Verlorenen: Von einer Toten* (1905), was presented in the form of a diary (*Tagebuch*). These supposedly "authentic" notes of a dying, confessing woman placed Böhme's work firmly in the *fin-de-siècle* female confessional tradition, whose authenticity was supposed to be guaranteed by the reality of a female body behind the text. While both Böhme and Grove drew on conventions that signalled to the contemporary reader a "true story" on female sexuality, Böhme's *Tagebuch* was a huge financial success, followed by reprints, a follow-up novel entitled *Dida Ibsens Geschichte* (1907), and even a film in 1929; *Fanny Essler*, in contrast, achieved only a very modest critical success and, after one reprint in 1907, was virtually forgotten in Germany until Douglas Spettigue rediscovered the novel in his search for the "real" FPG and had it translated into English. The fact that Grove's male version of a woman's life (and sexuality) did not find the popular success enjoyed by Böhme's *Tagebuch* may be indicative of (female) readers' growing suspicion of the (male) realist-naturalist version of female sexuality. Subtitled "a novel," *Fanny Essler* is firmly situated in the male European tradition of realism-naturalism.

Grove's literary models, to be sure, were all male. Arriving in Munich at the turn of the century and witnessing the lionizing of Thomas Mann after his success with *Buddenbrooks* (1901), Grove hoped to imitate his predecessor's social and financial success with his first naturalist novel.[6] Even more important for Grove's representation of female sexuality, however, was the influence of Gustave Flaubert, as the Baroness

---

5 E. D. Blodgett's review of the translated Fanny Essler is appropriately entitled, "Grove's Female Picaresque," *Canadian Literature* 106 (1985): 152.

6 "'Fanny Essler' we thought ... even I ... in my own and his favour ... should at least make as much impression as 'Buddenbrooks,'" Baroness Elsa writes in her "Autobiography," 35. I am using the typescript version of the autobiography (prepared by Djuna Barnes), of which the University of Manitoba Archives have received a copy. Further references will appear in the text, abbreviated *A*. On Mann's spectacular success in Munich (at a time when FPG was living in Munich), see Thomas Willey, "Thomas Mann's Munich," Chapple and Schulte 477–91.

confirms: "He esteemed Flaubert highly as stylist, which speaks for cultivated taste, he *was* cultivated, so he tried to *be* Flaubert" (*A* 34–35). The parallels between *Fanny Essler* and *Madame Bovary* are, indeed, striking. Like Emma, Fanny is driven by her sexual desire only to encounter disillusionment in every sexual relationship; like Emma, Fanny puts on male clothing but ultimately fails to change the male world around her. Using *Madame Bovary* as a dialogical intertext, Grove, though, did more than just pay homage to his French mentor. Grove's German Emma Bovary undergoes a significant metamorphosis into a *fin-de-siècle* figure, whose sexuality is authenticated by Elsa's confessional life-story. Energized by Elsa's adventurous life and daring voice, *Fanny Essler* sets out to challenge naturalist conventions, struggling to subvert the stereotype of the entrapped female and daring to "feminize" the genre from within – but only within limits.

While Fanny shares important features with Carrie Meeber (both are protean figures, always in transition and flux), Fanny is a much more radical figure. Always breaking out of confining normative systems and defying the very notion of (intellectual) docility encapsulated in Carrie's body, she assumes the (un-naturalist) position of an independent female subject with a new voice. Arriving in Germany's metropolis in May 1892 after an adventurous flight from the home of her tyrannical father in small-town Kolberg, Fanny is imbued with a deep sense of *Selbständigkeit*, a sense of standing on her own feet, of independence, especially when she walks alone through the streets of Berlin. "Spazieren" (going for a walk) is what connects Fanny with the city, and Grove's novel gives us a sense of the streets and the public places she connects with: the Brandenburger Tor, the Tiergarten, Friedensallee, and Leipzigerstraße. She always returns to Friedrichstraße, the street with the fashionable stores, where she is riveted to the display windows, or where she goes to Café Kranzler to sit at the window to see and to be seen, a scene that echoes Carrie's pleasure and obsession with sitting at windows and gazing outside. Later in the novel, Fanny comes to identify herself and her sense of independence with the city of Berlin: "Sie war Berlin":

> This large network of streets belonged to her; she considered it her own: this was Berlin, and the fact she owned it was thanks to no-one else but herself; she owned it as her realm and she wouldn't have given it up for the easiest, most carefree life. (*FE* 2: 8)[7]

---

7 "Diese große Straßenflucht gehörte ihr: sie empfand sie als ihren Besitz: sie war Berlin: und daß sie dies Berlin besaß, es als ihr Reich besaß, verdankte sie niemand als sich und sie hätte es nicht für das sorgenfreieste, glatteste Leben hergegeben" (*FE* 282).

Here the city connotes a breaking of spatial boundaries and social mores; it connotes the transition of the female from domestic into public space. Fanny has entered a new realm, adopting a new role, a new identity, and a new language for herself.

In her celebration of Berlin, Fanny deliberately uses masculine, territorial terms, terms of appropriation to describe her newly found freedom in the city. On one level, Fanny's language indicates that as a woman she is working within – she is adopting – the masculine terms that rule and structure the (female) city. But just as the city of Berlin cannot really be appropriated, Fanny's words have an ironic-parodic twist, especially since nothing is as foreign to Fanny as notions of ownership and possession. If anything, Fanny is ruled by the feminine economy of the gift that Hélène Cixous describes as follows: "If there is a 'propriety of woman,' it is paradoxically her capacity to depropriate unselfishly, body without end, without appendage, without principle 'parts.'"[8] Or, as Luce Irigaray puts it: "Le propre, la propriété sont, sans doute, assez étrangers au féminin. Du moins sexuellement. Mais non *le proche*" (*CS* 30). In her usage of the terms of appropriation to describe her closeness with the city spaces, Fanny parodically subverts the masculine language from within and implicitly signals that like the city, she herself cannot be (completely) owned or possessed by anyone.

And yet, despite the parodic note, this double discourse – the subsuming of the discourse of female independence in a masculine language of ownership, and domination – should make the reader suspicious. Even though the city is represented as a female icon, it appears to be ruled by a masculine order that inevitably reaches out to take control of the "independent" woman. Fanny Essler's picaresque journey towards independence is, not surprisingly, full of reversals. As she looks for accommodations in Berlin, the first sign Fanny is pointed to reads: "Advice and Protection for Young Women Travelling Alone" (*FE* 1: 61), a sign that is highly ironic if one considers that both Carrie and Fanny find their "protectors" in the first men they meet in Chicago and Berlin, Charles Drouet and Axel Dahl, who quickly become their lovers and without whom they feel alone, without courage, and overwhelmed by the city. Despite the nausea Fanny feels about the sexual relationship with Axel ("she had to close her eyes so as not to feel repelled" [*FE* 1: 82]), she needs his encouragement and jocularity: "The

---

8 Hélène Cixous, "The Laugh of the Medusa," trans. Marilyn A. August, *New French Feminisms: An Anthology*, ed. Elaine Marks and Isabelle de Courtivron (New York: Schocken Books, 1981) 259.

minute they parted, her courage failed" (*FE* 1: 81). Drouet and Dahl are similar characters: both are happy-go-luckies, and both are the archetypal male survivors in the city in diametrical contrast to the city's (male) sacrificial victims. As the self-proclaimed protectors of females they, in fact, conquer the women in the sexual relationships, so that the protectorship quickly takes on the overtones of pimping and sexual mastery.

Even as Fanny's linguistic play defies the naturalist confinement of the female within a fixed script, the novel frequently confirms the very naturalist conventions it calls into question, particularly in its treatment of female sexuality. Though Fanny's *spazieren* subverts the very idea of the naturalist streetwalker, prostitution is inevitably projected, and imposed as a role, on the female who ventures out into the city and claims the street or the night for herself. This recalls *Sister Carrie*'s treatment of the same motif. When Carrie stands at the foot of the stairs of her sister's apartment, she is immediately approached like a prostitute. On fashionable Broadway, Carrie discovers that "any one looking" at her and her friend Mrs. Vance "would *pick* Mrs. Vance for her raiment alone" (*SC* 340; emphasis added). While Carrie herself uses the language of prostitution, without even being aware of it, Fanny, in contrast, takes pleasure in acting "as if we're like one of those" (*FE* 1: 114). Here, Fanny's parodic mimicking of the role of prostitute takes on a rebellious, subversive edge, with the novel challenging the convention of the naturalist "fallen woman" by suggesting that for the "new woman," this is a role she can put on (in a provocative gesture) as easily as she can take it off again. And yet, despite Fanny's subversive edge, her language is doubly ironic, as it also anticipates her later need to appeal to lovers for money and parodically echoes the fact that later in the novel she is forced to recognize herself as a prostitute in these lovers' eyes. Thus the naturalist convention of the "inevitable prostitute" is simultaneously parodied (in Fanny's self-conscious play) and confirmed (as one of naturalism's male conventions).

In his comparison of *Fanny Essler* with Döblin's *Alexanderplatz*, Anthony Riley explores prostitution in a somewhat literal sense: "Young girls from the working classes or even the petite bourgeoisie, unable to make a decent living wage, are forced to resort to prostitution to make enough money to buy essential food and clothes."[9] Plausible though

---

9 Anthony W. Riley, "The Case of Greve/Grove: The European Roots of a Canadian Writer," *The Old World and The New: Literary Perspectives of German-speaking Canadians*, ed. Walter E. Riedel (Toronto: U of Toronto P, 1984) 46; see also Lawrence Hussman, "The Fate of the Fallen Woman in *Maggie* and *Sister Carrie*," *The Image of the Prostitute*

this argument may be, it glosses over the fact that Grove, like Dreiser, is concerned *not* primarily with the exploration of basic or essential human *needs* – the primary concern of nineteenth-century naturalism – but rather with an exploration of human *desire* in an emerging consumer society. (After all, Fanny's motto is not "Du pain! du pain! du pain!", as Émile Zola translates the essential need of the starving workers in the archetypal naturalistic novel, *Germinal* [1885].[10]) If Fanny wanted simply to fulfill her "needs," she would be happy in her own room in her father's house, or even with her Berlin aunt, Miss Blaurock, or her well-to-do friend Heinrich Stumpf, or her husband Eduard Barrel, all of whom are concerned with providing for her needs: "'I don't just want what I *need*'" (*FE* 2: 34) is how Fanny summarizes her desire for "more." Indeed, the naturalist preoccupation with need is parodied in Fanny's anorexic body: she is often hungry, even starving, but when offered food she frequently declines it and spends her last money on clothing and cigarettes. Similarly, she needs a wardrobe to be a serious actress on stage, but she quarrels with her aunt who might be able to finance this costly venture; when she finally receives money (through her mother's inheritance), she spends it on useless painting lessons.

Like Dreiser, Grove abandons the nineteenth-century focus on (instinctual) need to explore (psychological) desire, although Grove's evaluation of this sexualized drive is different from Dreiser's. While *Sister Carrie* presents an erasure of conventional forms of alliance in order to illustrate the deployment of sexuality in the modern consumer economy, Grove, in contrast, shows that the roots of desire are found in traditional forms of kinship. This difference in the conceptualization of desire can be attributed to Grove's earlier exposure to psychoanalysis. With its emphasis on the Oedipal family as the primary locus of sexuality, the novel highlights that Fanny's desire is born in the relationship with her mother and father, and thus is cathected with the conflicting emotions that she attaches to her parents. In Fanny's life, the desire "for more" energizes her journey into female independence, but it is simultaneously presented as a (naturalist) force of female subjection. These unresolved contradictions are a reflection of Grove's own ambivalent relationship towards (sexual) desire and the demands of the new woman.

---

in Modern Literature, ed. Pierre L. Horn and Mary Beth Pringle (New York: Frederick Ungar Publishing, 1984) 100, for a similar approach to Carrie Meeber, "who knows the agony of deprivation and knows that she must do anything to escape it, including using sexual favors for advancement."

10   Émile Zola, *Germinal*, Livre de Poche (Paris: Fasquelle, 1968) 335.

As a force of resistance, Fanny's desire is linked to her mother. Grove, significantly, uses the term "longing" ("Sehnsucht") rather than Lacan's favourite terms "wish" or "desire" (*Wunsch, Begierde, Begehren*) to describe the force that propels Fanny into action: "Her longing had almost changed into despair.... It was almost as if she sensed that her deep-rooted longing – a longing from which all other feelings, including her love of animals, stemmed – that this longing never could be satisfied" (*FE* 1: 37). "Longing" gains significance in Jane Gallop's feminist (re)reading of Jacques Lacan's theory: "Man's desire will henceforth be linked by law to a menace; but woman's desire will legally cohabit with nostalgia: she will not be able to give up her desire for what she can never have (again)," Gallop writes.[11] For Gallop, this nostalgia is grounded in a longing for the lost mother, "the mother as womb, homeland, source, and grounding for the subject." Since the mother (as homeland) is lost forever, the "subject is hence in a foreign land, alienated."

Gallop's Lacanian reading can be applied to Fanny's desire. Not only is Fanny's mother absent in the novel, but the novel is framed by Fanny's memory of her mother, a memory that is always accompanied by her desire to *return* to Berlin – "*Back* to Berlin" (*FE* 1: 40; emphasis added), "*Wieder* nach Berlin" (*FE* 31) – as if it were a home. Each time, this nostalgic desire to "return" is expressed in opposition to the dominating male figures in Fanny's life: the first time, it is her father who wants to keep her in Kolberg, her "Vaterstadt"; and the second time it is her lover Friedrich Karl Reelen, who wants to get her away from Berlin. Thus Grove inscribes Fanny's "nostalgic" desire (for her mother and Berlin) as a subversive force that becomes the root of her rebellion against male tyranny. At the same time, *Fanny Essler* also confirms the Lacanian point that desire is "an offshoot of that part of need which 'finds itself alienated.'"[12] Although her desire is for Berlin, once in Berlin Fanny often feels out of place; although her sense of identity is connected with Berlin (and her mother), her sense of identity in Berlin is highly precarious. It appears that the more Fanny's feels the splits and contradictions of her subjectivity, the more she feels the need to ground this subjectivity by yearning for a maternal home, for a space of origin (that she will never be able to recover). Here desire, then, is linked to homesickness, connected as it is with the memory of the lost mother.

---

11 Jane Gallop, *Reading Lacan* (Ithaca & London: Cornell UP, 1988) 146. The following quotations are from page 148.

12 Gallop 149.

While Fanny's desire for "more" is a desire for female independence emancipation, and self-determination, Grove deliberately sexualizes psychologizes, and problematizes this drive as that which ultimately confines Fanny within naturalism's textual boundaries. If Grove's original intent was to "free" the naturalist female from the traditional – genetic – entrapment, he does not really "liberate" her but further enchains her in new seductive psychological and socioeconomic snares, in which even her desire for female independence can be turned against her, used as an ingenious male tool of subjection. Like Flaubert, Grove conceptualizes female desire in terms of a sexual fantasy – the quest for the elusive fairy-tale "prince" who will be her "saviour," and who, in Fanny's case, is really a psychological father-ersatz. Whereas Emma Bovary remains caught in the romantic conventions of her readings, Fanny's emancipatory desire for "more" makes her intellectually recognize and criticize male constructions, but involves her nonetheless in a psychologized, compulsive search for the *Märchenprinz*-father-ersatz. Thus sexualized and recolonized, Fanny's desire for independence becomes the very force that enchains her in naturalism's conventions. These ironic reversals are a structural and thematic pattern of *Fanny Essler*, continually exposing the novel's ideological contradictions. The novel presents itself as a parodic spiral, which turns back upon itself, both challenging and confirming naturalist conventions.

The ambivalence of this parodic play is illustrated in Fanny's sexual relationship with men. On her first day in Berlin, Fanny is "seduced" by a stranger in a spontaneous theatrical street performance that both echoes and gives a parodic twist to Dreiser's motif of the city's scopophilic "eye of power." Window-shopping on Berlin's fashion street, Fanny becomes self-conscious when she recognizes a man gazing through his monocle at her reflection in a store window: "At that point the man flung his head back, which forced the hat to slip down his neck, his eyes and mouth popped open, the monocle fell and he stared at her. He held his hands under the collar in his cape pockets. Fanny saw all of this in the window and it was so comical that she turned away and giggled" (*FE* 1: 71). The voyeur-exhibitionist Axel Dahl parodies male scopophilia in this *mise-en-abîme* of gazes in the glass of a store window. Drawing attention to the theatricality of the city, Dahl displays a critical self-consciousness of the traditional specular pattern of male seduction. Such parodic subversion suggests the possibility of new roles between men and women, as well as the possibility of a rupture in naturalism's deterministic scopophilic economy.

Yet it is this very parodic play that initiates the rapist sex act that follows between Dahl and Fanny, the deliberate crudity of which reinscribes in *Fanny Essler* the naturalist topoi of female sexual subjection. For Dreiser, the city's imaginary quality is part of its never-ending potential ("The city of which I sing was not of land or sea or any time or place. Look for it in vain!");[13] Grove, in contrast, exposes the city's theatrical possibilities as a dangerous illusion. As soon as Fanny finds herself caught in the "reality" of sex, the possibility of playing a new role vanishes. Cornered by Axel, she undergoes a reverse metamorphosis into naturalist femininity: "she let him do with her as he pleased" (*FE* 1: 81), her "yielding" to his rapist sexuality always already predetermined in naturalism's textual web. Seduced by Axel Dahl, the "new woman" quickly finds herself back in the straitjacket of naturalist conventions, recontained in her role of sexualized victim.

To say that Grove draws attention to female complicity in her own sexualized subjection is, however, not enough. Highlighting the psychological interiorization of deterministic social structures, Grove's naturalism illustrates that the most ingenious jailer is often in the woman herself. In Part 3, for example, Fanny recognizes that she has undergone a pleasurable metamorphosis in her looks: she has become "großstädtisch," "citified," as she has become submerged in the big city's scopic economy.

> And if she came to a display window in which there were large mirrors she would stop and look at herself and try to see herself as a stranger would see her. And each time she was surprised all over again: this was Fanny Essler? (*FE* 2: 8; in the German text 282)

Not only has Fanny's own gaze been replaced by an internalized "stranger's" gaze, but the reflection she sees and falls in love with is literally in the place of the commodified object in the display window. This scene establishes a parodic dialogue with Zola's *Au Bonheur*, in which Denise and her brother admire in the display window of the new Parisian department store the headless mannequins, "portant des prix en gros chiffres, à la place des têtes" (*AB* 14). While *Au Bonheur* provides a male spectator who enjoys the spectacle of "ces belles femmes à vendre," in *Fanny Essler* the (male) gazer is present only in Fanny's own fantasy, suggesting how much the determining social structures have penetrated her body and mind. Here, the capitalist economy of desire not only seduces women into enjoying their own "fabrication" as specular objects of art, but it even seduces them into experiencing fe-

---

13 Theodore Dreiser, *Dawn* (New York: Horace Liveright, 1931) 156.

male "Selbstständigkeit" in their being seen, in their being a specular object for others. The internalized psychological constraints are thus revealed to be as powerful as the genetic determinants in Zola's novels. This internalization of an external spectator also aligns Fanny with the exhibitionist naturalist actress-prostitute. Zola's *Nana*, Dreiser's *Sister Carrie*, and Wharton's *The House of Mirth* illustrate that literal and metaphorical prostitution are often represented as a specular relationship between a male spectator and a female *tableau vivant*. *Nana* opens with an extended scene on the heroine's enactment of *La Blonde Venus* and ends with the audience's "orgasmic climax"; *Sister Carrie* offers to its male characters (and readers) a seemingly eternal scopophilic "foreplay"; and Lily Bart brings to the stage a high-class artistic sexuality, designed to arouse the (matrimonial) desires of New York's millionaire-bachelors. In her book *La Vie quotidienne dans les maisons closes, 1830–1930* (1990), Laure Adler has described the transformation of sexual practices in high-society brothels by emphasizing the increasing desire for – distanced – specular pleasures in the late nineteenth century: "Most observers of the period agree that the sexual demands of the rich were progressively transformed: consumption of the sexual act was abandoned in favor of visual orgasm. Certainly voyeurism had always been an essential component of desire, but the house of ill-fame began systematically to offer tableaux vivants."[14] Since the "visual orgasm" is a favourite naturalist topoi, as the examples of Nana, Carrie, and Lily illustrate, it is significant that Grove's new woman should be financially most successful in her "portrayal of marble statues," images that freeze her movement and life into highly sexualized statuesque objects, such as "'Ariadne riding on the panther' and 'Venus chastising Cupid'" (*FE* 1: 235).

Grove, to be sure, exposes the social and literary construction of the prostitute as a misogynistic convention. The novel satirizes its male figures in scenes in which Fanny is asked to provide such "visual orgasms." Fanny's fetishist-lover Nepomuk Bolle, a stained-glass artist in Berlin, derives sexual satisfaction from watching not so much Fanny's naked body as her hands. In fact, he creates a *Gesamtkunstwerk*, with Fanny on a church-like bench and the light falling through the stained-glass window (designed by Bolle): "'Those hands!' Mr. Bolle whispered in a sonorous voice, 'Just look at those hands!' Fanny looked at her hands in amazement: they looked very pale next to the dark stained oak. "'Truly, Miss Essler,' Madame Consul said quietly, 'You have authentic

---

14 Quoted in Apter 42.

Bolle-hands!'" (*FE* 2: 25).[15] Bolle typifies Freud's suggestion that "fetishist and voyeur alike, resisting passage to the Oedipal symbolic order, become fixed regressively in the anal-erotic stage."[16] While Bolle's scopophilic obsession is satirized as an infantile and unmasculine *idée fixe*, it also gives birth to his art, providing the male artist with a subject status that is denied to Fanny. A similar target of ridicule, his anal obsession – best encapsulated in his stinginess towards Fanny and his collectomania – gives him financial power over Fanny.

Presenting an overt critique of such patterns of sexualized power in his parody of male (and naturalist) scopophilia, Grove's parody also allows him to participate covertly in the very male specular obsessions that his narrative ridicules. Fanny's bedroom exudes the same sexuality as Nana's boudoir, and the dressing room in the Berlin theatre provides the same "pile-up" effect of women that Emily Apter describes as typical for the brothel's "composite of differences," or *l'hétéroclite*, in nineteenth-century French naturalism.[17] Peeping into Fanny's bedroom or into the dressing room at the theatre, the reader is turned into a complicitous spy who is invited to share this undressing of women, whereby the emphasis on clothing and underwear has the simultaneous function of keeping "the specter of the essential naked body at bay."[18] In his *Ways of Seeing*, John Berger distinguishes between nudity and nakedness: "To be nude is to be seen naked by others and yet not recognized for oneself. A naked body has to be seen as an object to become nude. (The sight of it as an object stimulates the use of it as an object.) Nakedness reveals itself. Nudity is placed on display."[19] The scopophilic obsession with nudity that characterizes Grove's males is one that is shared by the author himself. Like his male characters, the author maintains his male control by keeping his distance, "enjoying" Fanny as a specularized – naturalist – fetish.

In some ways, the author's complicity with naturalist conventions is also similar to Fanny's submission to the very conventions she rebels against. Often Fanny rejects valuable strategies of resistance, as she does when she works as a chorus girl in Berlin. Joking about their male

---

15 For a detailed discussion of this scene as a satire of German *Neuromantik*, see Blodgett, *Configuration*, 130–31.

16 Apter 52.

17 Apter 55.

18 Apter 86.

19 John Berger et al., *Ways of Seeing* (1972; London: BBC & Penguin, 1981) 54.

"souteneurs," the actresses satirically deflate the sexual attention they receive, particularly in their disillusioned but also refreshingly wicked language, in their dialect, their vulgarity, and their curses against their male lovers: "Those damn men!"; "They're shits ... all of them" (*FE* 1: 187). Though Fanny rejects these linguistic weapons of subversive resistance in order to show the world around her that she is more refined and "above" the common chorus girl, she does not reject the signifiers of female sexualization. The sight of the lace underwear and black silk stockings of one of the actresses – both paid for by one of her rich customers – arouses Fanny's desire to possess the same underwear and makes her conclude that "her [own] underthings were plain and unmistakably bourgeois" (*FE* 1: 191). Later, when her lover Ehrhard Stein wants to give Fanny a present, her only desire is for some silken slips.[20]

Conversely, when Fanny does resist her exploitation, this resistance is often articulated in forms that bring her close to the naturalist *femme fatale*. Just as Carrie verbally berates and then leaves Drouet once she has found a new lover in Hurstwood (only to leave Hurstwood once he becomes a burden), so Fanny often treats her lovers with an uncompromising and cold revenge for the humiliation she has suffered in the relationship. Not only does she drop lovers without blinking an eye, but she often confronts them with their own uselessness. As Hurstwood commits suicide after Carrie leaves him in the city, so Fanny's husband Eduard Barrel kills himself after Fanny takes off with Barrel's best friend, Friedrich Karl Reelen. This "tragic" ending, though, is one of Grove's deliberate making. Elsa's memoirs show that the real-life husband, the *Jugendstil* architect August Endell (1871–1925), not only "survived" his wife's adultery, but in an ugly divorce battle successfully stripped her of money that was rightfully hers. Grove's enforced "tragic" twist, then, exposes the author's deliberate conformity to the very naturalist conventions that he had set out to subvert.

Given the author's ambivalent resistance to and simultaneous exploitation of naturalist conventions, it should come as no surprise that Fanny herself becomes a living oxymoron. Fanny is bursting with energy: she acts, she paints, she is interested in literature and critical discussions, and she is determined to live life to the fullest. The narrator describes this desire for *Leben* as "eine ungeheure Lebenslust" (*FE* 79), which has been translated into English as "an incredible lust for life" (*FE* 1: 81). But

---

20 It is noteworthy that Grove's letters show his own obsession with underclothes. Numerous letters to his wife are crowded with references to his laundry, his shirts and underwear. See Pacey, *The Letters of Frederick Philip Grove*.

the German word *ungeheuer* literally translated means monstrous, unnatural, too much, connotations that describe how many characters (including the narrator) perceive Fanny.[21] Fanny is seen as a threat, as untamed energy and unnatural vivacity, which the males would like to direct, to channel and tame in order not to be conquered by it.

Just as Elsa Baroness von Freytag-Loringhoven complained in her autobiography that Grove dismissed her writing of the "story of my childhood" with "ironical derision" and with shoulder-shrugging contempt, so Fanny is not recognized as the artist she wants to be. Trying to be an artist, Fanny continually turns from artistic subject into object, into naturalist *tableau vivant*. Driven by a desire for art, Fanny becomes acquainted with various lovers and friends – painters, a stained-glass artist (Nepomuk Bolle), a sculptor (Heinrich Stumpf), and playwrights (Ehrhard Stein, Eduard Barrel). Though she is very capable of having intellectual discussions with them, her role is mostly that of a sexual consort from her lovers' and society's point of view. She does not succeed as an actress, and her painting remains essentially dabbling that is easily dismissed by her male friends. Like the author himself, who designed the original cover for *Fanny Essler*, Fanny also works on book designs, although they never find their way into any publication. Her art is always aborted, is only measured against a "superior" male art. Fanny is not the artist she yearns to be, but is often presented as a prostituted work of art to be looked at and subjected to the sensual specular touch of every character in the novel as well as the narrator and the author.

Although Grove satirizes the male artists who appropriate Fanny's *élan* and energy for their artistic productions, Grove's own transformations of Elsa's life-story also have the effect of making Fanny less of an artist, as well as of diminishing Elsa's artistic achievement on the stage

---

21 "Ungeheuer," the word that Franz Kafka chose to characterize Gregor Samsa's metamorphosis into an insect, is repeatedly applied to Fanny in the novel. She is playfully called "Ungeheuer" (little monster) by her aunt; she paints a picture of "the vast life" in Berlin, "das Bild von dem ungeheuren Leben," and her entrance into the city appears to Fanny as "ungeheuer erfolgreich," an "enormous success"; see *FE* 138, 54, 62; in trans. 1: 138, 60, 67. Similarly, Fanny's courage ("Mut") is often given a negative twist in the novel. Repeatedly, Fanny is linked to "Übermut" (57, 58, 65, 66, 70, 169, passim, in the German text), which the English text often translates by giving it the exclusively positive meaning of "high spirited." But "Übermut," like "ungeheuer," has a primarily negative connotation in German, implying a slippage into a dangerous situation (as in the German popular saying, "Übermut tut selten gut").

or as a writer. Grove's ambivalent oscillation between the demands of the new woman and his fear of her powers, between his desire to transform naturalism and his need for its secure gender boundaries, produces a self-deconstructive naturalist fiction that exposes its own (and its male author's) gender bias. This is most clearly illustrated in the novel's use and thematizing of the female sexual confession, which will be examined in the next chapter.

7

Fanny's Sexual Confession

Baroness Elsa's memoirs, written in the mid-twenties (when she was living in abject poverty in Berlin), highlight how much Grove was indebted to her for providing the raw material for his naturalist exploration of female sexuality twenty years earlier. "He had written two novels. They were dedicated to me in so far as material was concerned, it was *my life* and persons out of my life. He did the executive part of the business, giving the thing the conventional shape and dress," writes Elsa (*A* 34–35).[1] Since the female sexual confession had established itself at the turn of the century as a highly marketable, even best-selling, genre (as Margarete Böhme's work illustrates), Grove probably hoped to achieve a financial success by incorporating Elsa's sexual confession into his fiction.[2] That he was prepared to exploit the conventions of this newly

---

1 Elsa's original manuscript even says that the novels were "dictated by me." Preparing the typescript from Elsa's manuscript, Djuna Barnes probably misread these words; see Spettigue, "Felix, Elsa, André Gide and Others," 12 and 38, n. 5.

2 In a letter to André Gide (September 20, 1905), he claims that he is "certain of its success," quoted in Spettigue, "Felix, Elsa, André Gide and Others," 32.

emerging female genre is reflected in the fact that he even considered omitting his name from the novel. Gaby Divay has noted that Grove toyed with the idea of publishing *Fanny Essler* as an anonymous autobiography,[3] as he explains in a letter to André Gide: "L'un des romans de Mme Essler, qui paraîtra sans nom d'auteur et que M. l'éditeur croit une autobiographie, aura pour titre: *Fanny Essler*."[4] Determined to write a money-making novel, Grove may very well have thought of Laurence Housman's *An Englishwoman's Loveletters* (1900), which was published anonymously and became an immediate success as an "authentic" woman's story, until the author's male identity became known one year after the novel's publication. After all, the absence of the author's name on the book cover of a female confession is a signifier for its sexual content that stimulates the reader's projection of an authenticating female body behind the confessing voice.[5]

It is probably fair to say that *Fanny Essler* grew out of some kind of collaboration with Elsa. Whether she provided a written or an oral account of her life story is not known. With Grove, however, claiming exclusive authorship for the novel by putting his name on the cover, *Fanny Essler* exemplifies the problematic appropriation of the female sexual confession into *fin-de-siècle* naturalist fiction. This is all the more significant as the novel itself is concerned with the power effects of Fanny's confessions within the text. The novel provides a kind of *mise-en-abyme* of "confessor-fathers," with the male author, narrator, and characters all listening to, and exploiting, Elsa's sexual confessions. While Elsa's "collaborative" voice often becomes submerged in the novel's naturalist web, as often it erupts as a voice of protest and resistance against male (and naturalist) versions of truth.

My usage of the term *sexual confession* is borrowed from Michel Foucault, who writes that the "confession was, and still remains, the general standard governing the production of the true discourse on sex" (*HS* 63). Foucault has theorized this discursive practice in detail, arguing that it is part of a century-old social tradition: "This is the essential thing: that Western man has been drawn for three centuries to the task of telling everything concerning his sex; that since the classical age there

---

3 Gaby Divay, "Felix Paul Greve's Fanny Essler Novel and Poems: His or Hers?," unpublished ms, 7.

4 Grove, letter to Gide, October 17, 1904, quoted in Divay, 21, n. 45.

5 I am grateful to Lorraine Kooistra for bringing Laurence Housman's novel to my attention.

has been a constant optimization and an increasing valorization of the discourse on sex; and that this carefully analytical discourse was meant to yield multiple effects of displacement, intensification, reorientation, and modification of desire itself" (*HS* 23). The confession, Foucault argues, has become a modern ritual of sexualized power. "Having to tell everything, being able to pose questions about everything, found their justification in the principle that endowed sex with inexhaustible and polymorphous causal power" (*HS* 65). In this confessional spiral, the minutest detail of sexual behaviour, "whether an accident or a deviation, a deficit or an excess," is seen as part of a causal chain that eventually makes sex "cause of any and everything" (*HS* 65). While this causal network continually increases the desire to extract even more truths on sexuality, the sexual confession also gives the agencies of truth (science, medicine, psychoanalysis) a tool with which to "police" the sexual body.

If the male confession has had a centuries-long history, the female confession, in contrast, appears to be a relatively young phenomenon. It was the late-nineteenth-century psychoanalytic and sexological desire to map out the unexplored territory of women's sexuality that led to an increased effort to make women "speak" about their sexualities in confessional texts in order to capture women's "authentic" sexualities, to find out "what women really want," and to solve their sexual problems, such as anesthesia, or frigidity. These problematic areas of female sexuality are the very motifs that naturalist fiction had embraced as its favourite concerns. Foucault and poststructuralist feminists warn us that the confession is fraught with dangers for the confessing person. Where Foucault has discussed the confession in gender-neutral terms, contemporary feminists have emphasized that it is, above all, women who find themselves caught in confessional traps. To quote Rosalind Coward: "The pressure to confess does not, however, affect the sexes equally. Women bear the burden of speech in this area. ... Women are required to make sense of sexual relationships, they are meant to negotiate, explain, confess, keep the relationship in circulation."[6] Also, Rita Felski has noted that much of twentieth-century women's writing takes a confessional form, often drawing on the conventions of the diary or the autobiography. Skeptically questioning whether the female confession constitutes a "liberating step" for women, Felski has proposed to examine "the value and limitations of this trend toward self-disclosure."[7]

---

6 Coward 138–39.

7 Rita Felski, *Beyond Feminist Aesthetics: Feminist Literature and Social Change* (Cambridge, MA: Harvard UP, 1989) 86.

As Grove's use of Elsa's life story suggests, one danger of the confession is that it can be easily appropriated and recolonized by a male discourse. Given this danger of recontainment, the differences between Grove's naturalism and Elsa's memoirs deserve some close attention. If we follow the Baroness's memoirs, she had performed in very successful roles at the Central Theatre in Berlin, the "most fashionable stage." Grove's Fanny Essler, in contrast, never moves seriously beyond the amateur stage because she lacks the money to buy the expensive wardrobe necessary for a successful acting career. Also, while Elsa started posing for "Marble Figures" before she had any formal training at all, the "Marble Figure" episode in Grove's novel, significantly, follows rather than precedes Fanny's formal training and thus shows a (naturalistic) social fall and entrapment rather than an artistic development. Not only does Grove's naturalist transformation diminish Elsa's status as a serious artist, but the fictionalized Fanny Essler is also more strongly victimized compared to the young woman who emerges in the Baroness's memoirs of her Berlin years.

Fanny Essler has to be given credit for exposing the very confessional power play that the novel exploits. The novel draws attention to the confession as a ritual of sexualized power, in which "the agency of domination does not reside in the one who speaks (for it is he who is constrained), but in the one who listens and says nothing" (*HS* 62). To quote Foucault:

> The confession is a ritual of discourse in which the speaking subject is also the subject of the statement; it is also a ritual that unfolds within a power relationship, for one does not confess without the presence (or virtual presence) of a partner who is not simply the interlocutor but the authority who requires the confession, prescribes and appreciates it, and intervenes in order to judge, punish, forgive, console, and reconcile; ... [a ritual that] produces intrinsic modifications in the person who articulates it: it exonerates, redeems, and purifies him; it unburdens him of his wrongs, liberates him, and promises him salvation. (*HS* 61–62)

Fanny Essler is saturated with such rituals of sexual confession. The confessional question/answer pattern is what gives Fanny's first lover in Berlin access to her body: "Tell me the whole story," Axel Dahl says, and "Fanny started to tell him everything" (*FE* 1:74–75). She lays open how much money she has, gives him insight into her past, her desires, her seduction by the Baron in Kolberg, while her new acquaintance gazes deeper and deeper into the "secrets" of her life and prompts her revelations with further questions: "What sort of a baron is this?", "And what did he want?", "You didn't actually ...?" (*FE* 1:75). According to Foucault, there is a curious link of power and pleasure in the sexual confession; the person confessing is seduced by "all this careful attention, this caressing extortion of the most intimate details, these pressing explorations."[8]

How much this sexual confession is tied into the power relationship is revealed when, after the confession, Axel claims Fanny for sexual intercourse because, he argues, she had done it with the Baron as well. He has become the interpreter of her secret confession, imposing his own and society's view on her, namely, that once virginity has been renounced, the woman loses the right to decide over her body. Here, his language rapidly switches from questions to imperatives: "Now don't be stupid," Axel says, after which "she let him do with her as he pleased" (FE 1:81). The fact that Fanny accepts Axel's logic and dominance so quickly makes one wonder how much Fanny has really distanced herself from what she earlier dismissed as the old bourgeois ideas about seduction and dishonour.[9]

In *Fanny Essler*, female pleasure continually shifts from the sexual act to its transformation into discourse, a confessional pleasure that Grove's narrative exposes and satirizes as *ersatz*-pleasure that feeds on and reproduces hierarchical gender relations. Like her earlier sexual contacts with men, Fanny's sexual contact with her husband Eduard Barrel leads to frustration: "'But I don't feel anything,' she sobbed" on her wedding night (FE 2:121). As a result, Fanny and Eduard spend whole nights talking and analyzing her frustration: "So it came to pass that this couple who could not achieve a physical union found themselves in such a state, an almost feverish logic, as a result of their nightly theorizing, that Fanny was requiring her husband to scout around and find her the lover who would help her" (FE 2:141). As Eduard "suchte sie zu trösten, zu vertrösten" (FE 424),[10] this discursive pleasure feeds her desire but eternally defers satisfaction, and thus perpetuates her sexual confessions. She feels privileged to have a husband to whom she can confess her sexual problems, fantasies, and infatuations: "It really was very nice of Eduard to let her tell him all these things! How would other men have reacted!" (FE 2:171). Despite the torture of their lives together, Fanny and Eduard share a sensual pleasure in discussing their relationship and her "secret" sexual passion for Eduard's friend Reelen, a passion that

---

8 Dreyfus and Rabinow 173.

9 See FE 1:46–47. Right after her sexual initiation with Baron von Langen, Fanny realizes that "she had done something that 'dishonoured' her," but "she did not feel sullied," which suggests that she rejects the verdict of her society.

10 While *trösten* means "to comfort her, to console her" (FE 2: 121), *vertrösten* means putting off (even with empty promises).

Eduard does not suppress. On the contrary, he fuels and channels it to his own advantage, because it allows him to maintain his relationship both with Fanny and with his friend Reelen.

Foucault has analyzed such discursive sensualizations as "the pleasure in the truth of pleasure, the pleasure of knowing that truth, of discovering and exposing it, the fascination of seeing it and telling it, of captivating and capturing others by it, of confiding it in secret, of luring it out in the open – the specific pleasure of the true discourse on pleasure" (*HS* 71). Fanny's sexual truth-telling, of course, is not an isolated practice, but belongs to the larger social dissemination of procedures of confession at the turn of the century: "Campe, Salzmann, and especially Kaan, Krafft-Ebing, Tardieu, Moll, and Havelock Ellis carefully assembled this whole pitiful, lyrical outpouring from the sexual mosaic. Western societies thus began to keep an indefinite record of these people's pleasures" (*HS* 63-64). Indeed, many of the new studies were concerned with female sexuality, reflected in Krafft-Ebing's *Psycho-pathia sexualis* (1886), Albert Moll's *Das nervöse Weib* (1898), and August Forel's *Die sexuelle Frage* (1905), often promising "liberation" through sexual truth-telling. Foucault takes pleasure in parodying this liberationist logic: "Confession frees, but power reduces one to silence; truth does not belong to the order of power, but shares an original affinity with freedom: traditional themes in philosophy, which a 'political history of truth' would have to overturn by showing that truth is not by nature free – nor error servile – but that its production is thoroughly imbued with relations of power" (*HS* 60). Theorizing the sexual confession as a modern ritual of power, Foucault inverts this psychoanalytic logic of sexuality and truth-telling, arguing that the "repressive hypothesis" itself is part of the larger proliferation of sexualized power.

Foucault's point is illustrated in the power relationships that emerge through Fanny's confessions. Listening to Fanny's sexual life story and interweaving it with the contemporary discourses on sexuality, Eduard, in fact, finds the perfect tool to define Fanny's identity. By adopting a psychoanalytic discourse Eduard convinces Fanny of his telling the truth about her state: "She believed him when he told her that she was sick" (*FE* 2:141), which in turn gives him the power to suggest methods for a cure. In his analysis she becomes a psychopathological creature who has to be sent to the sanatorium in order to be treated for her "disorder" by having her uterus massaged. While Fanny secretly accuses Eduard of her sexual problems, and later imposes her own psychoanalytic argument, namely, that Eduard is a "half-man" because he has given all his energy to his art, she nevertheless accepts the fact that it is she who needs treatment. Here Grove's text is very evocative of Charlotte Perkins

Gilman's *The Yellow Wallpaper* (1892), in which a doctor-husband analyzes his wife and orders a rest cure that ultimately drives her into madness. But while Gilman's text criticizes the doctor's analysis as a complete misreading of the state of mind of his wife, Grove's is only in part critique, as the narrator is in "secret communion" or at least partially complicitous with the amateur psychoanalyst and husband Eduard when he imposes his interpretation on Fanny.

Throughout the novel, the narrator appears to play the role of amateur psychoanalyst himself, who sets the stage so that Fanny can speak her (sexual) self into being. The novel starts out with a focus on Fanny's daydreams which she experiences seemingly in free association on her *chaise longue* in her bedroom, with the narrator as an apparently impartial and objective analyst looking over her shoulder and "listening" to her sexual fantasies as they pass Fanny's half-conscious mind in free indirect discourse. The scene of Fanny's sexual initiation with Baron von Langen is related in confessional language, brought to the surface through Fanny's *Erinnerung* (FE 14; remembrance, memory). In *Fanny Essler*, the confession always comes "from below, as an obligatory act of speech, under some imperious compulsion [that] breaks the bonds of discretion or forgetfulness" (*HS* 62).

"It is through sex," Foucault writes in his discussion of the Freudian conception of sexuality, "that each individual has to pass in order to have access to his intelligibility" (*HS* 155). We look for our identities in our sexualities, so that sexuality "has become more important than our soul" (*HS* 156). Similarly, Fanny Essler participates in the sexualization imposed by the male "confessor-fathers" by locating the search for her identity into the sexual realm. The free indirect discourse that describes her sexual initiation is very telling:

> Sie hatte nur gewußt, wenn ich jetzt gehe, so tue ich etwas Entscheidendes, etwas was mich von allem abtrennt, das ich bisher war, und dann kommt, kommt es, das Ungeheure, das Geheimnisvolle, das, was alles in ihr lösen mußte, was alles erlösen mußte; das Geheimnis des Daseins würde ihr offenbart. (*FE* 13)[11]

In Fanny's language ("erlösen" and "offenbaren"), the sexual act takes on a religious, even an apocalyptic quality, an inflated language that has

---

11 "She had only known: if I go to him now, I'll be doing something crucial, something that will separate me from all that has gone before, that I previously was, and then it'll happen, it'll happen, that immense something, that mystical something that would have to release everything within her, which would save her: the mystery of being would be revealed to her" (*FE* 1:26).

a parodic effect, especially in light of the frustration she experiences in the sexual act itself. At the same time, the decision to be sexually active is a decision through which Fanny consciously defines, creates, and proudly affirms herself as an active subject ("wenn *ich* jetzt gehe, so tue *ich*"). And yet, in the middle of the same sentence, the grammatical, speaking subject ("ich") is displaced by the gender-neutral "es" (it), the "Other," the subconscious, which disrupts her sense of (a unified) self: the "ich" of Fanny's sentence turns into a thing of the past before the sentence is even complete ("das *ich* bisher *war*"). "Es" is unnamed and unnameable in Fanny's confession, but it is personified as "das Ungeheure," a word that accompanies her like an epithet throughout the novel.

In contrast to Fanny, Grove's real-life model Elsa von Freytag-Loringhoven presents irreverent neologisms in her memoirs that simultaneously express her sexual pleasure and parody the Freudian obsession with sex, as when she calls one lover her "sexsun" or insists on her "sex rights" when faced with an impotent husband. In fact, Baroness Elsa identifies her younger self with her "sexattraction" and confesses that the "enlargement of experience – knowledge – personality – was with me reachable only through sex" (*A* 148). Like Elsa, Fanny perceives her own subjectivity as inextricably interwoven with her sexuality. This connection between self-knowledge and identity is not surprising, since sexuality has become, as Foucault has shown, the paradigmatic domain of truth in Western culture. Knowing one's sexuality has become equivalent with knowing oneself; finding the key to one's sexual secret means finding the key to self-knowledge and personal identity: "We demand that sex speak the truth ... and we demand that it tell us our truth, or rather, the deeply buried truth of that truth about ourselves which we think we possess in our immediate consciousness" (*HS* 69). For both Fanny and Baroness Elsa, sex appears to be the (illusory) key to self-knowledge and liberation.

While male seduction is a predominant motif in Dreiser's sexualized world, Fanny, in contrast, rejects the idea that she has been seduced, deliberately assuming responsibility for her sexual desire: "Seducer! She hadn't needed a seducer!" (*FE* 1:47). Nevertheless, *Fanny Essler* also draws critical attention to the fact that the "normal" form of sexuality she experiences is a male mastery over the female body. Fanny actively seeks the sexual initiation with Baron von Langen but in the act itself stops being an active subject and acquiesces to becoming a masochistic object: "her whole body had cried out for him. And she had had the feeling: now he can take me and do with me as he pleases. Whatever he wishes, that's what I'll do; and even if he beats me, even if he murders me – he can do all that, and I'll sink down in front of him and still be his" (*FE* 1:27–28). The reader witnesses these events after they have taken place, as they pass Fanny's consciousness, a narrative technique that reaffirms the impression of a strange female passivity, because when reminiscing, Fanny finds herself in a state of "weariness," exhaustion, and semi-sleep.

Thus the unrelenting search for the truth of sexuality is a double-edged sword because sex becomes the anchorage point for the female's continued imprisonment. While Fanny Essler hopes for sexual enlightenment, Grove reveals the protagonist's lack of self-awareness and self-knowledge in her confessional voice, which is inevitably self-contradictory: "Had she loved him? Oh yes, she still loved him – or, no – she really didn't know" (*FE* 1:29). The confessional yearning for a single truth deconstructs itself, revealing Fanny's entrapment in the confusion of her feelings, while readers are invited to draw their own (psychoanalytic) conclusions. Fanny is, as Freud would have it, tied to her father, and hence compulsively rejects every lover as an insufficient *Ersatzmann* (who is unable to satisfy her sexually).[12] While Fanny is incapable of drawing these conclusions herself, the reader is invited to take an ironic perspective on this character – the typical perspective offered to the reader in the traditional naturalist novel – and simultaneously to participate with the author-narrator and the (male) characters in the (psychoanalytic) search for the key to Fanny's sexuality.

Like many naturalist females, Fanny is represented not only as hypersexual but also as hysterical – defined on the basis of her reproductive organs. Discussing the historical "hysterization of women," Foucault reminds us that "one of the first to be 'sexualized' was the 'idle' woman": "Thus there emerged the 'nervous' woman, the woman afflicted with 'vapors'; in this figure, the hysterization of woman found its anchorage point" (*HS* 121). Though the eighteenth-century French *Encylopédie* had revived the Greek conception of the womb as "the source, cause, and seat of an infinite number of diseases,"[13] Sigmund Freud's twentieth-century "achievement" lies in showing that hysteria is not a physiological but a psychological disease. Continuing the hysterization of women by claiming the unconscious as a new site and source of hysteria, Freud argued that this typically female neurosis is caused by the repression of incompatible wishes. Brilliant though Freud's insights into Victorian sexuality may have been, they largely glossed over the gen-

---

12 See Freud, "Das Tabu der Virginität," *Gesammelte Werke*, vol. 12, 174.

13 Quoted in Terry Smiley Dock, *Women in the "Encyclopédie": A Compendium* (Maryland: José Porrúa Turanzas, 1983) 17.

eral mental and social repression of women in patriarchal society, as Susan Bordo has observed. In *Studies in Hysteria* (1895), for instance, Freud describes nearly all of the female subjects as unusually intelligent, creative, energetic, independent, and often as highly educated, yet "Freud never makes the connection (which Breuer had begun to develop) between the monotonous domestic lives these women were expected to lead after their schooling was completed, and the emergence of compulsive day-dreaming, hallucinations, and hysterical conversions."[14] Also, as Foucault notes in his critique of Freud, the hysterization of women in the course of history has entailed women's subjugation and social docility, since the danger of this "psychological disease" requires that she be placed under the supervision of a husband, a doctor, or a psychiatrist. In the Western history of sexuality, the potential pathology of sex created "the urgent need to keep it under close watch and to devise a rational technology of correction" (*HS* 120).

Indeed, it is the psychoanalytic discourse of the idle and hysterical woman that allows the men to define Fanny. According to Eduard Barrel, his wife "was hysterical, that is to say, she had an incredibly exaggerated sensual need that remained unfulfilled for fear of not being able to fulfill that need, which in turn engendered her nervousness. This sensual need was nothing else than a secret longing for motherhood" (*FE* 2:140) – "ein verborgenes Verlangen nach Mutterschaft" (*FE* 449). Eduard's claim for the naturality of motherhood, without which a woman becomes hysterical or psychologically sick, is an argument that is diametrically opposed to Fanny's own conscious rejection of domesticity and her desire for independence, as it glosses over her own desire to be an artist. This "scientific" discourse furthermore glosses over the fact that Eduard, like every other male in the novel, directs, criticizes and ultimately suppresses Fanny's creative impulse (as it detracts from Eduard's own problems with sexual impotence). At the same time, *Fanny Essler* exposes that in each case, male analyses and "cures" are linked to intense relationships of sexualized power in which Fanny is dominated and defined on the basis of her problematic sexuality. When Ehrhard Stein hits her and pours water over her in order to stop her hysterical crying fits,[15] Fanny's reaction is that "his brutality was a comfort to her.

---

14 Susan Bordo, "Anorexia Nervosa: Psychopathology as the Crystallization of Culture," *The Philosophical Forum* 17 (1985–86): 89.

15 This act of humiliation is figuratively repeated in her relationship with Reelen, who stops her laughter by telling her, "Das darf man nicht," which prompts the following reaction: "Fanny war wie von Wasser übergossen" (*FE* 521).

All of a sudden her behaviour did seem like theatrics" (*FE* 2:70). Although Grove's narrative criticizes Ehrhard Stein as insensitive and even brutal (*Stein*, stone, as well as *hard* underscore his brutality; *Ehre*, honour, is his *idée fixe*), the fact remains that the narrator also projects Fanny in the role of a hysterical woman whose symptoms are correctly analyzed by the male characters and who is brought back to her senses by her male partners.

Though it continues the problematic "hysterization" of the sexualized female in twentieth-century naturalism, *Fanny Essler* nonetheless has to be credited for making a direct connection between the suppression of female creativity and a woman's dissatisfaction, frustration, growing tyranny, and hysteria, a connection that feminist critics often accused Freud of not making. Subjected to degrading working conditions as a chorus girl in the theatre, Fanny responds with hysterical crying fits and has to be sent to a doctor for treatment. Once married to Barrel, Fanny adopts the role of the idle and sexually frustrated bourgeois housewife, whose husband has no time for her. Grove demonstrates that this role turns her inevitably into a tyrant figure who becomes obsessed with monitoring, supervising, criticizing, and discharging her various maids. As a household tyrant, Fanny becomes another Mrs. Hurstwood, but while *Sister Carrie* criticizes Mrs. Hurstwood as a "castrating" character, Grove's sympathies lie with Fanny. Her obsession with household cleanliness and her growing tyranny are juxtaposed to scenes that describe her sexual frustration. Despite the hysterization of the protagonist, *Fanny Essler* does not continue the literary cult and glorification of female invalidism that is so prominent in nineteenth-century writing.[16] Ultimately, the novel exposes that Fanny's frustrations and psychological problems are created by degrading living and working conditions and by the male refusal to acknowledge and take seriously a woman's intellectual and artistic creative energies.

Striving for sexual liberation, Fanny Essler ultimately remains entrapped in her sexuality, whereby naturalism's genetic determinism is replaced by a Freudian *Wiederholungszwang*, the compulsion of repetition. Drawing critical attention to the sado-masochism of Fanny's sexual life – not only are many of her sexual relationships a repetition of the first sado-masochistic act with Baron von Langen, but the protagonist remains unsatisfied and tortured in her sex life – Grove's satire of such

---

16 See Bram Dijkstra, *Idols of Perversity: Fantasies of Feminine Evil in Fin-de-Siècle Culture* (New York & Oxford: Oxford UP, 1986) 37.

male sexual dominance culminates in a very pessimistic view. Unable to break out of a circle of giving herself to "rapist" (or impotent) lovers, Fanny is finally "cured" of her sexual frustration by the ultimate sexual dominator, Friedrich Karl Reelen, ironically the author's double, whose eyes are "like frozen lakes"[17] and who claims that "You have to have something to hit, or to tame" (*FE* 2:146–47). "Was he a sadist?", Fanny indeed asks herself about Reelen, before she experiences a new "ecstasy" by being sexually "mastered" by him (*FE* 2:160, 195). Given the novel's Freudian subtext, it should come as no surprise that it is an archaeologist who manages to "unlock" the secret of her sexuality, thus providing a release of sexual tension. But Fanny's sexual experience also echoes French feminist Luce Irigaray's point that in patriarchal society women are often forced to mimic male desires if they want to experience any desire at all:

> Elles [les femmes] s'y retrouvent, proverbialement, *dans la mascarade*. Les psychanalystes disent que la mascarade correspond au désir de la femme. Cela ne me paraît pas juste. Je pense qu'il faut l'entendre comme ce que les femmes font pour récupérer quelque chose du désir, pour participer au désir de l'homme, mais au prix de renoncer au leur. Dans la mascarade elles se soumettent à l'économie dominante du désir. (*CS* 131)

By the end of the novel, Fanny finally becomes adapted to a sexuality which completely subjugates her as a woman and that is seen as "normal" by almost every character (including the narrator) in the novel. Irigaray, however, warns us not to misread such orgasmic satisfactions for a transcendence of hierarchically structured gender relations. She reminds us that often, "[les] orgasmes [de la femme] sont nécessaires comme démonstration de la puissance masculine. Ils signifient la réussite – pensent-ils – de la domination sexuelle de la femme par l'homme" (*CS* 198).

Thus Fanny's orgasm is not a mark of her female liberation but of a more subtle form of subjugation. Sexual *jouissance* does not really challenge the boundaries of naturalism but recontains the female body within the genre's traditional conventions. After all, Fanny's orgasm is the ultimate triumph of a normalized sexuality of male mastery, and it should come as no surprise that Fanny reflects about it in a strange fascist language. She realizes that the sexual act did not work with her former

---

17 If we see *Fanny Essler* as a *roman à clef*, Reelen is Grove himself and thus a satire of himself: Reelen is a satanic creature, whose eyes evoke the frozen lakes that immobilize Satan in Dante's *Inferno*.

lovers because they *"had* no race" (*FE* 2:195). *Fanny Essler* exposes that the controlled, mechanical, goal-oriented, masculine form of love-making not only negates pleasure but also ritually reinscribes the binary oppositions between self/Other, active/passive, masculine/feminine, racially superior/racially inferior. To be sure, even as she acknowledges these binary divisions, Fanny identifies herself with the second category and also finds in this position the impetus to resist Reelen and recognize him for what he is. Thus, the experience of orgasmic satisfaction does not end Fanny's quest; she is as disillusioned as ever and yearns for her mother, turning her attention (back) to women.[18]

Grove signals Fanny's lack of true liberation in the circles of repetition that characterize this novel. He satirizes Fanny's relationship with Reelen by constructing this character as a double of the sadistic *Neuromantik* Ehrhard Stein. Also, Fanny's act of leaving Barrel for Reelen is a repetition of her earlier leaving of Nepomuk Bolle for Ehrhard Stein. And Reelen is also a double of Fanny's father. Not only does Fanny become "Mein liebes Kind" in Friederich Karl's discourse,[19] but both men are *Kerkermeister* in her life who impose the constraints (*Zwang*) of bourgeois conventions. In both relationships, Fanny's rebellion is rooted in the memory of a mother–daughter alliance against the father-lover. The relationship of the nineteen-year-old Fanny with her father has explicitly Oedipal overtones: Fanny understood "that one could fall in love with Papa. He was strong, incredibly strong, and so blond and – yes, in fact, he was truly handsome" (*FE* 1:25). This language is echoed in her later description of Reelen. Not only does she emphasize how much other women desire Friederich Karl, but she also sees him as blond, blue-eyed, and incredibly strong. It is through these doubling devices that Grove reinforces the satire of Reelen by indicating that in Fanny's life this man is not the ultimate "saviour" but just another circle of repetition and another twist in the spiral of power. Like Foucault and de Beauvoir, Grove draws attention to the fact that the construction of the hysterical woman is tied into relationships that are inevitably saturated with power.

By the end of the novel Fanny turns emotionally away from Reelen and yearns for female rather than male companionship. And yet, Grove

---

18 *Fanny Essler* thus satirizes the "maschinenmäßige Liebe" ("machine-like love-making") celebrated by some *fin-de-siècle* writers, among them Hermann Bahr; see Jens Malte Fischer, *Fin-de-siècle: Kommentar zu einer Epoche* (München: Winkler Verlag, 1978) 111; also 53–65.

19 See *FE*, 518, 522, 523, 531, 532, 533.

chose to link this feminine, maternal alternative to her "peaceful" death rather than to a new beginning, with the last sentence of the novel emphasizing that if the end of desire means pleasurable peace, it also means death: *"Thus a calm death saved Fanny Essler from the greatest disappointment of her life"* (FE 2:232). The italics should be seen as a warning signal not to take this sentence at face value. Considering that Fanny spent her whole life in search of a "saviour," it is ironic that she should be "saved" in death. It is Grove himself who becomes here the "authorized" saviour and gives his protagonist peace by putting an end to her desire and "allowing" her to die. Here, the saviour-author, freezing Fanny's life forces into the absolute stasis of death, becomes the last in a series of male artists all of whom try to appropriate, to channel, and to neutralize Fanny's creative energies. The parody thus turns full circle back to the author who has succeeded where his character Reelen has failed: he has finally tamed Fanny's desire by containing her voice, body, and sexuality within naturalist conventions.

8

Fanny Essler in
(A) Search for America

"Throughout his writing Grove has been moving in the direction of an androgynous society, in which roles are no longer sex stereotyped," writes Lorraine McMullen in her analysis of Grove's Canadian fiction.[1] This emphasis on androgyny, however, marks less a telelogical "direction" in Grove's Canadian fiction than a feature already anticipated in his German novels. Fanny Essler is a precursor of the twenties androgynous "flapper," whose sexuality is expressed less in eroticism than in nervous energy. Although contained within a naturalist narrative, Fanny's female body stubbornly rebels against its "natural" destiny: she wears male clothing, is called a "lad" by one of her lovers, and plays male roles on stage. When asked to play female roles in the theatre, she forgets her lines. This continual crossing of gender boundaries – indeed, her refusal to conform to traditional notions of "femininity" – challenges naturalism's traditional assumptions about the innateness and

---

1 Lorraine McMullen, "Women in Grove's Novels," *The Grove Symposium*, ed. John Nause (Ottawa, U Ottawa P, 1974) 75.

"naturality" of male and female identities. The novel's conceptualizing of the female body and sexuality, then, suggests a mode of social determinism that moves far beyond the social Darwinistic frameworks of Spencer and Huxley. Through Fanny's deliberate play with gender roles, her body becomes, to use Judith Butler's poststructuralist words, "a peculiar nexus of culture and choice," whereby "'existing' one's body becomes a personal way of taking up and reinterpreting received gender norms."[2] Thus, the construction of Fanny's body occurs through what Foucault has termed "technologies of self," via practices and codes, through which she becomes submerged in the social network of power.

This point is highlighted in Fanny's relationship with Friedrich Karl Reelen, the author's persona, in Parts 4 and 5 of the novel. Reelen can only "construct" his masculinity by coercing Fanny into the role of traditional femininity, so that – like the male naturalist narrator – he appears in the role of the Mephistophelian manipulator of the sexual "technologies" provided for Fanny's "self-construction." Just as traditional naturalism insists on clear-cut boundaries between male and female nature, so Reelen proceeds to "rewrite" Fanny in the social network, insisting on transforming her from a sexually ambiguous "lad" into a respectable "lady." In long dresses, Fanny's body "achieves" the statuesque look, and on Reelen's advice she also transforms her formerly "boyish" hairstyle:

> She now wore her not very full-bodied but curly dark blond hair tied back loosely, without a part, so that both her ears, in which she wore two costly pearls, were left exposed; and the large knot that in part consisted of a wide false bun to back her own hair, hung loosely from the middle of the back of her head and reached far down to the nape of the neck, which set off the face by adding a full frame of hair around her shoulders when seen from the front. (*FE* 2:212)

The arrangement of her hair as a deliberate frame for her face reinforces the impression of Fanny as a beautiful picture – a (male) work of art, or a sexualized body-construct inscribed on the material body of the female. This new hairstyle, significantly, corresponds very closely to what Ursel Lang has analyzed as the female hair-model ordained by the fascists in Hitler Germany, thirty years later: "Some women have their hair waved in careful ridges, kept well in order. The face, and above all the forehead, is always completely exposed."[3] Reaching the pinnacle of

---

2 Quoted in McNay 72.

3 Ursel Lang, "The Hair Project," Frigga Haug et al. 100.

"femininity," Fanny thus carries the signs of her relationship with this tyrannical "god" imprinted on her body, as her hairstyle, clothing, and body language reflect Reelen's obsession with discipline and control of the body.

Relying on such processes of "feminizing" the female body in relationships of power, male identity and sexuality are shown to be conditioned by and "constructed" on the basis of, social, psychological, and normative determinants. Though Reelen uses a language of Nietzschean will power and self-sufficiency to describe himself, the novel exposes how much his "self-construction" as a desexualized, "strong man" depends upon his "disciplining" and sexualizing of the female body. Grove subverts Reelen's *Übermensch*-persona, by showing that he is as much a *Schablone* as the other male characters in the novel. Reelen can only create his masculinity by defining himself against Fanny's femininity, representing himself as "complete" by defining her as "lacking," the incarnation of voracious desire. Fanny becomes quite simply his "Other," his negative mirror image (which explains why Reelen's obsession is not with her change and "improvement," but with her flaws). Hélène Cixous' Hegelian gender critique is very appropriate to describe Fanny's specific relationship with Reelen, but also describes the male narrator's more general relationship with the female body in naturalist fiction: "We know the implied irony in the master/slave dialectic," Cixous writes, "the *body* of what is strange must not disappear, but its force must be conquered and returned to the master."[4]

However, the sexualized female victim is by no means a literal "slave." While Fanny exults in her sexual satisfaction, she stubbornly resists the price she is asked to pay for sexual pleasure. Resisting total "feminization," she embarrasses Reelen in public through her mistakes and her moods, which remind him that she cannot be absolutely appropriated, as she continually disrupts his scheme of order. But Fanny's mistakes also present a target through which Reelen maintains his male dominance in this relationship because they indicate that his "orthopedic," "educational" process has to be intensified.[5] Fanny and Reelen

---

4 Cixous, "Sorties: Out and Out: Attacks/Ways Out/Forays," *The Newly Born Woman*, Hélène Cixous and Catherine Clément, trans. Betsy Wing (Minneapolis: U of Minnesota P, 1988) 70.

5 In the style of free indirect discourse, Fanny herself thinks of her attitude in terms of "Trotz" (*FE* 527, 529, 530), a word that denotes resistance ("obstinacy"), but like "Übermut" this word has a negative twist in that it implies an infantile obstinacy. "Trotz" is also a strategy Fanny uses in her relationship with her tyrannical father.

become involved in a sadomasochistic power play, which is inscribed on her sexualized body, whereby, to use Susan Bordo's words, "the attempt to subdue the spontaneities of the body in the interests of control only succeeds in constituting them as more alien, and more powerful, and thus, more needful of control."[6]

By refusing to be metaphorically "corseted" by Reelen, Fanny rejects not only his "technologies" of feminization. She also rejects what Susan Bordo has described as the social function of the corset: "the nineteenth-century corset appears, in addition to the actual physical incapacitation it caused the wearer, as a virtual emblem of the power of culture to impose its designs on the female body."[7] By the same token, Fanny also resists the sexual-textual constraints of traditional male naturalism. By rejecting the culturally sanctified "technologies of self" and with it the reality of a "natural" femininity, Fanny challenges naturalism's generic "corset" for women.

Recognizing in Fanny nothing but the raw material, the female force of nature that can be transformed and tamed according to his male vision, Grove's Reelen is a Grovian self-parody in more than one sense. If Grove ridicules himself in his cold dandy persona, he also parodies himself as a male naturalist author who disciplines, tames, sanitizes, or freezes excessive or unconventional female sexuality and behaviour within the textual boundaries of his narrative. Just as Reelen fails in his efforts to feminize Fanny, so Grove realizes that her voice often explodes the framework of his narrative. Throughout Reelen's attempts to transform Fanny into a "lady," she continues to re-emerge as an androgynous "lad" who successfully refuses to become a *Schablone*, defying the corset that Reelen and naturalism wish to impose on her sexual body.

If Felix Paul Greve's parodic treatment of Reelen marks the beginning of his critique of stereotypical sex roles, Frederick Philip Grove continues this exploration of sexual identities in his Canadian fiction, as Lorraine McMullen's quotation at the beginning of this chapter suggests. Writing his Canadian classic, *A Search for America* (1927), almost twenty-five years after the publication of his first German novel, Grove recontextualized his German characters and motifs by situating Fanny's journey into *fin-de-siècle* North America. Like *Fanny Essler*, *A Search for America* is a picaresque, featuring a European intellectual dilettante who struggles to find a new identity in the new world culture. Grove's "Od-

---

6 Bordo 78.

7 Bordo 76.

yssey of an Immigrant" presents the first-person narrator Phil Branden, a young pseudo-aristocrat from Europe, who works in turn as an omnibus waiter in Toronto, an encyclopedia salesman in New York, and an itinerant labourer on western prairie farms before becoming a teacher in Winnipeg. Grove's inscription of his autobiographical self into his Canadian novel is reminiscent of *Fanny Essler*: in both, fact merges with fiction in typically Grovian ways. It should come as no surprise, then, that Phil Branden shares many features with the author's European persona, Reelen, as his impeccable clothing, his high-society flair, and the mask of the arrogant and cold dandy suggest. Furthermore, the Canadian novel echoes *Fanny Essler*'s self-parodic tone, as when Phil Branden charges his younger self with being a "presumptuous pup," an "insufferable snob and coxcomb," who speaks in "nonsensical prattle" and indulges in "artificial poses."[8]

More interesting than the parallels, however, are the differences between the two novels, which frequently echo ideological shifts in Grove's conceptualizing of sexual identity. While Reelen used Fanny as a foil that allowed him to confirm his role as a "master," Branden himself encounters a deep identity crisis in his odyssey across America, so that his experience doubles Fanny's. In North America, Branden finds himself entrapped in the typical naturalistic plot, often occupying a "female" position as he becomes victimized in his journey across America. In fact, in the course of his cultural and linguistic crisis, in his personal experience of entropic disorientation in a new culture, the new Canadian immigrant experiences a precarious sense of his own "feminization." The cultural and linguistic uncertainty experienced in the new country, and the accompanying "loss" of power and masculinity, prove so unsettling for Branden that he can only articulate this loss of control by impersonating a female role in the naturalist plot of decline, eventually to exorcize both his "femaleness" and his "sexuality" when he is reborn as "a new man" in Canada. Transforming his "search for America" into narrative, Branden in many ways impersonates Fanny Essler – her anorexia, her fear of slipping into prostitution, her hysteria, her reduction to her body under the gaze of others. He can only overcome his crisis by distancing himself from Fanny Essler, by repressing her, and by eventually asserting himself in his "male" identity.

---

8 Frederick Philip Grove, *A Search for America: The Odyssey of an Immigrant* (Toronto: McClelland & Stewart, 1971) 3–4. All subsequent quotations will appear in the text abbreviated *ASA*.

This "translation" of *Fanny Essler* into *A Search for America*, then, has to be seen in the larger context of Grove's life and adventurous biography. In her memoirs, Baroness Elsa von Freytag-Loringhoven gives some interesting insights into the emotional and ideological changes FPG underwent after his emigration to America in 1909 (and after inviting her to join him in his new world adventure). Absorbed in his "primitive struggle for life" on his farm in Kentucky between 1910 and 1911, Grove distanced himself from Elsa sexually, telling her "*I don't need any woman*" (*A* 72) before leaving her altogether. Unbeknownst to her, he travelled to Canada to become a teacher and a writer in Manitoba in 1912. Yet *A Search for America* is not only a continuation of but also a reworking of – perhaps even a Freudian *Durcharbeiten*, a "working through" – *Fanny Essler* in a new context; consequently, this preoccupation reflects FPG's problematic attachment both to Elsa (the "real" woman) and to *Fanny Essler* (the novel left behind in Germany). Though in his first Canadian novel, *Settlers of the Marsh* (1925), Grove "kills" an Elsa-like (and Fanny Essler-like) character in Clara Vogel, in *A Search for America* the male narrator impersonates her, absorbing her into his own persona. If this "ingestion" is part of the author's psychological separation process, it also highlights the self-contradictory sexual ideology inscribed in Grove's Canadian fiction.

Branden's odyssey of an immigrant is set in the early 1890s, which does not coincide with the author's biography, but significantly overlaps the time of Fanny Essler's European odyssey (thus emphasizing the parallels between Branden and Fanny Essler).[9] Like his female predecessor, Branden moves to the big cities, to Montreal and New York, where he relives (Fanny's) exhilarating possibilities of self-construction, but also experiences a sense of naturalist subjection as he becomes enchained in America's norms. Like the German *picara*, he moves from one adventure to the next, trying to maintain his integrity in naturalist episodes that ritually torture and mutilate his body. Like Fanny, Phil Branden searches for his identity, but unlike Fanny he finds the key to

---

9 Also, in his fictionalized autobiography *In Search of Myself* (Toronto: Macmillan, 1946), Grove describes a personal life that closely overlaps *A Search of America*. He reiterates that between 1892 and 1893, he "had successively been a waiter, a book agent, a factory hand, a roust-about on board a lake steamer ... and a hobo or itinerant farm-labourer in the West" (181), when in reality he went to school at St. Pauli (Germany) during this time; see Spettigue, *The European Years*, 39. For a study of the time framework and composition history of *A Search for America*, see K. P. Stich, "Beckwith's 'Mark Twain' and the Dating of Grove's *A Search for America*," *Canadian Literature* 127 (1990): 183–85.

his identity not in his sexualization but in his desexualization, as he tries to detach himself from the status of the naturalist victim. Thus, in *A Search for America* Grove's naturalist fiction undergoes a significant shift: the (androgynous) female protagonist that characterizes his German fiction is replaced by a (feminized) male, who is subjected to painful but equally exciting adventures; consequently, the narrating (male) subject merges with the narrated (feminized) object. This gender configuration, in turn, challenges the typically naturalist separation between powerful male spectator and powerless female object.

Although silenced and repressed in his Canadian life and identity, *Fanny Essler* is thus covertly incorporated into Grove's Canadian art. Just as Branden remains attached to his past throughout the novel, so the author turns back to his earlier fiction and to the German naturalist conventions to produce his new Canadian fiction in an act of creative translation and transculturation. Although he yearns to leave his marital and artistic "failures" behind in Europe (the relationship with Elsa was a personal "failure" leading to public scandal, just as *Fanny Essler* was a financial disappointment), FPG fabricated his own rebirth as a writer of fiction by secretly resurrecting *Fanny Essler* in his Canadian naturalism (albeit as the novel's silenced "discourse of the other"). As a new world writer, Grove "confessed" his identity by simultaneously withholding significant information about his German past and the Fanny Essler subtext that energized his new world fiction. While the Canadian author's *Versteckspiel* with his readership thus marks the birth of the immigrant-author as a trickster, even as a "pathological liar," it also continues the German author's self-parodic naturalism and allows him to inscribe into the gaps of his new world fiction an elegiac subtext – his separation from (and simultaneous assimilation of) Elsa/Fanny Essler.

Margaret Stobie has appropriately discussed *A Search for America* in terms of a Rousseauistic romance, a "fable of identity," in which the protagonist undergoes a true metamorphosis, descending into "the depths" in order to ascend to a higher level and to be reborn as a new human being. Following in Thoreau's footsteps in an experiment of self-isolation, Branden takes off his "mask" and his clothing in his American odyssey in order to find his "essential self" underneath the artificial poses of the European dilettante. According to Stobie, then, the key to the novel lies in its Rousseauistic undercurrent: "As Rousseau insisted, the essential man, the 'I, myself,' existed independent of the social order or of vocation."[10] While the novel frequently alludes to Thoreau, the nov-

---

10 Stobie 67.

el's transcendental frame of reference is put into question by the novel's naturalist framework. If anything, the novel deconstructs the notion of a transcendental self that can be "found" underneath layers of clothing, just as it deconstructs the notion of a "natural" sexual identity. Branden's "search for America" is as illusory as Fanny's search for the fairy-tale prince. Just as Branden never solves the riddle of America, so his search never leads to the discovery of an "essential" core of sexual identity, or manhood. After shedding the mask of the male dandy, Branden discovers his (female) identity, his connection with Fanny Essler, a connection that is too troubling even to name or explicitly identify.

In a more general sense, Branden travels through North America not so much to discover (or become alienated from) a true (innate) selfhood, but rather to create himself as a subject. Distancing himself from society in general and from women in particular, he eventually appropriates Thoreau's technologies of desexualization in order to escape the sexualization that subjugated Fanny Essler and that jeopardizes his sense of self in the beginning of his journey. In his desire to find new technologies of self on the American "soil," Branden not only discovers the immense "labour" involved in this undertaking, but he also becomes aware of his deterministic subjection to the cultural norms of the new society. Foucault has argued that the individual cannot produce a self without producing the self's subjection, "their constitution as subjects in both senses of the word" (*HS* 60), which echoes a naturalist sense of social determinism. While Foucault writes that "the subject constitutes himself in an active fashion, by the practices of self," he also emphasizes that "these practices are nevertheless not something that the individual invents by himself. They are patterns that he finds in his culture and which are proposed, suggested and imposed on him by his culture, his society and his social group."[11] The "technologies" available for the individual's self-construction vary from culture to culture, from time period to time period, but they always assign the individual a place in the network of power. Illustrating Foucault's point about the polymorphous power effects on the individual body, a myriad of social practices shape the direction of the new immigrant's actions, engineering his new identity while encouraging the subject's active participation in this self-construction. Grove draws attention to this transformation of self as a process of "Americanization"; the word "America" is repeated at least one hundred and thirty times in the novel in order to emphasize

---

11 Foucault, "Ethic of Care," 11.

that Branden becomes a new subject, a "social man" who is absorbed into America's social practices and discourses. Just as *Fanny Essler* becomes "citified" in Berlin's metropolis, so Phil Branden becomes "Americanized" through a host of technologies that embrace and "penetrate" his body.

As the intertextual dialogue with *Fanny Essler* reveals, *A Search for America* conceptualizes Branden's "subjection" to – and "submersion" in – American culture by drawing on naturalism's sexual and feminine tropes. Like Fanny, Branden speaks a confessional language. Highlighting the feminization of Branden's speech, all chapter titles start with the pronoun "I" or "my," and the first paragraph of the novel presents seventeen counts of the first person personal and possessive pronouns. Caught in a struggle for survival in America's social Darwinistic universe, Branden is transformed into "that impersonal neuter thing called help" when he becomes a waiter in Toronto, in a chapter appropriately entitled "I Submerge." Ready to don his apron, he descends into a naturalist, "excessively dirty subterranean room" (*ASA* 41) that echoes Fanny's dressing room in the theatre. From here, he emerges to serve an "ever-thickening mass of humans" (*ASA* 52) in the cheap Toronto restaurant, thus occupying the feminized waiter position of other naturalist males (e.g., the saloon employee Hurstwood or the bellhop Clyde Griffiths), which is inevitably linked to the plot of decline. Grove's description is Zolaesque in his evocation of the human masses that absorb Branden's younger self in a living, pulsating machinery of bustling waiters, hungry customers, and swinging doors: "I felt like a drowning man, swamped under the crushing flood of humanity" (*ASA* 53).

Moreover, like Fanny (and like the typical female in naturalist fiction), Branden experiences his own objectification and victimization as metaphorical prostitution. Entering the "new world" with neither sufficient money nor adequate job experience, he soon finds himself in the typical position of the specularized, naturalist female who is "stared at," like Carrie Meeber, when he travels by train to Toronto in search of his first job. Faced with the probing eyes of Bennett, the Simpson's worker, Branden's formerly powerful gaze is emasculated and impotent: "I should have frozen him, annihilated him with one of those glassy stares for which I had been famous among my former friends, one of whom used to say, 'Phil can put more opprobrium into one of his fish-eyes than you can cull out of an unemasculated Shakespeare in a day'" (*ASA* 21). Thus unsettled, the immigrant-narrator is in the process of losing his sense of control, particularly when, later in the novel, he becomes the specular object of male "desire": "I felt a pair of eyes which brushed over my body and seemed to touch it, now here, now there."

Courted by two males, Branden occupies Fanny Essler's position in a triangle of male desire, mimicking her female sexual submission: "I yielded to its invitation, at first reluctantly, then not without pleasurable readiness" (*ASA* 109). Like Fanny, he is punished for his complicitous submission: he is fleeced in a con-man game and soon finds himself in prison.

It is small wonder that Branden, experiencing his cultural crisis as a crisis of (sexual) identity, should feel "embarked upon things desperate and suicidal" (*ASA* 19) as he enters the new world. The new gaze he encounters fills him with a sense of bottomlessness, of the abyss, or what Martin Heidegger has called *Abgrund*. Subjected to a process of feminization and victimization, Branden senses the danger of disappearing altogether, of finding his masculinity – and thus his positive subjectivity, according to the logic of naturalism – completely shattered on the new continent. He provides a strong image of male emasculation in the figure of Whiskers, an old waiter, an aged Hurstwood figure, whose hollow cheeks and eyes stand for "Old Age," "tragedy," and "failure" (*ASA* 59). That Whiskers should terrify Branden with the giggle of "a silly girl" reveals how much Branden conceptualizes his own loss of power in feminized terms. For Branden, Whiskers is a demonic double, whose disintegrating body signifies the victimized, objectified, and castrated naturalist male.

Reluctantly playing the role of a feminized male, Branden finds himself inevitably slipping into the position of the naturalist prostitute (if only in a metaphorical sense). Early in the novel, he discovers that in order to survive in the new world and get a job, "I had to sell myself to this man" (*ASA* 35), and from this early struggle to get a job, Phil, like Dreiser's Clyde Griffiths, learns the techniques of selling services and goods by "selling himself." Yet his struggle is, like Fanny's, to maintain his own integrity in order not to be drawn into the deterministic fate of the naturalist female. In contrast to Fanny, who sees the key to her identity in her promiscuous sexuality, Branden makes an effort to distance himself from sex through various strategies: the novel is virtually without any sexual relationships; he speaks about sex only in the distanced, Latinized form of "rebus sexualibus" (*ASA* 72); and his friendship with Ella, the only female friend, is clearly asexual. Thus it is not his sexuality but his aversion to sexuality that deserves further critical attention, since Branden's desire in overcoming his "feminization" is related to naturalism's conceptualization of female sexuality in terms of excess and lack of control.

The body of the sexualized female in naturalism is often driven by excessive hungers and voracious desires. This feminized body, best encapsulated in the physical weakness of *la chair molle* with its predictable "yielding" to the demands of the flesh, is naturalism's privileged signifier for female lack of control and will power. Feminized and sexualized as naturalist figures, Branden and Fanny struggle for control over their bodies, both driven by the urge to conquer in an act of will power the body's hunger and voracious desires. Obsessed with stripping the body of its precarious weakness, its femininity, both Branden and Fanny are anorexic figures. For Fanny, fasting is a life style, an activity that she indulges in. While starving herself, she feels "her body so heavy" and is tortured when "feeling the weight of her body" (*FE* 2:8). In her Foucauldian analysis of anorexia nervosa, Susan Bordo has made a connection between anorexia and the female's desperate desire to control her body: "In this battle, thinness represents a triumph of the will over body, and the thin body (i.e., the non-body) is associated with 'absolute' purity, hyperintellectuality and transcendence of flesh." In contrast, "Fat (i.e. becoming *all* body) is associated with the 'taint' of matter and flesh, 'wantonness,' mental stupor and mental decay."[12] The anorexic is often dominated by a "deep fear of 'The Female,' with all its more nightmarish archetypal associations: voracious hungers and sexual insatiability."[13]

As Branden enters the new country and impersonates the naturalist female, he struggles against his "descent" into naturalism by divesting himself of (female) desire and physicality. Moreover, the narrator tries to maintain textual control by preventing his metamorphosis from narrating (male) subject to narrated (female) object, from manipulator of language to manipulated physical and sexual body. Determined not to allow American society to seduce him by appealing to his desire, he becomes a tramp and an itinerant farm-labourer, a role that dissociates him from sexuality. As he divests himself of his clothing (and his language), he also divests himself of food, trying to impose his will on his body by denying it vital nourishments; he follows Carlyle's formula of increasing the value of the "fraction of life" by "lessening the Denominator" (*ASA* 223). Appropriately nicknamed Slim, Branden inscribes into his narrative the pleasure of starving: in his odyssey across the country he feels not only a perpetual hunger, but "a weird intoxication with hunger" (*ASA* 250), like Fanny Essler. Moreover, the adult anorexic's ideal of eternal adolescence is reflected in his impersonation of Huck Finn. The novel explicitly alludes to Mark Twain, and, like Twain's "uncivilized" orphan, Branden survives by eating the leftovers of civilization, such as the corn he purloins from fields or the ham he finds along the

---

12 Bordo 80.

13 Bordo 87.

river banks after a flooding. The latter, however, is a "rich" food that his
stomach instantly rejects, so that Branden is caught in the bulimic's
self-imposed binge-purge cycle, as eating becomes a secretive, isolated
activity. While he takes pleasure in denying his body vital nourishments,
this compulsive rationing of food corresponds to his deliberate efforts
to eliminate desire and to escape the lure of a seductive consumer
economy.

Like the naturalist female who yields to the demands of the flesh, so
the anorexic is characterized by a sense of powerlessness and desperately tries to regain control of her body: "Most strikingly, there is the
same emphasis on *control*, on feeling one's life to be fundamentally out
of control, and on the feeling of accomplishment derived from total
mastery of the body."[14] Bordo's description of the anorexic applies to
both Branden and Fanny. In his desire to gain control over his new situation in a new country, Branden dominates his body, and identifies in
anorexic fashion with "the mind (or will), ideals of spiritual perfection,
fantasies of absolute self-control." But in trying to master his (feminized)
body (just like Reelen tried to master and subdue Fanny's body), Branden
paradoxically ends up in Fanny's position: his anorexic mindset echoes
her lack of control. Like Fanny's, Branden's anorexic condition, then, is
a no-win game, or to cite Bordo on the anorexic's typical entanglement
in contradictions: "caring desperately, passionately, obsessively about
attaining an ideal of coolness, effortless confidence, and casual freedom,"
the anorexic remains caught in "powerlessness."[15]

Branden, significantly, reaches the bottom of his naturalist "descent"
in Book 3, "The Depths," where he encounters his own – feminized –
mirror image in the figure of a hermit, a true androgyne.[16] The hermit's
alien body is part female (he has long hair, "like that of a woman") – and
part male; he is also a Cyclopean monster, without an expression "in his
vacant bold eye." The uncanniness of this encounter, to be sure, is based
on Branden's own projections. The chapter title, "I Come Into Contact
with Humanity Again" (*ASA* 250–64), is deeply ironic, since Branden
does not connect but recognizes in this physical body nothing but the
threat of his own internal emptiness and hollowness. Feminized and
"reduced" to the experience of "body," the male narrator, like the her-

---

14 Bordo 84.

15 Bordo 94, 85.

16 This title could also be seen as an intertexual nod to Oscar Wilde's *De Profundis*, a
work Grove had translated into German.

mit, has lost control and speech with which to "master" his experience. Both face each other, unable to connect through words. Speaking becomes a painful bodily activity, as the hermit, "twisting his whole body into the act," produces a word of farewell, "heaving the words up from, let me say, his abdomen and ejecting them forcibly" (*ASA* 259). At the same time, this scene also suggests a birth-giving of language through the body (just as the naturalist narrative itself is born and energized through the language of the body).

Branden's feminized body dies metaphorically in a fever attack to be reborn as a male and as a desexualized farm "hand" in a chapter conveniently entitled "I Become a 'Hand'" (282–93). This "death" in a foreign land echoes Fanny Essler's death of a malaria fever attack in Portugal, where she dies, like Branden, far away from her *Heimat*. But in contrast to Fanny, Branden's "death" marks the beginning of a "rebirth" and a new life beyond the realm of naturalist femaleness. Indeed, the death of the female and the rebirth of the male is a recurring motif in Grove's fiction: the female's violent death (e.g., Clara Vogel, Frances Montcrieff) often marks the end of a plot of decline, while the male is frequently allowed a comic "rebirth" (e.g., Niels Lindstedt, Harold Tracy). Branden initiates his own rebirth by rescuing the androgynous hermit from drowning and by forcing this alien body to eject the first words; thus he becomes his own midwife as he is born into a new culture, speaking a new language and moving beyond victimized femininity. But the fact that Branden, as a "new man," insists on his maleness also shows that Grove's conceptualization of sexual identity continues to operate within naturalist conventions, in which the position of control is automatically associated with the male.

Since Branden's "descent" is characterized by his feminization, anorexia, and aphasia, it should come as no surprise that his "levelling" entails a new male identity, an acceptance of essential food, and his transformation into a writer. Accepting that his place is "with the men," he follows Dr. Goodwin's commission that the "real man longs for production" (*ASA* 289) and becomes an itinerant worker on the large western farms, celebrating the new community of "hoboes" as a male community of "desublimated Thoreaus." If the "theme of Grove's *A Search for America* is the narrator's search for a North American pastoral myth in its genuinely imaginative form," as Northrop Frye has argued,[17] then

---

17 Northrop Frye, *The Bush Garden: Essays on the Canadian Imagination* (Toronto: Anansi, 1971) 240.

Branden appears to have found his ideal in what Grove describes as a pastoral of the fields. As a simple field worker on the Mackenzie Farm, the mecca of "hobodom," the narrator's earlier anorexic vision gives way to a catalogue of food, an Odyssean banquet of essential nourishments:

> We went to the cook-house for dinner. The food was good, consisting of soup, meat, vegetables, and pudding. Plenty of pies were scattered over the tables which were covered with white oil-cloth; there were large stacks of fresh bread, both white and brown, dishes of butter, pitchers with milk, and pots full of coffee and tea. As once before in similar surroundings I marvelled again at the capacity for eating which these workers of the soil displayed. (*ASA* 347)

And yet, just as Grove does not abandon the narrative strategies of the naturalist genre, as the descriptive catalogue suggests, so Branden continues to adhere to the naturalist position of (male) narrative authority. In this context, the gaps are as important as what is said in the text. While Branden overtly celebrates his identity as a farm "hand," he silences the fact that he has become "a voice," as well, a narrator who controls his experience through manipulation of language, through story-telling. The identity assumed by Branden, then, is one that echoes the traditional male – desexualized – narrator in naturalism, who hovers above the text as a bodiless authority, endowed with immense powers.

The contradictions of Branden's different roles underscore this point. Even as an itinerant worker he does not really merge with the community of field workers he celebrates, but is separated from them by a distinct difference in consciousness. *A Search of America* is a "novel of double consciousness," as Tom Henighan defines this genre in *Natural Space in Literature* (1982); it is a narrative in which "field is polarized with the city" and in which the narrator is generally a sophisticated outsider who tries to reach some kind of identification with the peasant world.[18] Just as pastoral myths "do not exist as places," as Northrop Frye has observed,[19] so the idyllic picture of the workers' Odyssean banquet clashes with Branden's naturalist consciousness of the reality of social problems (such as gambling, vermin-infested houses, dependency on employers). As the social problems reintroduce a naturalist leitmotif, so Branden presents himself as a sympathizing narrator-spectator, who enjoys a

---

18 Tom Henighan, *Natural Space in Literature: Imagination and Environment in Nineteenth and Twentieth Century Fiction and Poetry* (Ottawa: Golden Dog Press, 1982) 70.

19 Frye 241.

broader perspective and speaks with a voice of authority that others lack. As a naturalist narrator, he assumes control and narrative authority, and with it a clearly defined – male – identity.

Posing in his different roles as a pruner of trees and a teacher, Branden returns to the traditional orthopedic-didactic voice of the naturalist narrator. He uses the language of the early precursors of naturalism, the eighteenth-century French socialists, such as Saint-Simon and Charles Fourier, who voiced their social critiques in evocations of utopia. Branden's charge against the young farmer millionaire Mackenzie (who lives in a "white house"!) presents these two movements of naturalism: first, the social accusation – "You have taken [the small farmers'] land" (*ASA* 376) – and second, the projection of a socialist utopian order in which the millionaire should "divest" himself of his "property" and thus make possible "real democracy" based on an economy of "a greater number of independent farmers" (*ASA* 379–80). The closer Branden moves to his evocation of utopia, though, the more virulent and shrill are his accusations against "real" America. It is the very shrillness of his voice and the overly moralistic quality of his narrative that expose his personal involvement, insecurity, and the laboured effort to speak in a "male" voice of authority.

Indeed, the novel continues to undercut the naturalist separation between empowered (male) narrator and impotent (feminized) victim. The narrator-observer (having superior knowledge and the power to manipulate language) and the narrated naturalist object (being blind, impotent, and without language) are shown to be one and the same character, with the novel deliberately blurring the boundaries between the two. It is Branden himself who participates as an active, *eironic* agent in the satiric-naturalist dissection of his younger *alazonic* self. Splitting his self into young and old, naive and mature, Branden creates what W.J. Keith has called "a curious 'double-view' effect in which first- and third-person intermix, and Branden can present himself as both the personal 'I' and the objective 'young man,'" or what Frances Kaye has discussed as Branden's "biformity," his tendency "to propagate opposing points of view."[20] This dialogical principle is an ironic technique of self-subversion that allows the new "I" to put the old self on trial and to play the role of vicious, critical prosecutor at the same time that both

---

20 W. J. Keith, "Grove's Search For America," *Canadian Literature* 59 (1974): 59; Frances Kaye, "Hamlin Garland and Frederick Philip Grove: Self-Conscious Chroniclers of the Pioneers," *Canadian Review of American Studies* 10 (1979): 34–35.

young and old narrator put America on trial, testing the American reality in their odyssey across the country.

The dissection of his younger self tortures and mutilates the body, so that the narrative takes the form of "*sparagmos* or tearing to pieces," according to Northrop Frye "the archetypal theme of irony and satire," or naturalism.[21] Branden's (naturalist) adventures are painful ones, in which the male body is ritually dissected and crucified in bodily tortures that carry the overtones of Sadeian pains. Travelling on train rods to the western hobo-land, Branden's body is crushed and metaphorically destroyed by a true torture machine: "I saw myself lying on the sleepers, a mangled mass of bloody flesh and crushed bones" (*ASA* 332). "Punishing" himself in a naturalist narrative is significant in two ways, signalling, first, the author's ritual destruction of his "female" self, and second, the author's guilt about his "killing" of Fanny Essler.

Unlike Dreiser's tragic figure, Clyde Griffiths in *An American Tragedy* (1925), who fails as "a historian of self" and lets others tell his story, Grove's naturalist victim rises phoenix-like out of naturalist ashes to tell his story. As Branden's youthful body is mutilated by "that part of America which had wounded and hurt me" (*ASA* 209), so a somewhat maturer Branden emerges from his passive victim status to put America on trial by dissecting it intellectually in naturalism's privileged mode of *sparagmos*. While Clyde is the naturalist victim of "an American tragedy," Branden turns his back on American society and becomes a "Canadian."

Just as Canada is described as a borderland in *A Search for America*, so Branden maintains a precarious borderline status: he is simultaneously subject and object, acting and acted upon, authority figure and victim, with the novel blurring the naturalist boundaries between knowing spectator and ignorant victim, between masculine and feminine. Like Fanny Essler, Branden deliberately speaks from the margins – as an immigrant, as a "hobo," and as a Canadian – which creates a distance between himself and the centres of power of the new society. His position on the margins of America also signals that his persona hovers on the margins of the naturalist genre. Although he assumes the authority of the male naturalist narrator, he also maintains Fanny Essler's female confessional voice up to the end, manipulating the conventions of the confessional genre. If it is true that Branden has not undergone a total metamorphosis into a "social man," but still shares the sense of superiority and arrogance

---

21 Northrop Frye, *Anatomy of Criticism: Four Essays* (Princeton: Princeton UP, 1973) 192.

of the European Reelen, it is equally true that he has not abandoned, nor totally repressed, Fanny Essler by the end of the novel. Opting for Canada as his new *Heimat*, the narrator continues to hover on the borderline between (stereotypical) masculinity and femininity, between narrative subject- and object-positions, so that the novel's overt claim of his re-birth as a new "man" is subverted by the novel's covert intertext. This intertext suggests a more feminized, Flaubertian identification, with the narrator "confessing" via intertextual dialogue: *Fanny Essler, c'est moi.*

IV. Eroticizing Bourgeois Power

9

The Male Body of Power:
The Titan

So far this study has mainly focused on naturalism's sexualization, co-optation, and on the complicitous docility of the female body in the social network of power. The next chapters, in contrast, will be devoted to the role and representation of the male "body of power" in naturalist fiction. *Sister Carrie*, I have argued, presents the reader with the spectre of the disintegrating male body in George Hurstwood, whose vulnerable physicality symbolizes his loss of social power. The feminization of Clyde Griffiths' body in *An American Tragedy* signifies his failure in writing his own history and his ultimate victimization as he moves through America's judicial institutions. In *A Search for America*, Grove adds a somewhat different twist, in that Branden's feminized body also suggests an androgynous challenge of naturalist gender boundaries. Though in these novels the male body is victimized, in their business novels, the Cowperwood trilogy and the *Master of the Mill* respectively, Dreiser and Grove conceptualize centralized capitalist power in terms of male power and dominance. They do not, however, inscribe this male power on the male body, but represent it in displaced forms, such as the female body or art objects. Conceptualizing submission to bourgeois power in sexualized terms, Dreiser describes the robber baron Frank A.

Cowperwood as a fantasy figure of male power, an imaginary construct, whose power wraps itself around the body of whole cities, "penetrating" and subduing them in a pleasurable embrace.

Dreiser's representation of the power of monopolist capitalism, to be sure, is related to historically specific developments. The Cowperwood trilogy is based on the life of the famous American robber baron and philanderer, Charles Tyson Yerkes Jr. (1837–1905), who made his name as a traction king, financier, and art collector in Philadelphia, Chicago, New York, and finally in London, England.[1] The trilogy presents an exploration of the art of manipulative speculation and fictive transactions at a time that marked both the triumph of the American robber barons and America's growing legal and political resistance to capitalist monopoly. In the first volume of the trilogy, *The Financier* (1912), Frank Algernon Cowperwood loses his entire fortune (including city money entrusted to him) in the stock market panic of 1871, only to regain it in true speculator fashion through the equally spectacular fall of another famous businessman, Jay Cooke, in the crash of 1873. The second volume, *The Titan* (1914), traces Cowperwood's rise as a street railway magnate in Chicago in the 1880s, an event that is followed by his downfall after Chicago's citizens and local politicians organize a popular crusade against him. The third volume, *The Stoic* (1947), describes his business ventures in England and his death in 1905.

Dreiser's treatment of big business capitalism raises some crucial questions concerning his naturalism's ideological underpinnings. The focus of the trilogy is not on the exploited "underdogs" (as they are represented in *The Titan* in Chicago's democratic populace), but on the robber baron, who emerges in *The Titan* in heroic stature, as an oxymoronic bourgeois *Übermensch*, continually appealing to the reader's sympathy and admiration. The question we have to raise, then, is to what extent naturalism's traditional claim to social criticism and solidarity with the working class "yields" to the seductive embrace of the robber baron in Dreiser's fiction. This issue, I will argue, highlights a deep tension within Dreiser's naturalism. The trilogy foregrounds naturalism's "entropic vision" in Cowperwood's unscrupulous business

---

1   For a discussion of Charles T. Yerkes's biography in relation to Dreiser's trilogy, see Gerber, 87–110, as well as Gerber's article "The Financier Himself: Dreiser and C.T. Yerkes," *PMLA* 88 (1973): 112–21; see also Pizer, *Novels*, 153–200. For a historical evaluation of Yerkes's spectacular business transactions in Chicago, see Sidney Roberts, "Portrait of a Robber Baron: Charles T. Yerkes," *Business History Review* 35 (1961): 344–71.

methods, which include the bribing of politicians, the overriding of other people's property rights, the overcapitalizing of stocks, and even blackmail. Yet the novel also suggests that the superman falls according to the logic of Dreiser's "equation inevitable" that brings down those who rise too high. While the trilogy condones the manipulative speculator's contempt for social and legal conventions, Cowperwood's capitalist excess appears to carry with it the seed of its own destruction, a point most clearly articulated in the second volume of the trilogy, *The Titan*, which will be my focus of analysis.

Continuing the displacement of sexuality onto economic relation that Dreiser had initiated in *Sister Carrie*, *The Titan*'s "entropic vision" deliberately interweaves Cowperwood's anarchic business methods with his equally "anarchic" sex life. As in the life of Dreiser's female "soldier of fortune," kinship and family alliance have been replaced in the capitalist's life by the deployment of sexuality and an economy of promiscuity. After his disastrous business failure and his scandalous affair with Aileen Butler in *The Financier*, Cowperwood displays a cold indifference to family alliances in *The Titan*: "He had a prison record to live down; a wife and two children to get rid of – in the legal sense, at least."[2] After his move to Chicago, Cowperwood's first family indeed disappears from the narrative as if they had never existed. Concepts such as genealogy, blood relations, or loyalty are nothing but obstacles to the financier's desire to create a new life for himself in Chicago's expanding economy.

As in *Sister Carrie*, this lack of family alliance is deliberate, allowing the author to highlight that modern bourgeois power is based less on lineage and paternalistic responsibility than on an eroticization of continually shifting power relations. Carrie Meeber's lack of true loyalties, combined with her characteristic high "self-interest," is echoed in the male speculator's equally narcissistic "I satisfy myself" (*T* 9). Dreiser, by the way, borrowed this formula directly from a newspaper interview with Yerkes: "Whatever I do," Yerkes declared, "I do not from any sense of duty, but to satisfy myself, and when I have satisfied myself, I know that I have done the best I can."[3] Dreiser shows that the modern technologies of sexualized power are not primarily interested in enslave-

---

2 Theodore Dreiser, *Trilogy of Desire, Vol. One: The Financier* (New York: Thomas Y. Crowell, 1974); *Trilogy of Desire Vol. Two: The Titan* (New York: Thomas Y. Crowell, 1974) 9. All further references to these works will appear in the text with *The Financier* abbreviated *F*, *The Titan T*.

3 *Journal*, January 29, 1898, quoted in Roberts 351.

ment of others but in "self-assertion." "Selfish" and "self-centred,"
Cowperwood "refuses to be a tool for others," and if the businessman's
"I satisfy myself" echoes the American tradition of self-sufficiency, as
Lois Hughson argues,[4] Cowperwood's pragmatic and manipulative strategies are more a parody than a confirmation of Emersonian virtuous
self-reliance. Indeed, the deliberately masturbatory implications of
Cowperwood's principle of action highlight how much the partners of
his business life (like his sexual partners) are only "tools" in his quest
for self-satisfaction. Endowed with a "magnetic" body, which has less
to do with his real, physical body than with the power fantasy projected
into it, he attracts men and women alike: women "yield" to his sexual
seduction, men "surrender" in business transactions, a defeat that is always accompanied by the typically naturalist sadomasochistic mixture
of pleasure and pain.

The primary goal of self-satisfaction in business and private action
encapsulates what Foucault has termed bourgeois autosexualization.
Dreiser's fiction thus instances Foucault's argument that the bourgeoisie should be seen not as a class that denies its sexuality, but as one that
makes clever use of it. In its historical establishment as the dominant
social class, the French bourgeoisie, for example, gave itself a body that
it cultivated and cherished, endowing itself with a class-specific sexuality. Foucault explains:

> Let us not picture the bourgeoisie symbolically castrating itself the better
> to refuse others the right to have a sex and make use of it as they please.
> This class must be seen rather as being occupied, from the mid-eighteenth
> century on, with creating its own sexuality and forming a specific body
> based on it, a 'class' body with its health, hygiene, descent, and race: the
> autosexualization of its body, the incarnation of sex in its body, the en-
> dogamy of sex and the body. (*HS* 124)

Dreiser expresses the same point aesthetically in his fictional exploration of America's late-nineteenth-century big business capitalism. It
was probably Yerkes's highly publicized, scandalous sex life that led
Dreiser to translate his story into naturalist aesthetics. Thus the trilogy's
very structure highlights that mechanisms of economic, bourgeois power
are interwoven with sexual concerns: chapters dealing with economic

---

4 See Lois Hughson, "Dreiser's Cowperwood and the Dynamics of Naturalism,"
   Studies in the Novel 16 (Spring 1984): 52–71.

power, with manipulation, speculation, and appropriation alternate with detailed descriptions of the protagonist's sex life.

Furthermore, Cowperwood's hyperactive sex drive is not only devoid of intimacy, but is a direct reflection of his poker-faced business life, as John O'Neill has noted: "In this sense his sexuality is linked to the abstract excitement he experiences in business, where he manipulates symbols whose meaning can never be entirely lost. Sex is energy, and it is not, in the end, very personal."[5] Indeed, despite the novel's emphasis on the protagonist's sexuality, Cowperwood indulges in very few bodily pleasures: he enjoys neither drink nor smoke, nor does he appear to relish food very much. It appears that in his willingness to suspend bodily pleasures Cowperwood is not very different from other famous contemporary capitalists: "I never had a craving for tobacco, or tea and coffee," John D. Rockefeller declared, "I never had a craving for anything."[6] While Cowperwood and Rockefeller may be psychological inversions of each other in the sense that Rockefeller was a saver, Cowperwood a spender, as Walter Benn Michaels has argued, Cowperwood echoes Rockefeller's emphasis on body control and will power. Just as Carrie's sexuality has an abstract quality and is mainly explored as a construct, Cowperwood's sex drive has the function of giving his economic power play an erotic charge that is reflected in the "magnetic" quality of his body image.

Focusing on promiscuity in *The Financier*, Walter Benn Michaels has argued that "Cowperwood's sentimental relations are hardly incompatible with his financial ones." The mistress and sexual promiscuity, Michaels argues, represent the speculator's mental manipulations and "fictitious dealings." Thus Michaels creates a binary opposition between Cowperwood's first wife, Lillian, "whose 'lethargic manner' and 'indifference' convey to [Cowperwood] a sexually charged sense of absolute security." But since, for Cowperwood, marriage allows no possibility of mental alteration or change, the financier turns to the mistress, to Aileen Butler, whose vitality and sexual generosity represent the instability and erratic quality of stock market speculation. Just as the mistress "gives" without attaching her gift to the idea of exchange, so the

5 John O'Neill, "The Disproportion of Sadness: Dreiser's *The Financier* and *The Titan*," *Modern Fiction Studies* 23 (1977): 421.

6 Quoted in Walter Benn Michaels, "Dreiser's 'Financier': the Man of Business as a Man of Letters," *American Realism: New Essays*, ed. Eric J. Sundquist (Baltimore: Johns Hopkins UP, 1982) 284.

stockmarket rejects the idea of security (implied in formal marriage ties).[7]

Despite Michaels's intriguing insights, the opposition between wife and mistress, between mental manipulation and production of tangible commodities, is not as clear cut in the trilogy as Michaels's reading suggests. Even more problematic is Michaels's monological equation of the narrative voice with the whole (deeply dialogical) text, as well as his assertion that the reader should not be concerned with whether or not Dreiser approved or disapproved of his economic culture, since it "seems wrong to think of the culture you live in as the object of your affection."[8] This somewhat categorical postulate is particularly puzzling in light of Dreiser's trilogy, which insists on conceptualizing monopoly capitalism in terms of love and hate, sexual conquest and sexualized yielding, seduction and rejection, always already cathecting power relations with deeply sexualized emotions. Indeed, the trilogy insistently points out that we cannot not think of our cultural economy without strong emotional reactions, since this economy appeals to human desire, continually awakening but also frustrating consumer fantasies of power and pleasure. Dreiser highlights this point by showing that even the narrator is, in part, drawn into Cowperwood's seductive economic universe. The readers, in turn, are presented with Cowperwood as a seductive icon of power that they can either "yield" to, by joining the narrator in a vicarious enjoyment of the robber baron's ingenious power play, or choose to distance themselves from, by reading "against the grain" of the narrator's comments and by focusing on the marginalized figures in the text.

While *Sister Carrie* is concerned with the seductive power of modern consumerism, *The Titan* translates naturalism's traditional social Darwinism into an eroticization of modern power, in which the bourgeois capitalist triumphs through techniques of seduction. In fact, Cowperwood's principle of domination is based not on a crude repression of the opposition, but on a clever appropriation of the people's interests, as the novel repeatedly underscores. When Cowperwood arrives in Chicago in the 1880s, the customers of the Chicagoan street railways are genuinely disgruntled with the bad quality of the service and the conservative owners who refuse to modernize Chicago's traction system. Cowperwood cleverly appropriates this public concern to his advantage. With the help of a powerful Irish "underworld" politician, the Democratic McKenty, he "infiltrates" the ranks of the representatives of the public "in order to

---

7   Michaels. "Dreiser's Financier," 279–80, 293.

8   For Michaels's full argument, see *The Gold Standard and the Logic of Naturalism: American Literature at the Turn of the Century* (Berkeley: U of California P, 1987) 18–19.

discredit the present management" of the street railway companies, who are opposed to his aggressive modernization scheme (*T* 179). Soon complaints are voiced and publicized by local aldermen, creating the impression of a "public uprising" against the bad quality of the railway service, a move that more or less forces the owners to sell out to Cowperwood. Donald Pizer interprets Cowperwood's consolidation of the Chicago street railways as the "paradoxical position of a man whose use of the Public for his own gain also eventually benefits the Public."[9] Thus, *The Titan* anticipates Foucault's point that capitalism's future and ever-increasing power is based not on "fighting against" but on appropriating the *élan* of the opposition.

Yet despite such accommodations of the opposition, the racist implications of Cowperwood's social Darwinism do not disappear behind such forms of sexualized power structures: on the contrary, Foucault explains that in the historical process of establishing its economic and social hegemony, the French bourgeoisie adopted a new kind of racism vis-à-vis the underprivileged classes, a racism very different from that manifested by nobility: "It was a dynamic racism, a racism of expansion, even if it was still in a budding state, awaiting the second half of the nineteenth century to bear the fruits that we have tasted" (*HS* 125). Racism also characterizes Cowperwood's relationship with the masses in *The Titan*. Although "temperamentally he was in sympathy with the mass more than he was with the class" (*T* 27), he also has an undisguised disdain for the masses that is expressed in his rejection of the working people as an externalized Other: "They were rather like animals, patient, inartistic, hopeless. He thought of their shabby homes, their long hours, their poor pay" (*T* 187). Cowperwood's universal denigration of the ethnically heterogeneous working class goes hand in hand with his misogyny, whereby his second wife, Aileen Butler, is presented as a double of the democratic mass. Not only is she linked to the people through her Irish background, but Cowperwood eventually sees her as "inartistic" and "slave-like" in her willingness to sacrifice herself for him. By conflating the Chicagoan people with Aileen, Dreiser highlights that both submit to Cowperwood's power (or rebel against it) in a very similar fashion; they are attached to Cowperwood in a love-hate relationship, always already yielding in oxymoronic pleasurable pain.

"What leads to power being desirable, and to actually being desired?", Foucault asked in an interview. For "the eroticizing to work," he an-

---

9 Pizer, *Novels*, 196.

swered, "it's necessary that the attachment to power, the acceptance of power by those over whom it is exerted, is already erotic."[10] In Dreiser's universe, those who are "weak" are magnetically, that is sexually, attracted to the strong, even to the social Darwinistic Machiavelli, who is "without a shred of true democracy": "Raw, glittering force, however, compounded of the cruel Machiavellianism of nature, if it be but Machiavellian, seems to exercise a profound attraction for the conventionally rooted. Your cautious citizen of average means, looking out through the eye of his dull world of seeming fact, is often the first to condone the grim butcheries of theory by which the strong rise" (*T* 189). This is how the narrator conceptualizes and universalizes the eroticization of power that creates Cowperwood's success in Chicago's booming economy: seduced like Aileen, the average (male) citizen surrenders his resistance to the eroticized fantasy of power projected by Cowperwood.

If there is a note of social criticism in Dreiser's trilogy, it is in the attention he draws to the construction of Cowperwood's fantasy image of power, which creates, shapes, and perpetuates the material reality of power relations. Lois Banner has described the evolution of such body images in her cultural history *American Beauty*. The American businessman in the 1860s was a "portly rotund male" who displayed prosperity in his figure, Banner writes, and continues: "By midcentury he was heavy and solid, even fat, a reflection in physique of the success for which American men strove."[11] At the turn of the century, America found its male models in businessmen and industrialists, who preferably represented themselves in their working place: "Writing about Newport society in the 1880s, George Lathrop described the industrialist's library as a private 'temple' of his religion of business. His immense desk was the 'high Altar,' and the 'incense of a cigar' was a regular tribute to the 'established cult.'"[12]

A photograph of Charles Yerkes (reprinted in Sidney Roberts' "Portrait of a Robber Baron") reflects a similar image. (The cigar smoke, though, is absent, reflecting the businessman's new health consciousness.) Yerkes sits at a wooden desk, so massive that it almost dwarfs his own enormous physique. Thus, despite Yerkes's imposing looks, the photograph inevitably exposes the physical human-ness of a man with a stout constitution and a pot belly who, sitting down, appears belittled by the massive paraphernalia with which he surrounds his body.

---

10 Michel Foucault, "Films and Popular Memory," Lotringer, 101.

11 Banner 112.

12 Banner 241.

Dreiser's trilogy translates this point into his naturalist aesthetics: the speculator's status as an eroticized icon of abstract power inevitably collapses when the viewer is confronted with the body's all-too-human reality. The only time Cowperwood's body is described in extensive physical detail is, significantly, when we witness his loss of power in *The Financier*, after his incarceration on a conviction of technical embezzlement. Once Cowperwood is imprisoned, the narrator dwells on his looks, which are filtered through the warden's inspecting eye as he notices the prisoner's silk clothing, his leather shoes and his manicured hands. Under the warden's gaze, the convicted embezzler strips naked to take a bath, after which his body is weighed, measured, and inscribed in the penitentiary's record book. Being thus "specularized" and reduced to his physicality costs the erstwhile speculator his sense of self-possession and identity. Alone in his cell, we see him for the first time look at himself in order to recognize what he has become and, like the metaphorically emasculated Hurstwood who is about to commit suicide, Cowperwood "stretched himself wearily on the bed" (*F* 442), adopting, if only for a few moments, the position of the naturalist victim.

Given the dangers involved in such acts of physical "specular–ization," it should come as no surprise that Cowperwood's body is absent over large parts of the trilogy. While this absence may be surprising in light of Cowperwood's obsession with self-representation, the disappearance of his body has to be seen primarily as a strategy of (patriarchal) power, as Jane Gallop's feminist theory suggests: "By giving up their bodies, men gain power," Gallop writes, "the power to theorize, to represent themselves."[13] Or, as Foucault explains the political-historical dimension of this phenomenon:

> Power in the West is what displays itself the most, and thus what hides itself best. What we have called "political life" since the nineteenth century is (a bit like the court in the age of monarchy) the manner in which power gives itself over to representation. Power is neither there, nor is that how it functions. The relations of power are perhaps among the most hidden things in the social body.[14]

The absence of Cowperwood's physical body in Dreiser's naturalist fiction, then, presents an aesthetic comment on the nature of modern power,

---

13 Quoted in *Refiguring the Father: New Feminist Readings of Patriarchy*, ed. Patricia Jaeger and Beth Kowaleski-Wallace (Carbondale: Southern Illinois UP, 1989) xii.

14 "End of the Monarchy of Sex," in Lotringer, 147–48.

which cannot be adequately represented in one (unified) body, since it is often anchored in polymorphous "economic infrastructures."

More specifically, the absence of Cowperwood's (physical) body is directly connected with his role (and power) as a speculator, a role that requires that he should never become a (sexualized and identifiable) spectacle himself. Whenever Cowperwood is in his element as a manipulating speculator, it is not his body but only his "deceptive eyes," which are "unreadable" yet at the same time "alluring," on which the trilogy dwells. Etymologically linked to "seeing" and "spying,"[15] speculation is based on an elaborate spy and surveillance system, in which everyone is engaged in collecting information about everyone else because the successful speculator-manipulators are those with some advance information over their competitors. *The Titan* is saturated with references to detectives who are hired to spy into the private lives of public figures because the gathering of information about those who are "the cynosure of all eyes" (*T* 334) means having power over powerful politicians, not so much in the sense of oppressing these people but in order to make use of them, to assign them a place and put them to work in Chicago's "Panopticon." After all, in "the Panopticon each person, depending on his place, is watched by all or certain of the others," as Foucault writes: "You have an apparatus of total and circulating mistrust, because there is no absolute point" (*PK* 158). Similarly, Cowperwood does not possess a god-like "eye of power," but is tied into a network of spying, inevitably being the subject and object of spying at the same time. While he operates successfully by keeping his name out of the business affairs he conducts, he suffers tremendous setbacks in Chicago when his enemies bring to light his Philadelphia past, his prison incarceration and his scandalous divorce from his first wife Lillian. In the social fabric's net of power, the status of the supposed superman is inevitably limited.

If Cowperwood's power relies on seduction rather than repression, on seeing without becoming the object of sight, this principle of mobile power cannot be adequately represented in his physical or sexualized body. According to the logic of Dreiser's naturalist aesthetics and ideology, the material body is always already a feminized, weak, and docile body – the antithesis of Cowperwood's immaterial body of power. Since his power principle is based on variability, his imaginary

---

15 Latin "speculator" means to spy, to scout; "speculor" means to observe, to spy out, to watch, to examine, to explore; to wait for.

and ever flexible body construct relies on a continual representational displacement of the capitalist's power into other material bodies: the city's body, the female body, and the body of his art collection. Exploring these displacements, *The Titan* highlights the power politics of capitalist self-representation as one of its *leitmotifs*.

Given Dreiser's naturalist conceptualization of male power as a net wrapped around a feminized, yielding body, it should come as no surprise that Cowperwood inscribes his power on the city's body, when taking control of Chicago's traction field in the 1880s and 1890s. In the course of his conquest, various parts of the city are absorbed and assimilated into his "body of power": "Within eight months after seizing the La Salle Street tunnel and gobbling four of the principal down-town streets for his loop, Cowperwood turned his eyes toward the completion of the second part of the programme – that of taking over the Washington Street tunnel and the Chicago West Divison Company" (*T* 221). Just as Cowperwood's power is conceptualized in Dreiser's naturalist aesthetics in spatial terms, so Foucault has emphasized the role of space as a key to modern procedures of power: "A whole history remains to be written of *spaces* – which would at the same time be the history of *powers* (both these terms in the plural) – from the great strategies of geo-politics to the little tactics of the habitat" (*PK* 149). In taking control of Chicago's public transportation system, Cowperwood lays down the city's spatial arteries, regulating the flow of people through the city, determining their pace and economic welfare. The traction lines spreading across Chicago's "body" become Cowperwood's material self-representation that make him very quickly "an attractive, even a sparkling figure in the eyes of the Chicago public" (*T* 223).

The construction of Cowperwood's eroticized body of power thus always depends on the appropriation and assimilation of an "alien" body and its simultaneous externalization as a sexualized "Other." Upon entering the windy city, Cowperwood perceives it in terms of a masculine body, as it is metonymically represented in a group of male workers that capture his attention: "Healthy men they were, in blue or red shirt-sleeves, stout straps about their waists, short pipes in their mouths, fine, hardy, nutty-brown specimens of humanity. Why were they so appealing, he asked himself. This raw, dirty town seemed naturally to compose itself into stirring artistic pictures" (*T* 4). What is striking in this scene is that Cowperwood, who professes to despise the workers as a class, endows their physical bodies with an homoerotic attraction. While this scene echoes Hurstwood's encounter with Drouet in Chicago's Fitzgerald and Moy's, it also foregrounds the ideological concern of Dreiser's naturalism with exposing the principles of eroticized power.

Homoeroticism is put in the service of Cowperwood's "I satisfy myself," as he anticipates the male bodies' "yielding" to his "embrace"; "penetrated" by his magnetic power, they, in turn, become his physical "arm of power."

Even more important to the construction of Cowperwood's magnetic body construct is the female body. Lois Banner has observed that in the late nineteenth century, American "men of great wealth were not the focus of the popular press" since "their complex businesses required the analytic skill of an Ida Tarbell, unravelling the doings of Standard Oil in a muckraking journal. Absorbed in the details of the intricate corporate structures they had created, they left the balls, parties, and other leisure-time activities of high society up to their wives." Indeed, the popular press featured "the wives and especially the daughters" of wealthy capitalists.[16] Thus it is no coincidence that the three "major" women in Cowperwood's life correspond to a succession of nineteenth-century American beauty icons. The financier's first wife, Lillian Semple, who possesses the "beauty of a vase," evokes what Banner describes as the beauty icon of the 1850s – a lady-like, frail, and delicate type of beauty. This American hothouse lily was challenged in the second half of the nineteenth century by a fleshy, voluptuous popular beauty icon. This is the very beauty that is reflected in Cowperwood's second wife, Aileen Butler, a true Venus figure, whose innate sensuousness displaces Lillian in Cowperwood's life by the end of *The Financier*. When in the 1890s the athletic, "natural" woman replaces the voluptuous beauty as the predominant American beauty icon, Cowperwood turns from Aileen to Berenice Fleming, who is both athletic and assertive, but "yields" her body to the speculator in the same way as Aileen and Lillian before her. Presented in such a line of heterogeneous beauties, the boundary between the role of the wife and the mistress becomes blurred, as Cowperwood cleverly appropriates the women's sexualized bodies into his power play.

This point is exemplified in *The Titan*, where Cowperwood's second wife Aileen, "truly beautiful herself – a radiant, vibrating *objet d'art*" (*T* 36), is presented to the "spectators" of Chicago, the socially prominent who comment and judge her as a representation. To emphasize the notion of the female as a representational art object even further, Cowperwood has Aileen's picture painted while she is "still young" and in the prime of her beauty, and this picture becomes part of his art

---

16 Banner, "American Beauty," 164.

collection, hung opposite "a particularly brilliant Gerôme, then in the heyday of his exotic popularity – a picture of nude odalisques of the harem, idling beside the highly colored stone marquetry of an oriental bath" (*T* 68). Gerôme's nudes are a very apt mirror image of Aileen's picture as well as of the real Aileen. Just as Gerôme's harem suggests a cornucopia of sex for the male potentate so its complement-mirror image, the picture of Aileen, celebrates sexual vitality and draws a whole number of male spectators – Cowperwood's business friends and rivals, who dream of sexual pleasure with her but are at the same time made conscious of the "lack" of this pleasure in their own lives because they feel that they are "chained" into "conventional" relationships with "cold" and "possessive" wives. The juxtaposition of the two visual representations draws attention to what is really absent in both pictures: the male as owner of the picture as well as "master" over the female body. Cowperwood triumphs over all the male spectators present, who are aware that he is the only one to have access to the beautiful body they admire in the picture. As the owner of the gallery, Cowperwood represents himself as a lover of beauty at the same time that his role as a powerful master-accumulator-owner is inscribed in the gaps of the representations he owns.

At the same time, Dreiser draws attention to the danger of being the centre of a representation, as Aileen is in the beginning of the *The Titan*. After Cowperwood's first social event in Michigan Avenue, in which Aileen is offered as the representational "centre-piece" (in a chapter that is significantly entitled "A Test" [*T* 66–73]), it is Aileen who is dismissed by Chicagoan society as "too showy" and "vulgar," and is cut in society. The Cowperwoods' social failure is repeatedly attributed to Aileen and she is sacrificed not only by the socially prominent but by Cowperwood as well, who distances himself from her. It is Aileen who becomes a social outcast, while her husband is occasionally excused and invited alone by Chicago's rich. Cowperwood's imaginary body of power survives, while Aileen, as his "official" wife, finds herself entrapped in the fate of the naturalist courtesan, who is reduced to the physicality of her aging body. By the end of *The Titan*, she is ostracized and is sexually no longer desirable.

Cowperwood's long line of mistresses and wives, suggestive not so much of sexual but of aesthetic variety, not so much of erotic intimacy but of sexualized power play, assumes the same function as the continually changing "body" of his art collection. Indeed, the trilogy makes a connection between power and art, since it is, as Berenice Fleming observes, "the spirit of art that occupied the center of Cowperwood's iron personality," just as Cowperwood recognizes that "the ultimate end of fame, power, vigor was beauty" (*T* 440, 470). Filling his houses with art collections from different periods and countries, while the houses themselves are built as works of art, he surrounds himself with museum-like interiors: not with a home but with an abstract body of art. On one level, his artistic representations are an intricate part of capitalist activities: Cowperwood knows very well that "the great pictures are going to increase in value, and what [he] could get for a few hundred thousand now will be worth millions later" (*F* 162).

Yet more importantly, Cowperwood anticipates the politics of capitalist self-representations of our own *fin de siècle*, most notably of Donald Trump. In his autobiography with the telling title *The Art of the Deal* (1987), Trump defines himself not as a lover of money but as a lover of art: "I don't do it for money. I've got enough, much more than I'll ever need. I do it to do it. Deals are my art form. Other people paint beautifully on canvas or write wonderful poetry. I like making deals, preferably big deals. That's how I get my kicks."[17] Similarly, Trump describes his fetishized obsession with collecting beautiful buildings in sexualized terms, echoing Cowperwood's sexual and aesthetic ethos. Making a personal statement with a hotel "can arouse passions faster than other possessions,"[18] Trump writes, celebrating the purchase of the New York Plaza Hotel as the acquisition of a sensualized and feminized "masterpiece – the Mona Lisa." Though Cowperwood is painfully aware of how much his success is based on what Trump calls "image-management," both financiers' strategy is to show the public their artistic side, one that yearns for aesthetic beauty and anarchic freedom. While obsessed with image management, both financiers profess not to care about public opinion.

And yet, *The Titan* exposes that the capitalist's self-representation as an "artistic center" and a "lover of art" is a double-edged sword, since the financier's fetishist obsession with accumulating works of art in his desire for a positive self-representation simultaneously draws (public) attention to capitalism's very principle of acquisition and accumulation. Cowperwood, like Donald Trump, cannot help but expose in the sheer excess of *objets d'art* accumulated over his life time the mechanics of his power. His chase for ever more sophisticated works of art becomes a circle of repetition, a bourgeois *idée fixe*, a collectomania that seems to

---

17 Donald Trump with Tony Schwarz, *Trump: The Art of the Deal* (New York: Warner, 1987) 1.

18 Donald Trump with Charles Leerhsen, *Trump: Surviving at the Top* (New York: Random House, 1990) 114.

ask for control and cure and is easily exploited by his enemies and rivals, quickly used as a tool against him. Indeed, Cowperwood's Chicagoan opposition eventually conflates the capitalist's spectacular – visible and physical, since excessively growing – body of *objets d'art* with his gargantuan body of power. Cowperwood's obsessive conflation of business and art thus deconstructs itself, exposing the mechanism behind his aestheticized and eroticized power play.

Much of *The Titan* is devoted to emphasizing the dynamics and flexibility of Cowperwood's bourgeois power. If Dreiser's *Titan* illustrates anything, it is Foucault's point on the instability of power, which refuses to stay in one fixed locus. As Foucault puts it: "The omnipresence of power: not because it has the privilege of consolidating everything under its invincible unity, but because it is produced from one moment to the next, at every point, or rather in every relation from one point to another. Power is everywhere; not because it embraces everything, but because it comes from everywhere" (*HS* 93). Since modern power energizes itself through appropriation of the opposition, Foucault argues that a chasm has opened up between the centralized monarchical power of the Middle Age feudal system and the modern power of the bourgeoisie: "This new type of power, which can no longer be formulated in terms of sovereignty, is, I believe, one of the great inventions of bourgeois society. It has been a fundamental instrument in the constitution of industrial capitalism" (*PK* 105). This new type of power "presupposes a tightly knit grid of material coercions rather than the physical existence of a sovereign" (*PK* 104).

While *The Titan* images this very point through numerous reversals and shifts of power, Cowperwood eventually emerges in the opposite image of the feudal-monarchical power, the titan, a construction that looms larger than life and, in its static greatness, makes a perfect target for oppositional attacks. With his art collections, mansions, and spectacular wives, he emerges as an ancient monarch-potentate who rules through his physical and spectacular presence and constitutes an exotic, alien body that can easily be turned into a scapegoat figure. Concerned with monopoly and the "trustifying" of companies in an advanced stage of capitalism, Dreiser, groping for an adequate metaphor to translate the modern phenomenon of centralized economic power, takes recourse to the popular metaphor of monarchical power, which, when framed within a naturalist narrative, carries with it the seed of the protagonist's destruction. John O'Neill appropriately discusses Cowperwood the titan as an "epic hero," while Donald Pizer writes that Cowperwood is "cast in a much more heroic role in *The Titan* than in *The Financier*."[19] Like a romance hero, Cowperwood becomes a static figure who polarizes people: for some an eroticized love object, he is for others an object of passionate hatred. In fact, *The Titan* culminates in a confrontation between what appears to be a spectacular monarchical power versus the mass of the people in a wild, rebelling mob. The newspapers, realizing that they can "increase their circulation, by attacking him" (*T* 528), manage to exploit this imperial stature and set up a public image of him as an ancient tyrannical emperor, who turns the democratic mass into slaves. Reading the newspapers, Cowperwood's new "feminine ideal" Berenice Fleming falls in love with the aging Cowperwood because "he came by degrees to take on the outlines of a superman, a half-god or demi-gorgon" (*T* 527). As she falls in love with his imperial stature, so does Cowperwood himself.

At the height of his power, in a chapter entitled "Mount Olympus" (*T* 422–35), Cowperwood becomes aware of his "inability to control without dominating personally" (*T* 438). He manages to triumph over his Chicagoan competitors by appearing like a sovereign king in person in front of all his rivals and threatening them from a position of majesterial greatness and power. But by using his body image to suppress and subdue his rivals rather than "seduce" them, Cowperwood provokes his own downfall. Cowperwood's fall is already anticipated in the novel's title, *The Titan*, which evokes the defeat of the mythological giants in their struggle with an even higher godhood. Assuming the status of a hero in Dreiser's naturalist world automatically dooms the protagonist to fall, according to the inexorable logic of the "equation inevitable" and the genre's plot of decline.

Cowperwood's magnetic, eroticized body of power, then, carries with it the seed of its own destruction, whereby the Mephistophelian seducer becomes seduced by his own image. By the end of *The Titan*, his self-image becomes his own narcissistic object of desire. His monumental houses turn into sepulchres, in which Eros merges with Thanatos, swallowing the titan alive. When the socially prominent refuse to frequent his Chicago mansion, it becomes a "costly sepulcher in which Aileen sat brooding over the woes which had befallen her" (*T* 381), masochistically waiting for (and perpetuating the fantasy of) Cowperwood's phallic love. Dreiser illustrates this point even more explicitly in *The Stoic* (1947). The narrator describes Cowperwood's funeral as the speculator's last and most spectacular self-theatricalization that raises a last – static – monument to his narcissistic-masturbatory love for himself:

---

19   O'Neill 419; Pizer, *Novels*, 189.

Above the doors of the tomb, in heavy square-cut letters, was his name: FRANK ALGERNON COWPERWOOD. The three graduated platforms of granite were piled high with flowers, and the massive bronze double doors stood wide open, awaiting the arrival of the distinguished occupant. As all must have felt who viewed it for the first time, this was a severely impressive artistic achievement in the matter of design, for its tall and stately serenity seemed to dominate the entire area.[20]

Although orchestrated from beyond the grave, Cowperwood's spectacular funeral presents the spectre of the male body frozen in its imperial greatness. Even more importantly, the tomb that awaits Cowperwood's body is represented through Aileen's perspective and evokes the image of a *vagina dentata*, as Elaine Showalter has described it: "the spectre of female sexuality, a silent but terrible mouth that may wound and devour the male spectator."[21] Dressed in Aileen's (revengeful) fantasy, the funeral scene in *The Stoic* thus ironically echoes the ending of *Sister Carrie*. Like Hurstwood, Cowperwood is supplanted by women, by Aileen and Berenice who survive him.

"'Endure! Endure! Endure!'" (*S* 272) are the ironic words that go through Berenice's mind at Cowperwood's funeral. The point of the trilogy is that nothing survives in capitalism – except the machinery of power itself. After Cowperwood's death, his fortune is quickly dismantled in legal battles; his last important business transaction has to be completed by others. *The Financier* and *The Stoic* present powerful scenes in which Cowperwood's carefully accumulated properties and art objects are auctioned off, the first after his downfall in Philadelphia, the second after his death. These fetishized objects are not suspended above time as representations of Cowperwood's power, but reenter the economic circle, immediately becoming signifiers of somebody else's success. By the end, Cowperwood's eroticized body of power inevitably collapses, exposed as a fantasy construction through Dreiser's naturalist aesthetics.

In her (Marxist) re-reading of the novel, Arun Mukherjee has argued that Cowperwood should not be mistaken for Dreiser's mouthpiece. Emphasizing the trilogy's contribution as a naturalist form of social criticism, she has pointed to the narrative's parodic undercurrents that

---

20 *Trilogy of Desire, Vol. Three: The Stoic* (New York: Thomas Y. Crowell Company, 1974) 272. Further references will appear in the text, abbreviated *S*.

21 Elaine Showalter, *Sexual Anarchy: Gender and Culture at the Fin de Siècle* (New York: Penguin, 1990) 146.

undermine Cowperwood's fictitious claims to heroism.[22] Yet these under-currents should not mislead the reader into turning a blind eye to the narrator's deep complicity with Cowperwood's eroticized power play. While the *Titan* culminates in the robber baron's defeat by the Chicagoan people, the narrator's sympathies are not with the people: by the end, the narrator, like Berenice, has surrendered his critical tools to Cowperwood's eroticized body of power. This narrative bias is all the more important if we consider the historical context treated in the novel. Cowperwood/Yerkes embodies monopoly capitalism and the corruption of municipal authorities. At the turn of the century, Yerkes appealed to the state legislature for a fifty-year extension of his street railway franchises, a move that would have allowed him to establish himself as a monopolist of national, if not international, stature had it been successful.

The narrator is complicitous with the monopolist's perspective when describing Chicago's democratic movement. While *Sister Carrie* pulls all the strings of empathy with the bad working conditions faced by Hurstwood, *The Titan*, in contrast, glosses over the public hazards of Yerkes's street railways. It has to be remembered, however, that Yerkes's railways were a public hazard, killing forty-six and injuring three hundred and thirty-six people through poorly strung overhead wires, which Yerkes refused to improve.[23] Furthermore, the narrator presents the protesting people as a disorganized, violent mob, echoing the capitalist's contempt for the masses in his description of "those sinister, ephemeral organizations which on demand of the mayor had cropped out into existence – great companies of the unheralded, the dull, the undistinguished – clerks, working-men, small business men, and minor scions of religion or morality" (*T* 539). What the text relegates into its margins, then, is the fact that Chicago's democratic movement against the unscrupulous traction king was successful in its spontaneous rebellion because it managed to appropriate the speculator's own strategies. Its strategy of success consisted in "specularizing" the speculator, in presenting him in the negative image of the capitalist as boodler and thief. The movement also singled out the corrupt politicians, naming them in public, displaying their names and faces on posters and pamphlets; its members became powerful spectators at the council meetings, levelling their newly empowered gaze on the (corrupted) members of the legislative house.

22   Arun Mukherjee, *The Gospel of Wealth in the American Novel* (London: Croom Helm, 1987) 96–97.

23   Roberts 352.

When retelling the Yerkes/Cowperwood story in *The Titan*, the narrator, thus, "yields" to his protagonist's seduction and is co-opted by the dominant power principle, dressing the defeated Cowperwood and his forces in heroic terms: "His aldermen, powerful, hungry, fighting men all – like those picked soldiers of the ancient Roman emperors – ruthless, conscienceless, as desperate as himself, had in their last redoubt of personal privilege fallen, weakened, yielded" (*T* 548). While Cowperwood's bribed politicians are thus elevated to the level of imperial soldiers, Chicago's democratic movement is dismissed as a violent mob and the anti-Cowperwood politicians satirically degraded to "a petty band of guerrillas or free-booters who, like hungry swine shut in a pen, were ready to fall upon any and all propositions brought to their attention" (*T* 533).

Yet despite the narrator's ideological bias, the novel is deeply dialogical, as it turns around to expose the narrative bias from within, from its margins. *The Titan* represents a somewhat different – much more positive – side of the democratic movement by significantly reducing narrator interference towards the end of the novel. Dreiser incorporates, for example, a page-long pamphlet that asks citizens to "Arouse and Defeat the Boodlers" (*T* 540). In order to represent this polyphonic voice of democratic resistance, Dreiser relies on naturalism's generic heterogeneity, as the novel moves from its prose discourse to the conventions of a dramatic play in order to convey a sense of the public debate in the city council:

> *Alderman Winkler* (pro-Cowperwood). "If the chair pleases, I think something ought to be done to restore order in the gallery and keep these proceedings from being disturbed. It seems to me an outrage, that, on an occasion of this kind, when the interests of the people require the most careful attention – "
> *A Voice.* "The interests of the people!"
> *Another Voice.* "Sit down. You're bought!"
> *Alderman Winkler.* "If the chair pleases – " (*T* 544)

Although the narrator interferes to provide information in parenthesis, Dreiser reduces the narrator's input to a minimum, and thus the three-page dramatic debate brings to the fore the dialogic heterogeneity of a democratic group united by their common goal to fight against exploitative capitalism and corrupted politicians.

David Baguley has argued with Philippe Hamon that in the novel's "lieux stratégiques," such as the beginning and the ending, the naturalist text strategically undermines a sense of mimetic order. In naturalism, "the conclusion of the text certainly does not fulfill the same familiariz-

ing function" that we find in realist texts.[24] The typical naturalistic endings are frustrating, as Baguley illustrates by identifying naturalism's
predilection for the deprivation ending, the banal ending, and the sententious ending. *The Titan* fits into this pattern in that it does not resolve
the Babel of ideological voices presented in the last chapters. As a result,
it is virtually impossible to determine whether the novel is "for" or
"against" capitalism. This is not to say, however, that this issue is suspended: rather, it is rendered problematic, leaving the reader with questions rather than answers, with different dialogical positions rather than
with ideological solutions. The hero's fall is more ironic than tragic, in
that the titan-protagonist does not undergo a significant *anagnorisis* or
change, but is revealed to be caught in the naturalistic law of the "eternal equation – the pathos of the discovery that even giants are but pyg-
mies" (*T* 551). The equation inevitable, which determines that the
capitalist's spectacular rise is inevitably followed by a downfall, has often been attributed to Dreiser's reading of Herbert Spencer. But the "equation inevitable" can be re-read in Foucauldian terms. A power relation
automatically creates its own opposition, so that there is no power without resistance or some form of freedom.

Finally, in the trilogy, and particularly *The Titan*, Dreiser is confronted
with his naturalism's ideological self-contradictions. As the object of a
naturalist novel, Cowperwood becomes inevitably "fixed" under the
narrator's and the reader's gaze. Operating in a naturalist framework,
the narrator cannot help but turn the speculator into a specularized body,
whose eroticized power also turns him into the narrator's (homoerotic)
object of desire. Thus specularized, the ever-flexible, cunning, and promiscuous speculator becomes frozen in an imperial stature and predict-
ably falls like the stone stature in *Don Juan*. Caught in naturalism's
conventions, even the superman is brought low, since everything in naturalism tends towards degraded repetition, parodically undermining any
serious notion of heroism. What deserves further attention, though, is
the implication of the male narrator's attraction to, as well as his problematic complicity with, Cowperwood, which will be the focus of the
next chapter.

---

24 Baguley, "The Lure of the Naturalistic Text," 278.

10

Naturalism's Specula(riza)tion: *The "Genius"*

Just as the narrative voice in *The Titan* is openly complicitous with, and seemingly seduced by, the speculator's principle of sexualized power, *The "Genius"* (1915), published only one year after *The Titan*, echoes the earlier novel's deliberate collapsing of the boundary between the naturalist expression of "hard facts" and the speculator's "fictitious" business dealings. In his autobiographical *Künstlerroman*, Dreiser examines his role as a naturalist writer in a modern consumer economy, tracing his own professional career as an artist and his private odyssey as a womanizer while detailing his mental breakdown and his traumatic bodily failings in the thinly veiled persona of Eugene Witla. Perhaps it was this autobiographical closeness, the blurring of the boundary between naturalist narrator and narrated object that created the problems in composing this naturalist tale of the artist's crisis and recovery. Contemporary readers, led by H. L. Mencken, were quick to condemn the novel as Dreiser at his worst: "The thing rambles, staggers, trips, heaves, pitches, struggles, totters, wavers, halts, turns aside, trembles on the edge of collapse."[1] But in its very shiftiness, its many repetitions, contradictions, and slippages, The *"Genius"* also presents a kind of Lacanian discourse of the Other, a language of the subconscious that gives insights into the repressed and silenced aspects of Dreiser's naturalism.

In his persona of Eugene Witla, Dreiser conceptualizes the modern artist as a clever money-maker whose wish-fulfillment dream is best encapsulated in his desire to imitate the success of the great American businessmen: "Here were Jay Gould and Russell Sage and the Vanderbilts and Morgan," Witla reflects when he arrives in New York and asks yearningly, "Would the city ever acclaim him as it did some?"[2] When Witla finally "makes it" as an artist, he finds his customers amongst businesses and corporations: he is commissioned to decorate a great bank, as well as public buildings in Washington. Dreiser conceptualizes this issue in similar terms in the sketch of "Ellen Adams Wrynn," in *A Gallery of Women* (1929), where a woman painter marks her first success as an artist by having her daringly exotic Parisian scenes exhibited permanently on four huge panels on one of the large department stores of Philadelphia. Here, art is assigned the function of advertisement, and the boundary between the consumption of art and that of other commodities becomes erased. At the same time the panels are an advertisement for the artist herself: "And each panel signed: Ellen Adams Wrynn,"[3] thus turning the artist's name into a representation of a capitalist success story, a signifier of an artist who has "made it."

While Walter Benn Michaels has argued that for Dreiser's financier, art is as speculative as the stock market, Rachel Bowlby has discussed the artist in The *"Genius"* as a capitalist "adman" and "businessman" who offers no resistance to capitalism whatsoever.[4] Indeed, as early as 1896, in a newspaper article on "Genius and Matrimony," Dreiser presented a psychological profile of the artist that anticipated Cowperwood's narcissistic principle of power: "But the artist, poor and proud, along with his endowment of creative power, is furnished with an aggressive egotism,"[5] a principle suggestive of the speculator's "I satisfy myself."

---

1 Mencken 87.

2 Theodore Dreiser, The *"Genius"* (New York: John Lane, 1915) 101. All further references will appear in the text, abbreviated *G*.

3 *A Gallery of Women*, Vol. 1 (New York: Horace Liveright, 1929) 145.

4 See Michaels, "Dreiser's Financier," 294; Bowlby 118–33.

5 Theodore Dreiser, "Genius and Matrimony," *Ev'ry Month* 2 (1896): 5–6, rpt. in *Theodore Dreiser: A Selection of Uncollected Prose*, ed. Donald Pizer (Detroit: Wayne State UP, 1977) 54.

Dreiser's naturalist aesthetics and ideology thus go counter to the grain of the American literary tradition. Many nineteenth-century American artists insisted on the arts as a realm of *Gedankenfreiheit*, as a space of imaginative freedom, inevitably outside and deliberately on the margins of American societal conventions and constraints.[6] Dreiser, in contrast, moves the arts into the economic centre, and with this shift the arts become a field on which are played out the tensions and struggles but also the seductive games of American capitalism. Indeed, the specific analogies Dreiser establishes between the naturalistic artist and the capitalist speculator are not only deliberate, but expose the ideological contradictions at the heart of his naturalism.

Naturalist fiction from the nineteenth century on articulated a commitment to social criticism in either overt or covert narrative forms. Yet the naturalist genre simultaneously perpetuates narrative positions of authority and power that echo in its very midst the (capitalist) tendency towards monopolization and centralization that it often criticizes in its thematics and structure. Although naturalist fiction frequently promotes social change, as often it confirms the ideological assumptions that help perpetuate a social and economic status quo. The working people in naturalism often emerge as a proletarianized, animalized Other, as the brute, the beast that can only be contained in acts of narrative exorcism, as June Howard has argued. These contradictions at the heart of naturalism are best illustrated by Dreiser's (seemingly incongruous but always deliberate) analogies between the naturalist artist and the capitalist speculator. A comparison of the Cowperwood trilogy and *The "Genius"* reveals that many of Cowperwood's strategies of gaining and maintaining power correspond to the epistemological, aesthetic, and ideological principles on which Dreiser's naturalism thrives.

To begin, in *The Titan* and *The "Genius"* the narrator's editorial voice shares the speculator's curiosity in and access to a world of privileged and complex knowledges; both the naturalist artist and the speculator are endowed with the ability to see ahead, to read what others are not able to decipher, and to accumulate bodies of knowledge. Philippe Hamon's theory emphasizes that naturalism's "stringing together descriptions like so many sections in the 'store of human documents'" generates "places to show off knowledge (of words and the world) and know-how (stylistic and rhetorical), and which are all carried out euphorically in enthusiastic lexical expansions."[7] The male narrator in *The Titan* typifies this point,

---

6   See Poirier 5.

7   Hamon 37, 38.

"showing off" his expertise by entering the complicated world of capital-ist manipulation, mental games, and speculative manoeuvrings. Sidney Roberts has noted that Yerkes's "bookkeeping methods and business tac-tics were so complicated that a clear account of how he captured control of Chicago's street railways can scarcely be made."[8] But by venturing into the complicated network of transactions and revealing to the reader Cowperwood's ingenious strategies of manipulation and financing, the narrator-author also draws attention to his own "superior" insight into such complicated procedures, presenting himself as the speculator's double and rival, by gathering and accumulating hidden and techni-cally sophisticated knowledges. Conversely, the narrator's ability to col-lect information about the speculator also makes him a potential oppositional force, since it allows him to "specularize" and to define Cowperwood. It is the narrator who exposes the speculator as a target for attack by making his imaginary "body" of power visible for the reader.

But as a "producer" of bodies of knowledge and naturalist plots, the authorial voice also reveals a slippery complicity with Cowperwood's role. Analyzing the first volume of the trilogy, Walter Benn Michaels has emphasized Cowperwood's fascination with "mental" facts, such as money, stocks, and bonds, and his obvious dislike for tangibles: "The financier's dislike of stability thus emerges even more explicitly as a distaste for [tan-gible] commodities."[9] Michaels, though, conveniently limits his argument to *The Financier*, where the speculator's love of "mental" manipulations leads to his incarceration on a conviction of technical embezzlement. In *The Titan*, in contrast, Cowperwood is not only "sick of the stock-exchange" but, from a lover of "abstract" tradings, he turns into a "builder" of tangibles and thus becomes a producer-figure who never abandons his manipulative strategies. Thus the binary opposition between the speculator's "fictitious dealings" and the producer's out-put of tangible commodities becomes blurred. Cowperwood's modern-ization of Chicago's street railway project entails the construction of (hundreds of miles of) extension lines, equipment of the horse-drawn streetcars with cable (and later with electricity), implementation of bet-ter cars, and improvement of the overall service for the customers. It is these contributions to the growth of the city and its very tangible infra-structure that make Cowperwood a productive figure in the eyes of the Chicagoan public.

---

8 Roberts 348.

9 Michaels, "Dreiser's *Financier*," 280.

Dreiser presents the same blurring of boundaries between artistic production and clever salesmanship in *The "Genius."* Not only in the title
but also in his middle and first names – often abbreviated to "Gene" or
even "Geni" – Dreiser presents Eugene Tennyson Witla as a producer-
artist (> Latin *gigno, genui, genitum* = to beget, to bring forth, to produce), so that on the surface the novel appears to echo Émile Zola's
conception of the naturalist artist as a producer-figure:

> Aujourd'hui, il nous faut produire et produire encore. C'est le labeur
> d'un ouvrier qui doit gagner son pain, qui ne peut se retirer qu'après
> fortune faite. En outre, si l'écrivain s'arrête, le public l'oublie; il est forcé
> d'entasser volume sur volume, tout comme un ébéniste par exemple
> entasse meuble sur meuble.[10]

Zola, then, identifies the naturalist writer as a producer-*labourer*, a skilled
craftsman, while Dreiser, in contrast, signals his reservations about such
an identification. As Amy Kaplan has pointed out, Dreiser "made an
effort to distinguish writing from labor," thus turning his back not only
on Zola but also on the American tradition represented by Edith Wharton
and William Dean Howells, who valued writing as productive work.
The idea of "making a splash, of promoting one's art" was more important for Dreiser than hard work, and "he also inverts a traditional causal
relation to show that labor itself did not generate recognition."[11] What is
needed for the artist to become a popular success in a competitive
twentieth-century market economy is not only productive genius but
also the speculative genius of salesmanship.

   Given this deliberate analogy between the artist and the speculator, it
should come as no surprise that naturalist creation (or production) is characterized by the same moral ambiguity that Cowperwood displays as a
"builder" of Chicago's traction system in *The Titan*. Contributing to the
construction of Chicago's infrastructure, Cowperwood's activities are interwoven with the speculator's mental manipulations. A whiz kid at making use of commodities already produced by others, Cowperwood
manages, for example, to lease for a nominal sum tunnels built years ago,
thus completing his street railway traction project without much effort.
Although this move is an ingeniously productive "recycling" of a commodity no longer used, which would otherwise go to waste, Cowperwood's
strategy is criticized by his Chicagoan opposition. If this criticism partly

---

10 Émile Zola, *Le Roman expérimental* (1880; Paris: Garnier Flammarion, 1971), 203.

11 Amy Kaplan, *The Social Construction of American Realism* (1988; Chicago: U of Chicago
    P, 1992) 116, 128.

reflects that the opposition has been outsmarted, it also highlights that Cowperwood's use of the tunnel exposes the speculator's parasitic quality, based as it is on the clever exploitation of somebody else's "labour."

It is the same principle of "productive recycling" that characterizes Dreiser's creative strategies as a naturalist writer. In his study on European naturalist fiction, David Baguley confirms that the typical strategy of naturalist plot composition consists in recycling *faits divers*, newspaper items, or extraliterary sources, so that the boundary between imaginative creation and parasitic appropriation, between fiction and document, becomes blurred: "The journalistic *chronique, conte, vignette*, the *risqué* tale, accounts of domestic crimes, of incest and adultery, descriptions of oddities of human behaviour from the macabre to the titillating, formed a huge subliterary generic stock of anecdotes on which naturalist fiction could draw and from which it is at times barely distinguishable" (*NF* 89). Heavily indebted to his collection, appropriation, and imaginative transformation of facts and documents, of newspaper articles, letters, personal stories, interviews, and autobiographies, Dreiser's fiction has even been described by Simon During in terms of "discursive cannibalization." During writes that "whole segments of his private correspondence were absorbed into *The Genius*, for instance, almost without alteration. He plundered other 'creative' writers too, being repeatedly accused of plagiarism."[12] While in *The Titan*, the boundary between the traditionally "honest" producer and the morally tainted speculator becomes blurred, Dreiser's own "production" of naturalist fiction is fed by the speculator's principle of "parasitic" appropriation, accumulation, and imaginative transformation. Just as Cowperwood assimilates and reorganizes different street railway companies to absorb Chicago's traction system into a larger corporate company, so for Dreiser writing partly was, as During has put it somewhat polemically, "a form of cutting and pasting."

All of these analogies, intersections, and deliberate connections converge to expose the problematic ideological underpinnings that help maintain the seductive power of both the artist and the capitalist speculator, a point highlighted in *The "Genius,"* in the artist's relationship with marginalized groups and women. Just as Cowperwood does not fight against but appropriates the interests of the people to create his own success at the beginning of *The Titan*, so the naturalist painter Eugene Witla turns to the working people as the subject matter of his art. "Creativity is

---

12 During 225.

not open to the lower classes; and yet it is working-class life – cities, factories, street scenes – which the modern artist takes as his subject matter," Rachel Bowlby observes in her discussion of *The "Genius"* and continues: "The artist's prospecting seems in one way to resemble the customary exploitation of 'millions of people' for the individualist end of capitalism."[13] Indeed, Witla shocks the bourgeois public in his first important exhibition with his painting of a black garbage collector, a painting that is selected by the narrator as an example of Witla's social *engagement*. Yet Witla's interest in the marginalized figures of America's urban slums simultaneously echoes Cowperwood's dubious alliance with the democratic movement in the beginning of *The Titan*. In both cases, the lower classes are only tools that help create the speculator-artist's own success.

The "Genius" reveals how the authorial voice's overt commitment to social criticism is contradicted by its covert advocacy of a social status quo. The narrator's description of Witla's picture of the garbage collector exposes how easily the signifiers of social criticism can be used to serve the opposite purpose. According to the narrator's description, this picture represents

> a great hulking, ungainly negro, a positively animal man, his ears thick and projecting, his lips fat, his nose flat, his cheek bones prominent, his whole body expressing brute strength and animal indifference to dirt and cold. ... He was looking purblindly down the shabby street, its hard crisp snow littered with tin cans, paper, bits of slop and offal. Dust – gray ash dust, was flying from the upturned can. (*G* 236)

Witla's painting is presented to the reader in a doubly mediated form: the visual signifier is translated into verbal ones, and the reader can only look at the picture by reading it through the narrator's eyes. And what we read is not so much naturalist social criticism but the representation of a social stereotype: we are confronted with the same picture of social "Otherness" that Cowperwood imposed on Chicago's workers in *The Titan*. In the narrator's description, the black man is an animalistic creature, a brute, the incarnation of the Other, whose place is (and probably will be) in the decaying garbage of white America. If Witla's painting really articulates social criticism, the painting as signifier is given a different twist in the narrator's discourse. If there is an indictment of social conditions, it is relegated to the gaps of the text.

---

13 Rachel Bowlby, *Just Looking: Consumer Culture in Dreiser, Gissing and Zola* (New York & London: Methuen, 1985) 124.

Equally problematic are the narrator's comments that frame the description of the painting. To describe the creative production process, he deploys the very metaphors of power that are used in *The Titan* to characterize the speculator's exploitation of the Chicagoan people. The narrative voice, for instance, celebrates Eugene's critique of contemporary power relations by linguistically reinscribing the master-slave dialectics on Eugene's own artistic production process: "Eugene was so cruel in his indictment of life. He seemed to lay on his details with bitter lack of consideration. Like a slavedriver lashing a slave he spared no least shade of his cutting brush" (*G* 236). The contextual framework signals a parodic twist: it is Eugene himself who is a labourer-slave, driven by his work. At the same time, however, Eugene's creative production reinscribes a master-slave relationship with the painter in a position of mastery and control, while the marginalized subject of his painting becomes objectified and appropriated into the capitalist machinery. It is significant that later in the novel when Eugene becomes marginalized himself (he falls sick and loses his fortune), he is no longer capable of painting. Witla's creation suggests very little solidarity with the marginalized subject; rather, on the canvas, Witla ritually exorcizes and externalizes the sense of Otherness that haunts the artist.

While Witla's art expresses sadness about the victims inevitably produced by capitalism, underneath its motifs of the margins his painting also affirms progress, movement, change, and growth, in short, the very ingredients of capitalism: "The paradox of a decaying drunkard placed against the vivid persistence of life gripped his fancy. Somehow it suggested to himself hanging on, fighting on, accusing nature" (*G* 729). The picture of the drunkard, significantly, accuses an abstract "nature," not a unjust social system. As the "priest" of the new aesthetics of ugliness, Witla celebrates the city in his paintings as an oxymoron, as beauty in ugliness. Maybe shocking at first sight, the naturalist art of Witla's pictures is by no means in radical opposition to, or subversive of, capitalism, but can be easily appropriated by the capitalist machinery, as *The "Genius"* demonstrates. Just as Cowperwood is obsessed with purchasing art in *The Financier* and *The Titan*, so Witla's rich customers use the new art as decorations, transforming them into signifiers of what they themselves stand for and what they would like to promote. This is reflected in the deliberate incongruity of the painting portraying a drunkard fetching a record price of eighteen thousand dollars (*G* 729). One of the first paintings Witla sells, for the wholesome sum of $500, depicts three engines and a railroad yard and sells to the vice-president of one of the great railroads entering New York.

Even more importantly, it is a sense of homoeroticized male solidarity that bonds the speculator and the artist. Cowperwood is associated
with the principle of fetishized accumulation, and so is Dreiser's (as
well as traditional French) naturalism. Just as Cowperwood is obsessed
with the pleasure of searching for, acquiring, and incorporating into a
collection precious *objets d'art*, so Dreiser's naturalism textually mimics
capitalism's collectomania and fetishistic obsession with material objects and facts by indulging in long narrative catalogues, repetitions,
and accumulation of similar scenes and stock characters (the doubling
and tripling of seduction and desertion scenes, of mistresses and wives).
Where Cowperwood collects works of art and women in an effort at an
adequate aesthetic representation of his variable body of power, the naturalist author textually participates in this sexualized collectomania by
indulging in descriptive accumulations and verbal hyperbole, in what
Emily Apter has called rhetorical fetishism. Similarly, William Berg has
noted that, although one might expect a reduction of rhetorical figures
in naturalism ("since these devices appear to be ultraliterary, blatantly
artificial, highly ornamental"), naturalist fiction in fact shows a profu-
sion of tropes such as metaphor, metonymy, and synecdoche, which are
privileged because they lend themselves to *visual* representation: "Zola's
figuration displays decidedly visual contents, mechanisms, and relationships, thus leading naturally to an exploration of the workings of the
visual imagination."[14]

The visual imagination is inevitably bound to the sexual world, and
it is in their sexual politics – in the long "galleries of women" – that
Dreiser's artist and his speculator insist on defending a biologically
"natural" and the psychologically "normal" expression of male sexuality. Dreiser's fiction conceptualizes male power in terms of sexual promiscuity; womanizing is a characteristic common to both the naturalist
artist and the speculator. Like Cowperwood's speculative genius, Eugene
Witla's productive gift is linked to a whole "gallery of women" (from
Margaret Dunn and Ruby Kenny to Angela Blue, Christina Channing,
Frieda Roth, Carlotta Wilson, and Suzanne Dale). Womanizing not only
creates a sense of male complicity, it creates a network of male power
that is integral to the world of Dreiser's naturalism and that is supported
by its aesthetic form and narrative manipulations. Naturalism's complicity with the male character's womanizing is reflected in its own
fetishized obsession with classifying, systematizing, and hierarchizing

---

14   William Berg, *The Visual Novel: Emile Zola and the Art of His Times* (State College, PA:
Pennsylvania State UP, 1992) 212–13.

specularized females. Supported by the narrative desire for taxonomical order, Cowperwood, for instance, professes to have a very clear notion of the hierarchy of art (and women). His hierarchy implicitly suggests the protagonist's teleological "growth" or "progress," as he moves through the different levels of the hierarchy. This, in turn, legitimizes his right to abandon one lover after the next, or to replace one painting with a better one, in order to move closer to an artistic "ideal." Donald Pizer as well as Lawrence Hussman have taken Cowperwood's "hierarchy" at face value, Pizer arguing that the women in *The Titan* are art objects in "an ascending order," and Hussman even recognizing underlying "religious dimensions" in Cowperwood's "mystical search" for the feminine ideal.[15]

Hussman's "transcendental" interpretation, however, seems in contradiction to Pizer's more convincing point on the "picaresque" quality of the novel, a quality that is reflected in the long line of often interchangeable mistresses, whose names are accumulated and catalogued in the narrative without ever attaching themselves as separate personalities in the mind of the reader, so that the novel also parodically undercuts the notion of Cowperwood's and Eugene's sexual, spiritual, or artistic "growth." In fact, the classification and cataloguing of different types of women in the course of Cowperwood's life corresponds to naturalism's predilection for the bordello's "pile-up" effect, as Emily Apter has identified it in the nineteenth-century French realist novel: "The fact that the juxtaposition of disparate nationalities, sensual temperaments, and body types characterizes artistic collection and bordello interior alike," writes Apter, "only reinforces the epistemological connection between the two species of cabinet."[16]

Focusing on Cowperwood's womanizing, *The Titan* reveals similar contradictions that unravel the genre's male bias from within. The narrator, for instance, states that Cowperwood's promiscuity implies disruption and excess:

> As has been said, this promiscuous attitude on Cowperwood's part was the natural flowering out of a temperament that was chronically promiscuous, intellectually uncertain, and philosophically anarchic. (*T* 201)

The narrator's (manipulative) comment thus makes an implicit connection between Cowperwood's womanizing and naturalism's "entropic

---

15 Pizer, *Novels*, 173; Hussman, *Theodore Dreiser*, 85–86.

16 Apter 53.

vision." But while Dreiser's authorial voice conceptualizes male sexual promiscuity in terms of anarchy and disruption, the text itself frequently demonstrates the opposite: other (more conservative) businessmen also take their "human pleasure secretly" (*T* 8). Indeed, as Lois Banner's social history reveals, male promiscuity amongst America's business elite was not antibourgeois, but rather the bourgeois norm: "In their memoirs," Banner writes, "members of New York high society protect their privacy, but their indignation makes them unanimous on one issue: the men of their class were not faithful to their wives." Banner illustrates her point with the example of Caroline Astor, whose "husband spent much of his time on his yacht entertaining chorus girls." Similarly, "Alva Vanderbilt, to shame her husband, divorced him in New York on the grounds of adultery so that his infidelity would be publicly known."[17] Considering this social backdrop of "normalized" promiscuity and infidelity, the narrator's comments have to be seen as a clever manipulation of naturalism's gender ideology. While readers have made much of Cowperwood's refusal to be hypocritical, the fact is that, like the other married capitalists, he lies to and cheats on his wife Aileen in order to enjoy both the advantages of marriage and the thrill of extramarital adventures.

Conspiring to "normalize" male womanizing within the aesthetic and ideological boundaries of naturalism, the male narrators and their womanizing characters engage in some "fictitious dealings" of their own to convince the reader of the "naturality" of such male sexual politics. Although this male ethos is supported by the naturalist conventions, it also creates uneasy contradictions, as *The "Genius"* demonstrates in its exploration of Witla's relationship with his wife. Feeling entrapped in his marriage, Eugene Witla is obsessed with what he claims to be physical overindulgence in his sexual relations with his wife Angela, a notion the narrative voice supports:

> He had no knowledge of the effect of one's sexual life upon one's work, nor what such a life when badly arranged can do to a perfect art – how it can distort the sense of color, weaken that balanced judgment of character which is so essential to a normal interpretation of life. (*G* 246)

The word "normal" strikes a particularly false note in this quotation, especially since earlier in the novel, Eugene's art – like Cowperwood's business strategies – is celebrated for its disruption of "normal" perspectives and its emphasis on a deliberate foregrounding of disruptive

---

17 Banner 191.

Otherness. Similarly odd and contradictory is the narrator's claim that Eugene lacks "knowledge" of the pernicious effect of sexuality, since it is Eugene himself who worries about the negative influence of his sex life on his art (just as Cowperwood attributes his own social failure in Chicago to Aileen's daring sexuality).[18] This scene exposes how much the promiscuous Eugene and the male narrator are in secret communion with each other to manipulate and convince the reader of the pernicious influence of a monogamous sexuality in which the woman insists on her pleasure.

Finally, womanizing was the driving force not only for Cowperwood and Witla but for Theodore Dreiser as well, as the sexual confessions of his diaries indicate. Condoned, legitimized, and even celebrated by the male narrative voice, this principle of fetishized accumulation of women as sexual and epistemological objects is both a logical expression of naturalism's male power politics and a space that exposes its gender bias, deconstructing its claims to "objectivity" and "naturality." The pleasure of womanizing and of masculinizing the genre inevitably unravels naturalism's in-built structures of male solidarity and male power. Dreiser's naturalism is a "male club," in which a woman's appearance places her almost automatically into the bordello's *l'hétéroclite*. Yet, oscillating between anarchy and convention, between chaotic excess and obsessional taxonomical order, the naturalist speculator and the "specularizing" naturalist cannot help but expose the eroticization of male power in their naturalist club. In its politics of male promiscuity, then, Dreiser's naturalism inevitably deconstructs itself, showing that the (homo)eroticized male complicity relies on its subjugation (and, perhaps, its continued fear) of the female body.

---

18 Some readers have been quick to note these contradictions. See, for example, Philip Gerber's reaction to this passage in *Theodore Dreiser*: "To ask a reader to accept this nonsense, in the face of Cowperwood, to whom sex was an essential spur to full living, is asking a good deal indeed. But it is asking much more to swallow it in the face of Dreiser's own life which, if we are to believe the legends he himself inspired, directly refutes everything he says about Eugene" (119).

V. Grove's Sexualizing of Patriarchal Power

11

Sovereign Power, Bio-Power and the "Inevitable Form" in *The Master of the Mill*

Although Grove establishes a Dreiserian connection between art and economic relations, he moves in a different direction by focusing on what one might term an economy of hyperproductivity. The publication of his late business novel *The Master of the Mill* (1944) thus has to be seen in the context of the *Künstlerroman* that followed, *In Search of Myself* (1946). Opposing Dreiser's ethos of male sexual promiscuity, Grove associates both the artist and the businessman with the traditional producer figure – the family patriarch. Grove's ideal of aesthetic production, as he expressed it in *In Search of Myself*, is encapsulated in the artist-persona as a patriarchal father figure who gives birth to his fictional sons. The author's relationship with his "sons," in turn, is conceptualized in terms of struggle and rivalry, energized and determined by psychoanalytic structures, in particular by the Oedipal conflict. Thus, the aging narrator-author in the fictionalized autobiography has a vision of himself as a godlike paternal creator, a patriarch who rules as an omnipotent and omniscient father-sovereign over his fictional characters, who looks down "as though, from the summit of a mountain" on the "empire" of his creation, a master over life and death.[1] While Cowperwood slowly freezes to a static figure of sovereign power in *The Titan*, Grove's autobiographical *Künstler*-persona is always already caught in the image of a larger-than-life figure of power.

With the artist's persona thus echoing the Virgilian imperial view from above, Grove's conceptualization of authorial power is suggestive of what Foucault has described as the Roman model of patriarchal power:

> For a long time, one of the characteristic privileges of sovereign power was the right to decide life and death. In a formal sense, it derived no doubt from the ancient *patria potestas* that granted the father of the Roman family the right to "dispose" of the life of his children and his slaves; just as he had given them life, so he could take it away. (*HS* 135)

Similarly, in *In Search of Myself*, the artist sees his fictional characters as his fictional sons, who are doubles of himself and who come into being because he is willing to "distil my blood and infuse it into two creatures who had no right to exist on this earth except what right I had myself bestowed upon them" (*ISM* 373). Small wonder that in twentieth-century Canada this dream of absolute omnipotence over his creation is complemented by a negative flipside – the artist's vision of himself as an absolute failure who is drained of his life forces and then cast aside by his fictional characters, who claim their independence from their creator-father: "The trouble was that, after all, I *had* given them birth in my mind and, therefore, power to dispose of my substance" (*ISM* 373). The negative flipside of the omnipotent artist is the impotent artist as a complete failure, who is sacrificed by his fictional sons.

Foucault has argued that, starting from the end of the nineteenth century, "we can trace the theoretical effort to reinscribe the thematic of sexuality in the system of law, the symbolic order, and sovereignty," a phenomenon that Foucault links to the advent of psychoanalysis. After all, Freud's endeavour was "to ground sexuality in the law – the law of alliance, tabooed consanguinity, and the Sovereign-Father, in short, to surround desire with all the trappings of the old order of power" (*HS* 150). With the discovery of the Oedipal triangle, Freud reinserted sexuality firmly into the family, connecting it with the "law" in his emphasis on the incest taboo. But according to Foucault, this "new" psychoanalytic conception of "the category of the sexual in terms of the law, death, blood, and sovereignty" is "in the last analysis a historical

---

1 *In Search of Myself* (Toronto: Macmillan, 1946) 262. Further references will appear in the text, abbreviated *ISM*.

'retroversion'"'; in other words, it is part of the reason that in its representation of modern power, Western society has not yet "cut off the head of the king."

It may come as no surprise that this "historical retroversion" is a characteristic feature of Grove's novels of the soil, yet we also find it at the heart of his futuristic big business novel, *The Master of the Mill*. Sam Clark, the main narrator, obsessively turns backwards to examine his and his family's involvement in the mill's construction, his thoughts continually circling around his father and his son. Reflecting the author's preoccupation with the role of the patriarchal family in twentieth-century Canada, this "retroversion" has several functions: first, the father as a bourgeois monopolist is a figure echoing the productive, rather than the repressive, aspects of modern power; second, the patriarchal figurehead of power reflects Grove's grappling with an adequate representation of the contemporary Canadian centralization of finance and industry; and third, the novel's simultaneous focus on the patriarch's loss of power signals Grove's continued preoccupation with the crisis of masculinity, which leads to a defensive inscription of traditional models of masculinity into his fiction. Indeed, Grove's representation of modern power in terms of a monarchical-patriarchal power creates fascinating contradictions between the centralized power of the family patriarch, on the one hand, and his modern (Foucauldian) conception of mobile power that is dispersed in all levels of the social hierarchy, on the other. The author can only "resolve" these contradictions by giving his realism-naturalism, eventually, a twist into naturalist dystopia.

Focusing on the construction and automation of the monumental Clark mill, *The Master of the Mill* explores Canada's transitional age, namely, the period between the 1880s and the 1920s that witnessed the economic and cultural consolidation of Canada as a nation. In this period, Canada's economy shifted from a postcolonial, agricultural state towards industry and finance. Looking back on the mill's history, the protagonist Sam Clark traces the development of the Clark flour empire in Langholm, Manitoba, as it grows from Rudyard Clark's small family business in 1888 into Edmund's huge, fully automated corporate machinery with international connections in 1923.[2] Ousted from his posi-

---

2   Since the novel's chronology is not linear, here are some of the crucial dates. In 1875, the railway net connects with Langholm, giving birth to the original mill. In April 1888, the old mill conveniently burns down, prompting the building of the new mill, which harvests the benefits of the 1888–89 economic boom. When Rudyard dies in 1898, Sam follows his father's plans and completes the first phase of the mill's automation in 1901, causing a massive workers' strike.

tion of power by his son, Edmund, after the First World War, Sam resumes control of the mill in 1923, after his son's death, and "narrates" the mill's history shortly before his own death in 1938. In light of this historical chronology, it has been argued that Grove's novel offers "an allegory of the development of Canada as a nation," with Rudyard Clark representing a pioneer type of capitalism, Samuel a "more liberal generation," and Edmund a "new breed of corporate executive obsessed with an abstract concept of power."[3] While this teleological perspective highlights the differences between the three "masters of the mill," the fact remains that the three men, who profess to be radically different from each other, are driven by the same goal to expand the mill and increase "the demands of production," using similar strategies of power to achieve their common telos.

Conceptualizing his Canadian big business novel as a "historical retroversion" while inscribing an Oedipal psychodrama, Grove in his exploration of power heads in two opposed directions: he is obsessed with what Foucault has described as "cutting off the head of the king" while simultaneously refusing to dispense with the concept of patriarchal-monarchical power. Indeed, Grove tenaciously holds on to that concept. For instance, in the succession of the three male Clarks, it is always the sons who set out to take over the father's power, an idea that reinforces the patriarchal-monarchical notion of power, in which the son can only assume power after the old king is dead or removed from his position. This pattern of *Le roi est mort, vive le roi* is further emphasized in the novel's two-part structure and those parts' titles: "Part One: Death of the Master"; "Part Two: Resurrection of the Master." In a gesture of Oedipal rivalry, Sam opposes his father's ruthlessness in dealing with the workers. He even sees himself as a socialist who is mentally much more attuned to the workers' problems than his father ever was, and he dreams of workers' participation, of raising their wages, of profit for all. Yet once Sam takes over control of the mill, no changes are implemented; Rudyard's legacy is handed over like the sovereign's crown to the son. Enchained in a generational *Wiederholungszwang*, Sam's psychological submission is further reinforced through the mechanistic constraints imposed by the mill. While Edmund and Rudyard pay homage to the mill – indeed, they die for the mill – Sam frequently struggles against the mill's unscrupulous demands, only to yield, in turn, to its law like his father before and his son after him.

---

3 Spettigue, *Grove*, 124; Keith, "F.P. Grove's Difficult Novel: *The Master of the Mill*," *Ariel* 4 (1973): 37.

While Sam dismisses his father, Rudyard, as a tyrant-father who manipulates the son even from beyond the grave, Edmund recognizes in Rudyard the mill's mythological and eroticized origin of power. For Edmund, Rudyard is the opposite of his physical – real – father, Sam, whom Edmund despises and rejects as weak and impotent and whom he easily ousts from his position of power after the First World War. Mythologized as the creator of the powerful mill, Rudyard becomes conflated with the mill itself in the eyes of his grandson, who thus resurrects the grandfather in his life as an icon of power and the ultimate love object. For example, while Edmund is presented as a sexually sterile character, his attachment to the mill and the grandfather has (homo)erotic undertones, suggestive of Cowperwood's relationship with Chicago's workers. In an earlier version of the novel, this connection is made in more explicit imagery. Edmund sees the mill as "populated by giants naked to the waist and toiling with superhuman expenditure of energy. Their toil consisted in a fight with machines, forcing them to a pace hardly to be endured. These giants were his father's slaves; but in some incomprehensible fashion they were held in subjection by his grandfather who was dead."[4] The homoerotic signals are accompanied by equally sadistic ones: the workers' (physical) bodies are both gigantic and enchained, impotent, enslaved, emasculated, subdued by the machine. Behind this sadistic image of bondage, Edmund recognizes the traces of his dead grandfather, who emerges for the grandson as a fantasy figure of omnipotent power.

Given *The Master of the Mill*'s emphasis on patriarchal power, the question arises to what extent it really departs from Grove's earlier novels of the soil. The thematic focus and structural devices in Grove's pioneer novels often rely on opposing the leisure- and money-loving, manipulating speculator-capitalist with the honest, hard-working producer-farmer. (*The Yoke of Life* [1930], for example, explores this opposition in a tragic mode, while *Two Generations* [1939] translates it into comedy.) In *The Master of the Mill* (1944), however, Grove shifts his focus radically from the agrarian producer ideal to its apparent opposite – the speculator figure. This may be an indicator that, for Grove, the binary opposition between speculator and producer is not as clear-cut as it appears on the surface of his agricultural novels. Grove, in fact, dealt with manipulative salesmanship as early as 1927 in *A Search for America*, and he presented a

---

4 Quoted in Robin Mathews, "F. P. Grove: An Important Version of *The Master of the Mill* Discovered," *Studies in Canadian Literature* 7 (1982): 249.

true speculator in the Americanized businessman Jim Alvin, Jane's husband in the unpublished "Jane Atkinson," but in both novels manipulative speculation is not only morally condemned but leads to unhappiness if not disaster in the speculator's life. In *The Master of the Mill*, in contrast, crooked ways go unpunished: speculative trickery and manipulation lead to lasting economic success. Thus the moral rigidity of the earlier novels seems to be replaced by moral relativism, although even here the protagonist Sam Clark engages in a typically Grovian soul-searching of why and how he "has failed."

In contrast to the Machiavellian philosophies of his father and his son, Sam shares the moralistic vision of Phil Branden in *A Search for America*. But like Branden, Sam "yields" to what his moral vision condemns, succumbing to the demands of the mill, whose power principle he cannot resist. Looking at the mill in the beginning of the novel, Sam sees it standing "behind a veil" (*M* 7). Veiled and fetishized like the Lacanian phallus, the mill emerges as an abstract signifier of power, with which Sam is involved in a love-hate relationship that, in turn, echoes the relationship with his tyrannical father. In psychological terms a fetish is a cover for a knowledge that cannot be faced easily and that Sam can lay open only in the face of death. Sam "unveils" the mystery of the mill in his confession, determined to set "his house in order" by piecing together the mill's history and his family's involvement in it. And just as Lacan asserts that "the demon of *Aidos* (*Scham*, shame) arises at the very moment when, in the ancient mysteries, the phallus is unveiled" (*E* 288), so Sam is filled with a sense of shame and humbleness when he obsessively highlights the moral tainting of those who "yield" to the phallic mill in reluctant submission.

Yet despite Grove's concern with the protagonist's moral complicity, the novel also makes a Dreiserian point. In making the Clarks "return" so obsessively to the mill's shady origins, Grove emphasizes the idea that the monumental mill originates not so much in hard labour as in the manipulator's ingenuity in turning a paper fiction into a material reality, a very "real" corporate machinery, which in turn produces vital commodities without end. Through Sam we learn, for example, that the gigantic mill has its origins in "fictitious dealings," an ingenious paper fiction, very similar to Cowperwood's "technically illegal" money transaction that has him convicted and incarcerated for "technical embezzlement" in his early Philadelphia years in *The Financier*. Just as Cowperwood made profits for his own pocket by speculating with city money before the stockmarket crisis in 1871, so Grove's master financier Rudyard Clark managed to build his new mill in Manitoba in 1888 by using money cleverly drawn from a fraudulent insurance scheme.

With one single stroke in his bookkeeping Rudyard declared a massive amount of his wheat "destroyed" by a fire which he himself had set, only to resell this same wheat at a huge profit after collecting the insurance premium. Like Cowperwood's city money, Rudyard's insurance money may be seen as a "loan" because years later Sam pays back the sum plus the interest on it, ironically to discover that his father had already reimbursed the insurance company with an anonymous money payment right after he had made his fortune. This dark origin and the desire to cover it up binds three generations of male Clarks together in an incestuous bond that is invested with secrecy and mystery. The revelation of the mill's dark origin is like the confession of a sexual secret that has been hidden and repressed over decades. The ethical ambiguity surrounding the mill's origin becomes erotically charged, as it becomes an object of obsessive veiling and of simultaneous voyeuristic curiosity.

Examining both the published and the unpublished manuscript of *The Master of the Mill*, Robin Mathews has observed that the sexuality of the Clark family "is related to some idea, not completely clear, that Grove has about technology, power and the psychological effects of power relations."[5] Indeed, the mill not only produces psychological effects, but Grove uses psychological structures and subtexts to explore modern relationships of power. He examines the monopolization in the contemporary Canadian economy by locating it within a single – patriarchal – family, tracing the contributions of three generations to the building of a monumental mill. Lacan has observed that the phallus, "by virtue of its turgidity," is "the image of the vital flow as it is transmitted in generation" (*E* 287); the mill-phallus takes hold of the three Clarks, so that together they become a composite Cowperwood-superman figure. While Dreiser locates the modern deployment of sexuality and power deliberately outside the close-knit family unit by invoking Cowperwood's spiral of wild promiscuity and his continual breaking of the marital bonds, Grove, in contrast, reinserts sexuality within the family structure by repeatedly invoking an incestuous circularity that binds the three Clarks to the mill and to each other.

This incestuous bond is particularly evident in the Clarks' relationships with the women in their lives, all of whom are called Maud and become somewhat interchangeable in their relationships with the different Clarks. Indeed, the male Clarks' sexual desires are never firmly attached to the one Maud they are married to; desire circulates freely

---

5 Mathews 250.

within the family. Rudyard Clark, for example, embraces Maud Carter as more than a daughter-in-law, lavishing presents on her that he jealously begrudges his own son. Similarly, when Edmund starts an affair with Sam's secretary, Maud Dolittle, the public seduction scene is closely watched by a sexually jealous Sam, the rival father. When three years later, after the end of his affair, Edmund marries Maud Fanshaw, it is only to discover that his father has not just participated in the son's courtship, but has outtricked his son by handing over shares in the mill to Maud, so that Edmund is dependent on his wife's collaboration and goodwill in his operation of the business. Sam eventually chooses Maud Carter as his heir, sharing with her a complicitous affection, which is expressed not in words but in "tones which vibrated with unspoken things" (*M* 20).

The dispersal and simultaneous containment of sexuality within the family boundaries represents a sexualization of power that is radically different from Dreiser's exploration of this motif in his trilogy. Like Dreiser, Grove uses his big business novel to inscribe the ingenious workings of sexualized power in his twentieth-century Canadian naturalism; but Grove gives this exploration a more specifically psychological dimension. In this process, sexuality assumes an even more abstract quality than in *The Titan*. While sexuality is strangely omnipresent in the Clark household, neither of the male Clarks is a very physical or sexual person. Sam is described as small in stature, Edmund has a disability from the war. "Divorcing" herself from the mill, Sam's daughter Ruth eventually marries an old European aristocrat to escape sexual relations altogether; she can only exorcise the powerful hold of the mill in her life by renouncing sexuality. Assimilated by the mill, male and female sexuality assumes a symbolic function, representing the mill's hyperproductivity. Invested with male and female sexuality, the mill emerges as an hermaphroditic machine, endowed with monstrous reproductive powers.

Given the mill's mixed blessing of cornucopian productivity, Grove's point on modern power is, in part, a Foucauldian one. The mill's power principle cannot be simply dismissed as negative and exploitative because it is committed to production, the ultimately positive principle of Grove's novels of the soil. Based on Sam Clark's genial plan "whereby the mill could go on growing and growing,"[6] the mill takes on a life of its own to the point of becoming self-procreative. Nature-like, it produces

---

6 Frederick Philip Grove, *The Master of the Mill* (1944; Toronto: Macmillan, 1945) 65. Further references will appear in the text, abbreviated *M*.

vital commodities – flour and bread – in unimaginable quantities, enough to provide not only the national demand but also the demands of other countries. Birk Sproxton has discussed the mill in terms of a plant, a living organism,[7] which is appropriate in that the mill, as a huge, futuristic machine, becomes capable of producing its own abundant harvest.

This principle of production, however, is also the mill's secret of seduction. The mill's productivity is linked to the laws of nature, creating a naturalist framework that subjects everyone to its inexorable laws. Sam presents the mill as a "fact of nature," emphasizing that, like nature, the Clark mill has its own laws, which go beyond a sense of good and evil, and are indifferent to morality. Indeed, presented as an independent, larger-than-life organism through the different narrators' perspectives, the mill comes to occupy a position similar to Père Colombe's demonic tavern, *L'Assommoir*, another all-embracing machine that deterministically rules the characters' lives, involving them in the naturalist plot of decline, degradation, and death.[8]

The ambiguity associated with the mill as "a fact of nature" is one that Grove recognizes at the heart of naturalism itself, in which nature is either indifferent or destructive. Walter Benn Michaels has demonstrated in his reading of Dreiser's *Financier* that "nature" is in alliance with the speculator, not with the producer,[9] a point Grove never tires of dramatizing in his agrarian novels (and that he makes most poignantly in *Fruits of the Earth* [1933], where the pioneer-patriarch's constructions are immediately followed by nature's work of decay). Grove's prairie pioneers are engaged in endless and sometimes apparently pointless struggles against the arbitrariness of nature and its power to destroy what is built by human toil.[10] Floods and drought work against the producers' ideal of a regular harvest as compensation for their "honest" work. Nature's principle of providing cornucopian excess in some years and withholding its harvest arbitrarily in others evokes the pattern of sudden disruption

---

7 Birk Sproxton, "Grove's Unpublished MAN and Its Relation to *The Master of the Mill*," Nause 50.

8 For a detailed discussion of American naturalism's interest in the "procreative force of the machine, see Mark Seltzer, *Bodies and Machines*, especially his chapter "The Naturalist Machine," 24–44.

9 Michaels, "Dreiser's *Financier*," 288.

10 For a discussion of the (inevitable) conflict between prairie pioneer and nature in Grove's works, see Pacey, *Frederick Philip Grove*, 123–29. Stanley McMullin, in "Evolution Versus Revolution: Grove's Perception of History," Nause 78, links Grove's vision of nature and culture to the influence of the German philosopher Oswald Spengler (1880–1936), who argued that "What man strives to build, Nature tries to destroy."

and arbitrary fluctuations that the speculator thrives on. Thus, the nature-analogy in Grove's conceptualizing of the mill highlights both the productive and destructive aspects of capitalism. Capitalism in *The Master of the Mill* dismisses the former producers – the mill-hands – as useless unemployed, a burden to society. By turning the mill into "a fact of nature," Sam (and Grove) appears to have found an appropriate metaphor to suggest that capitalism with its trickery manipulation has become all-pervasive, like a law of nature that embraces everyone and that is fundamentally indifferent to human welfare.

The mill's principle of seduction, its hyperproductivity, is, significantly, reflected in its capacity to create discourse without end: all those involved with the mill inevitably talk about it, theorize its functioning, and write their histories about it. Rudyard Clark keeps his secret journal that throws light on the genesis of the mill; Maud Clark and Odette Charlebois fill their hours with stories of the mill; Mr. Stevens writes the mill's history between 1898 and 1924; and Mr. Arbuthnot writes a proletarian novel about it, reflecting the workers' perspective. And yet, the production of continually new discourses on the mill hides as much as it reveals. The networks of narration reflect the deliberate confusion and complexity of the mill's own organization.

In *In Search of Myself*, Grove speaks of the "inevitable form" of *The Master of the Mill*, as "the only form in which the book can convey its message" (*ISM* 438). With the shift of manipulative speculation into the foreground of the novel, Grove's traditionally linear narration – the mark of his agrarian novels with their "honest" characters – changes to incorporate discontinuous shifts in time, flashbacks, and unreliable narrative perspectives, which seem not only appropriate but very successful in highlighting his theme of "discontinuous," disruptive, arbitrary, and manipulative speculation, as well as the shifting, mobile workings of power. Dreiser's *Trilogy of Desire*, by contrast, follows the traditional chronological narration and has been negatively criticized because it "lacks a genuinely innovative strategy" for representing the "new man," the superman-speculator F. A. Cowperwood.[11] Grove's Canadian business novel is more innovative than Dreiser's trilogy in representing in

---

11 See O'Neill 419–21. Although Beverley Mitchell entitled her essay "The 'Message' and the 'Inevitable Form' in *The Master of the Mill*," *Journal of Canadian Fiction* 3.3 (1974), 74-79, she never really addresses the question of why this form should be "inevitable." In "Grove's 'Difficult' Novel," 34–48, W. J. Keith compares the work formally to William Faulkner's *Absalom, Absalom!* and thematically to D.H. Lawrence's *Women in Love*, emphasizing the paradoxes and moral ambiguities of the characters' relation with the mill.

its narrative form both the mobility of the speculator's power and its limitations.

Just as the mill has no ultimate centre of power, the novel has no single narrative centre. Sam, the main narrator, is senile, and other narrative centres are needed to fill the holes left in his history. Just as the complexity of the mill's structure consists of a play of presences and absences, so the novel presents a double discourse of "official" and "unofficial" history, the latter reflected in Sam's act of remembrance in his state of senility. The mill's complex administrative organization thus is echoed in the complexity of the novel's narrative structure; both are based on the same kind of *Versteckspiel*.

Consisting of a system of interlocking subsystems, the mill is "a marvel of organization," designed with the deliberate intent of "disguising and dividing the profits of the huge concern, profits which in a single aggregate would have been monstrous" (*M* 93). After Rudyard's death in 1898, Sam's secretary Maud Dolittle becomes "nominal vice-president" of the company, but as such has only a few "qualifying shares" in it, which limits the power of this office drastically. At the same time Miss Dolittle's "real" power lies in her function as sales manager of the company, but in this function her power is disguised (and controlled) by the fact that she does not sign her letters with her own name but puts the secretary treasurer's, Mr. Stevens, stamp under her letters, a formality that again creates confusion for the outside observer about who is in charge. Frequently, the presence of a name signifies the absence of any real power.

Echoing this deliberate confusion in the mill's network, Sam relates its history from the perspective of his growing senility, so that his state of mind partly disqualifies him as a reliable historiographer. Yet it is Sam, in his state of mental disintegration, who revises the "official" history of the mill, "confessing" its dark secrets, if only to himself. Conversely, the supposedly reliable historiographers in the novel frequently reiterate the "official" history. Grove signals to the reader to be suspicious when Mr. Arbuthnot, the writer of proletarian novels, is exposed as Edmund's master spy who helped put the workers out of work in the last stage of the mill's automation in 1923. Similarly, the two female narrators (Maud Fanshaw and Ottilie Charlebois) appear to be reliable witnesses, who lived through some of the events without being fully in charge, and therefore should be expected to offer a critical, revisionary account. Yet their histories eventually turn out to be tainted by their own complicitous involvement in the mill's construction. Maud Fanshaw, Sam's chosen heiress, collaborated in Edmund's unscrupulous business ventures (*M* 307), while her function as a historiographer is coloured by her belief that extraordinary men "cannot be measured by ordinary standards" (*M* 264). With the women thus willing to "suspend judgement," they perpetuate the official version of events. Naturalist and modernist techniques thus converge to present a narrative network of manipulation and complicitous silence that echoes the mill's administrative complexity.

The mill as a naturalist machine without a true "centre" illustrates Foucault's notion of the workings of power in modern institutions: "One doesn't have here a power which is wholly in the hands of one person who can exercise it alone and totally over the others. It's a machine in which everyone is caught, those who exercise power just as much as those over whom it is exercised" (*PK* 156). Foucault also makes use of the image of the pyramid, which happens to be the architectural structure of the mill:

> It's obvious that in an apparatus like an army or a factory, or some other such type of institution, the system of power takes a pyramidal form. Hence there is an apex. But even so, even in such a simple case, this summit doesn't form the "source" or "principle" from which all power derives as though from a luminous focus (the image by which the monarchy represents itself). The summit and the lower elements of the hierarchy stand in a relationship of mutual support and conditioning, a mutual "hold" (power as mutual and indefinite "blackmail"). (*PK* 159)

Similarly, the hierarchically structured mill "towered up, seventeen stories high, at the foot of the lake, like a huge pyramid whose truncated apex was in line with the summits of the surrounding hills" (*M* 2). Significantly, the apex is "truncated," metaphorically illustrating Foucault's point that those who are at the top are by no means the ultimate centre of power. As an old man approaching senility in 1938, Sam Clark nominally wields power as the mill's president and principal shareholder, but he realizes that it is really not he but "the engineers who did what they judged should be done" (*M* 18). Conversely, those who make important decisions in the running of the machine remain somehow faceless and unnamed individuals in the background of his narrative.

On the novel's psychological level, the truncated apex thus emerges as an image of metaphorical "castration," suggestive of Sam's lack of power: he is not "the master of his house" but is submerged in the larger machine. Feeling that his power as the head of a monopolist company has been "an empty shell" for many years (*M* 18), Sam dresses his history in a naturalist language, presenting himself as a naturalist victim caught in an all-embracing machine that holds him in bondage and predetermines his action: "He could never get away from the feeling that, whatever he had done, he had done under some compulsion. Yet it was he who had determined the development of the mill; but it was, first his father, then his son who had chosen the time for every change proposed, thereby twisting his own purpose" (*M* 4). As Foucault emphasizes that power has become "a machinery that no one owns" (*PK* 156), so even Sam, the president of the mill, is dominated by a sense of being out of control, of being only a tool in the workings of the anonymous machine. Grove makes much of the fact that those who work in the mill somehow become an inseparable part of it, or, as W. J. Keith puts it, "those who are associated with the mill tend to give up their individual traits and, to adapt a phrase from W. H. Auden, forget themselves in a function."[12] Enchained in a text of psychological and mechanistic determinism, Sam, who had the lion's share in the construction and administrative direction of the monumental mill, presents himself as acted upon, as a small cog in the large machine, even at the very moment when his decision inaugurates the first phase of the mill's automation.

Naturalist discourse, then, has a very ambiguous function in the novel. On one level, it constitutes a self-critical analysis of the capitalist figure of power, who recognizes his own limitations. Indeed, the protagonist's sense of Virgilian telos is subverted by the intrusion of his deliberately ironic, degrading perspective, designed to undo his vision of greatness and teleological progress. The subversion of capitalist beliefs in progress and continuity has been one of the traditional functions of naturalist fiction, as David Baguley explains: "It offered images of disruption to an age that desperately sought continuity, failure to an age bent on success, disorder and atrophy instead of regularity and progress, chinks in the chains of cause and effect, the rotting foundations of proudly constructed edifices" (*NF* 218).

But if the naturalist voice in Sam's narration is designed to poke holes into his capitalist success story, it also serves the opposite function, paving the way for the mill's monopolization. Indeed, the naturalist subtext of Sam's story illustrates Foucault's point that a discourse of opposition can easily be recolonized and put in the service of the dominant power principle. Just as Sam is seduced into subjection to the mill's demands, so Sam himself becomes the mill's tool, co-opting oppositional forces. Sam makes much of the fact that he is a man with socialist leanings, who is in sympathy with the lower classes. While there is no doubt that his own ideological position is deeply split, it is his sympathy for the

---

12 Keith, "Grove's Difficult Novel," 43.

workers that gives Sam the flexibility to succeed in his capitalist ventures, where Dreiser's inflexible titan fails. Sam cleverly assimilates oppositional voices, as illustrated by the example of Bruce Rogers, whose agitation amongst the disgruntled workers jeopardizes the implementation of the first phase of the mill's automation. Voicing an official complaint about the bad working conditions, Bruce Rogers is turned from a proletarian agitator into a capitalist accomplice, a tool in the mill's monopolization, expansion, and automation. "I'm telling [the men] that the whole thing can't be helped; that it is nobody's fault; that strikes and walk-outs are of no use" (*M* 219), Rogers says before leaving Sam after an extended discussion. The supposed agitator ends up reflecting the position advocated by Sam himself, his voice reluctantly supporting the master's plans for complete automation. As Sam listens to Rogers's complaints about the "inhuman grind" of assembly-line work, this criticism is embedded in Sam's "official" narrative, signalling by its context Sam's clever assimilation of the worker's opposition.

Sam Clark's strategy of power corresponds to what Foucault has theorized as bio-power, whose methods are subtler and more effective than the capitalist's open confrontation with the opposition. Describing the bourgeois commitment to philanthropy in Canadian society between 1870 and 1920, Mariana Valverde has explained the mechanics of bio-power as deployed in Canada as follows:

> As historians have pointed out, one important aspect of the growth of modern Canada was the development of an urban-industrial working class. The correlate of that was the development of an urban bourgeoisie, certain sectors of which initiated a philanthropic project to reform or "regenerate" Canadian society.[13]

According to Foucault's analysis of the French bourgeoisie, its usage of bio-power involved a "calculated management of life," subsuming measures of population control and demography:

> This bio-power was without question an indispensable element in the development of capitalism; the latter would not have been possible without the controlled insertion of bodies into the machinery of production and the adjustment of the phenomena of population to economic processes. (*HS* 140–41)

In *The Master of the Mill*, this "gentle," life-affirming bio-power is conveniently represented by women. It is theoretically expressed by Maud

---

13 Mariana Valverde, *The Age of Light, Soap, and Water: Moral Reform in English Canada, 1885–1925* (Toronto: McClelland & Stewart, 1991) 15.

Dolittle, who explains the demands of the machine for an increased or reduced labour force:

> Population will dwindle as its task disappears. The enormously increased population was needed to nurse the machine in its infancy, to teach it its paces till it could walk by itself. As the population dwindles, it will live in ever greater abundance and ease till comfort smothers it, and it becomes extinct; for ease and comfort do not make fruitful. (*M* 390–91)

Indeed, Edmund envisions a future in which the population is kept in submission through material comfort, whereby charity becomes the major bourgeois strategy to keep "docile" the former workers, who, disgruntled and frustrated, might otherwise attack the machines and disrupt production. Similarly, when Sam Clark dies toward the end of *The Master of the Mill*, he stipulates in his will that a large amount of his money will go to create a charitable fund for the unemployed, the victims of the mill. In its last volume, *The Stoic*, Dreiser's trilogy culminates in a similar pattern: in his will, Cowperwood sets up a charitable fund for a hospital in which people should be treated regardless of colour and creed. Prompted by the demands of bio-power, these charitable activities are, however, not in opposition to the spirit of capitalism, as many readers have argued, but make its smooth functioning possible (as Donald Trump's more recent publicizing of his charitable activities shows).

Just as the reflection of the mill is "shattered and broken into a million luminous shards" (*M* 7), so the sexualized representations of the mill change, according to the demands of bio-power. Given the traditional secrecy of the male Clarks, the women are offered as representations of the mill to the public eye, especially when the male Clarks prefer to retreat into the "not to be seen." The women, then, are not just "useless adornments," as Nancy Bailey has argued,[14] but sexualized representations of the mill's bio-power. They make its smooth running possible by acting as important catalysts in the economic and social power plays. In times of peace, the mill is represented in its static timelessness by the three "regal" and "aristocratic" Mauds. Like the snow-white mill, Maud Carter appears in "snow-white" at the important social event in Langholm (*M* 140), just as the "virginal" Maud Dolittle appears in a "white fur" at a party at Langholm House many years later. While this circular doubling and tripling of Mauds suggests that they fulfill a similar function in their relationship with the mill, the representations of the mill are by no means

---

14 Nancy Bailey, "F. P. G. and the Empty House," *Journal of Canadian Fiction* 31–32 (1981) 189.

stable but continually shifting, depending on the mill's demands. The two important stages of the mill's automation in 1901 and 1923 are, significantly, represented by figures who signify excess and rebellion.

Grove highlights how much Sam's capitalist monopolization process makes use of images of sexual disruption. A figure of daring promiscuity, Sibyl Carter emerges at the turn of the century as a woman who articulates the new woman's sexual rights. Unlike the images of "ideal" and "regal" femininity, such as Maud Carter and Maud Fanshaw, Sibyl looks very boyish and androgynous, very much like Fanny Essler. Set up as the archetypal, *fin-de-siècle femme fatale* through the eyes of both Sam and his housekeeper, Odette Charlebois, Sibyl's aim is not only to seduce the master of the mill, Sam, but also to flirt with the mill-hands. Her sexuality, then, crosses class boundaries and, on the surface, disrupts the boundaries of Langholm's social and economic order. Indeed, Sibyl's indiscriminate promiscuity seems to infiltrate and sexualize the whole apparatus of the mill, a mill that towers up in front of her as a huge phallic symbol:

> Leaving the office, followed by her sardonic and overpowdered maid, she went down to the carriage, stopping a moment to stare at the mill which, though an unfinished torso, was at the centre towering up to almost its present height. (M 174)

Like the other sexual relations in the novel, though, Sibyl's wildly promiscuous and aggressive sexuality takes on an incestuous quality when associated with the mill. Trying to seduce Sam, her sexual desire is directed back to the head of the patriarchal family, the male icon of power, back to her brother-in-law, who conveniently resists physical seduction, but does not resist the temptation to exploit Sibyl's sexuality and put it in the service of the mill in the first phase of its automation in 1901.

As a sexualized object of sight, Sibyl is allowed to displace the "regal" and dignified Maud Carter as the predominant representation of the mill in the minds of the public just before the first stage of automation. Given her image as a seductive siren, she becomes associated with the mill's destructive aspects in the workers' minds, so that the workers' wrath against the exploitative mill culminates in a public chase in which Sibyl is stripped of her clothing:

> All the time such of her pursuers as fell behind were replaced by fresher and younger ones. But she knew now where she was: in a moment she would be skirting the park of Clark House. Meanwhile new hands were reaching for her. Her petticoat fell; her vest; her drawers; and just as she was topping the hill, coming into the direct light, she ran naked, save for her corset. (M 177–78)

Culminating in this satirized assault, the spreading sexual aura in Langholm is accompanied by a hectic boom in land speculation that leads to a bust in 1901. This scene, narrated by Odette Charlebois, makes a logical connection between the spreading sexual promiscuity, the speculation bust, and the first workers' strike in Langholm. In fact, the "official" history holds Sibyl responsible for the ensuing "chaos" at the mill, that is, the growing liberality that culminates in the rebellious strike of otherwise submissive workers. In this official history, Sibyl is conceptualized in the (stereo)typical terms of the naturalist female, whose body "infects" the whole social order.

Yet Sam deconstructs this stereotype in his revisionary history. While the official history (ironically related by Sam's housekeeper) identifies Sibyl's "contagious" promiscuity as the cause of the workers' strike, Sam's revisionary history exposes this sexualized "disruption" as part of his own larger plan. Sam was the real instigator of the speculation bust and cause of the workers' unrest, and he was conveniently absent when Sibyl was ritually assaulted and driven out of town. The moment Sibyl left town, Sam returned to workers who were, once again, willing to make peace and comply with the management's call for order. Sibyl's promiscuity hence is not disruptive of capitalist processes but is a clever strategy that helps the apparently innocent Sam to implement the first stage of the mill's automation in 1901. "Unveiling" the mill, then, means exposing that its power principle is based on such "unheroic," sexualized acts of co-optation, which fill the narrator with humility and shame.

Thus it should come as no surprise that Sam survives the other excessive figure in the novel, his own son Edmund. While the clever capitalist survivor Sam remains modestly in the background, refusing the honours of knighthood, his rebelling, excessive son eagerly accepts the old titles in lieu of his father, insisting on being called by his aristocratic title of "Sir Edmund." By the end Edmund dies, when he bravely steps into the limelight of a mill surrounded by rebelling and chaotically shooting workers, a display of old-fashioned valour reminiscent of Cowperwood's display of "titanic" greatness. Trying to subdue the rebels by his sheer presence, he believes himself magically protected by the mill's "veil." Signalling the last disruptive phase in the mill's automation, his fall, like Cowperwood's, does not mark a setback in the mill's monopolization but ensures its survival and consolidation, illustrating Foucault's point that removing the apex of the pyramid does not necessarily destroy the system.

In psychoanalytic terms, the conceptualizing of modern power in the image of a "truncated" pyramid carries with it undertones of sexual castration and impotence. While Edmund is metaphorically "castrated" (the novel emphasizes his sterility and his premature death), Sam's limited powers and his eventual slippage into senility evoke the same concept. On the surface, these recurring images of emasculation and impotence suggest the Foucauldian idea that the old sovereign-patriarch has been stripped of his power in Canada's twentieth-century economy. Yet the novel's ending simultaneously suggests the opposite. By resorting to an utterly fictional, dystopian, and static future state in which the corporate machine can completely dispense with labour, Grove creates a whole group of unemployed who become like children in their dependency on the charity of a fabulously rich patron. This provider of necessary tangible commodities, in turn, echoes the patriarchal father as well as the generously giving producer figure of Grove's agrarian novels. It appears that Grove's nostalgia for a paternalistic power principle emerges in the midst of his dystopia of modern bio-power. Evoking a modern paradise without the curse of labour, the ending reveals Sam's (and Grove's) longing for an archaic patriarchal power, which holds the strings even from beyond the grave.

The novel reveals the same ideological contradictions in its gender politics. After creating the monumental mill, the males die, leaving the legacy of the mill to three women, Maud Dolittle, Odette Charlebois, and Maud Fanshaw, whose function it is to distribute charity to the unemployed – the "victims" of the mill. If the novel thus ends on the ascendancy of women to (nominal) power, this ending simultaneously suggests the opposite. The women, always already metaphorically "castrated" in a world of male "masters," represent a final – aestheticized – feminine submission to the demands of the phallic mill. This suggests less an increase in women's powers than an ultimate containment of female powers within the boundaries of Grove's naturalism. The women continue their complicitous participation in the economic process, while propagandistically mimicking Edmund's earlier vision on the mill's absolute self-sufficiency: "'What,' Lady Clark asked at a given stage of the discussion, "'am I to do with the mill now I own it?' 'Nothing,' Miss Dolittle said promptly" (*M* 390). Returning to the image of the naturalist wheel, history is conceptualized as an eternal circle of repetition in which everyone is caught. This voice is contradicted by Maud Clark's optimistic re-reading of the wheel imagery in terms of teleological progress: "A wheel does not rotate in empty space: it moves forward" (*M* 392). While the three interchangeable Mauds are thus occupied in the same circles of repetition, as they quietly participate in and are co-opted by masculine versions of power, their narratives inevitably confront them with their ideological complicity and self-contradictions. But before they can move on to a truly dialogical exploration of their different positions, the author ends their debate, by arbitrarily and abruptly ending the novel.

Finally, in radical contrast to Dreiser's novel, here the three women who survive are not primarily sexualized mistresses but fetishized mother-figures: Odette Charlebois raised Maud Carter's children, Edmund and his sister Ruth; Maud Dolittle was a mother as well as a mistress to Edmund; and Lady Clark mothered Senator Clark in the last years of his life. As the mill continues its nature-like production, so the women's function is to "shelter and feed the unemployed," as Maud Clark puts it (*M* 390); as the mill is suspended above good and evil in their narratives, so the three women seem serene and impervious, above the disruptive forces of physical sexuality. And yet, it is the man-made mill that triumphs as the image of production; the three women are child-less. Female childbirth has been usurped as the ultimate image of pro-ductive energy. It is significant that *The Master of the Mill* presents two mothers who die in childbirth; first Sam's mother and then Sam's wife Maud, when she gives birth to her daughter Ruth. As the fetishized and aestheticized representations of the maternal functions of the mill, the three women in nominal power over the mill have been stripped of their own productive capacities. The novel's final view of three fetishized "mothers" without children presents an indirect ironic triumph of "mas-culine" productivity in the form of the machine, just as Cowperwood's long line of sexualized mistresses functions as a representation of his "masculine" manipulative genius.

12

The Father's Seduction
and the Daughter's Rebellion

In Grove's German and Canadian fiction, the patriarchal family is saturated with sexuality and power. Hence, it is also a privileged locus for
his exploration of naturalist determinants. While *The Master of the Mill*
examines the workings of psychological and social determinants through
the father-son bond, many of his earlier novels explore the daughter's
position in the family network and her problematic relationship with
her father. Indeed, the father-daughter relationship lends itself to a naturalist exploration of power relations since, within the family, daughter
and father are "the most asymmetrically proportioned" in gender, age,
authority, and cultural privilege.[1] In Grove's fiction, the family has all
the trappings of an imprisoning institution, perpetuating hierarchically
structured gender relations from generation to generation. But if the
daughter finds herself at the bottom of this hierarchy, she also challenges

---

1 See Lynda Boose, "The Father's House and the Daughter in It: The Structures of
  Western Culture's Daughter-Father Relationship," *Daughters and Fathers*, ed. Lynda
  E. Boose and Betty S. Flowers (Baltimore & London: Johns Hopkins UP, 1989) 19–74.

the determining structures of the family institution, just as she challenges the naturalist plot that frequently predetermines her sexualization and victimization. As often as in nineteenth-century naturalism, her desire for change is frustrated, though, as she finds herself caught in a naturalist plot of circular repetition in which the institutional framework triumphs, recontaining the daughter's rebellion and exposing the limits of her power. *Maurermeister Ihles Haus* (1906), *Settlers of the Marsh* (1925), and *Our Daily Bread* (1928) explore the father-daughter relationship by highlighting such deterministic constraints.

The focus of this chapter, then, is twofold. I will first explore the daughter's strategies of rebellion, her search for new alliances and new discourses of resistance against the patriarch's principle of sexualized power. By rebelling against the determining structures of the patriarchal family, the daughter, I will argue, simultaneously challenges the naturalist conceptualization of the female as always already seduced, enchained, and subjugated through her body and sexuality, rendered docile in the social networks. Given this emphasis on change, Rita Felski's feminist theory provides a useful starting point, since Felski has urged feminists to think of the relationship between social structures (institutions) and agency (the individual) as dynamic, not static: "Human beings do not simply reproduce existing structures in the process of action and communication, but in turn modify those structures even as they are shaped by them."[2] This will serve as a springboard to explore the extent to which women's (feminist) voices manage to poke holes in the father's "law" and to defy his seductive power.

By locating the daughter's struggle in a naturalist context, Grove signals that the women's struggle to subvert the "symbolic order" of the patriarch's house does not occur in a linear fashion but is full of reversals, illustrating Michel Foucault's point on the polyvalence of discourse. As Foucault observes, discourses can be "both an instrument and an effect of power," but also "a point of resistance and a starting point for an opposing strategy" (*HS* 101). Drawing attention to the shiftiness and flexibility of discourse, the German and the Canadian novels alike emphasize that the daughter's struggle against patriarchy is often a strategic game that involves a cautious manoeuvring between slippery discourses. While such manoeuvres allow her to defy the father's authoritative word, it is only rarely, if ever, that the daughter manages to change the patriarchal rule of the house. While Grove's twentieth-century vision emphasizes that the daughter must dethrone the word of

---

2 Felski 56.

the father in order to resist its assimilation, the author also points to the limits of her discursive resistance. The naturalist frame frequently recontains the daughter, as her discourse of resistance is reappropriated and recolonized within the larger patriarchal institution.

Secondly, this chapter explores the father's strategies for holding on to his patriarchal power at a time when women demanded new rights for themselves. As the head of a patriarchal and sexualized institution, the father employs strategies ranging from his psychological "seduction" of the daughter to his use of sexualized violence against women, including physical and sexual abuse, both of which are condoned and silenced within the family. If in Grove's early fiction the daughter is frequently attached to her father in what Freud described as the Electra complex (*Fanny Essler*), in his late fiction the father-daughter plot is determined by a King Lear subtext (*Our Daily Bread*), in which the daughters come to occupy a male position and "punish" the senile and impotent father for the abuse they have suffered. But in both cases, the tenacious structures and practices of the patriarchal family predetermine the pattern of the daughters' lives. Grove's father-daughter novels reveal the author's deep concern with the institutionalization of patterns of sexualized power within the family, which allow the father's dominance to continue.

Grove's father figures are all naturalist types, characterized by a typical misogyny, rigidity, tyranny, and intellectual blindness. "Basically, Master Mason Ihle despised everything that was female," is how Grove describes the German patriarch in *Maurermeister Ihles Haus*,[3] and if Richard Ihle is Grove's most blatantly misogynistic character, he is also, as E. D. Blodgett has noted, "the prototype of Grove's fathers."[4] Focusing on the marginalized female characters in Grove's fiction, Blodgett has persuasively argued that Grove's prairie patriarchs – Abe Spalding, Niels Lindstedt, and John Elliot – are immobilized and somewhat static in their epic greatness, and that it is the women in Grove's German and Canadian fiction who are not only capable of change but also challenge the frozen systems of order set up by the men: "where the males always seem to be who they are – unchanging, hopelessly teleological – it is the females who must act."[5] The males are comic "blocking characters," who

---

3 *The Master Mason's House*, ed. and intro. A. W. Riley and D. O. Spettigue, trans. Paul P. Gubbins (Ottawa: Oberon Press, 1976) 99. All further references to this novel will appear in the text, abbreviated *MI*. Citations from the German original are from Felix Paul Greve, *Maurermeister Ihles Haus* (Karl Schnabel: Berlin, 1906).

4 Blodgett, *Configuration*, 134.

5 Blodgett, *Configuration*, 126.

are caught in an *idée fixe*, in a monomaniacal chase for a particular goal. Richard Ihle is presented as an irate self-made man in Bismarck's Germany, and the young Swedish immigrant-pioneer Niels Lindstedt in *Settlers of the Marsh* and the old Manitoban homesteader John Elliot in *Our Daily Bread* are formed from the same mould; both are obsessed with conquering and imposing their will on the Canadian wilderness. In their discourses and practices, they all share and perpetuate the very deterministic structures that victimize the women who share their lives.

Grove's naturalism, then, targets these discursive determinants, highlighting the father's inflexible language of authority through which he establishes himself as the representative of a rigid, patriarchal law. The language of Grove's German and Canadian father figures is "indissolubly fused with its authority," to use Mikhail Bakhtin's words; fused with the family "institution," this language "stands and falls together with that authority."[6] Exploring the Bakhtinian "word of the fathers"[7] as a naturalist determinant, Grove's fiction also illustrates the Foucauldian conceptualization of discourse as an instrument of both power and resistance: "Discourse transmits and produces power," Foucault writes, "it reinforces it, but also undermines and exposes it, renders it fragile and makes it possible to thwart it" (*HS* 101). While the father's language perpetuates the structures of female submission in the family framework, the female characters struggle against these linguistic determinants by experimenting with discourses of resistance designed to undo the father's word of authority. Yet, trying to change the deterministic course of their lives, the daughters' resistance is frequently recontained, with the naturalist plot and the "word of the father" triumphing in Grove's fiction over their demand for change.

Grove's translation of physiological determinism into discursive determinism was without a doubt influenced by the turn-of-the-century philosophical interest in language crisis (*Sprachkrise*) associated with Friedrich Nietzsche, for example, whose work Grove knew well. In the *Gay Science* – a book "of the greatest importance," according to Grove (*ISM* 166) – Nietzsche has a section entitled "Of the sound of the German language" in which he criticizes "the militarization of the German language," a German that has turned into *Offiziersdeutsch*: "welches wütende Autoritätsgefühl, welche höhnische Kälte klingt aus diesem

---

6 Mikhail Bakhtin, *The Dialogic Imagination: Four Essays*, trans. Caryl Emerson and Michael Holquist (Austin: U of Texas P, 1981) 343.

7 Bakhtin 342.

3ebrüll heraus," Nietzsche writes, "what raging sense of authority, what cornful coldness speak out of this roaring."[8] "*Wütendes Autoritäts-*ɡefühl" is precisely what characterizes the language of master mason Richard Ihle in *Maurermeister*; Ihle is attached to the word *Wut* (rage, wrath, ire) like an epithet (e.g., *MI* 45–46; 48–49 in translation). Not only s Ihle's *Offiziersdeutsch* stripped of all music – it is pure command. Simiarly, in Grove's Canadian fiction the male language of barely contained violence is echoed in Niels Lindstedt's reductive voice of command in his relationship with his wife Clara Vogel, and in John Elliot's autocratic language that intimidates his children. Yet this authoritarian language inevitably stirs up disgust ("Widerwillen") at the same time that it provokes resistance ("Widerstand"),[9] not only in the language philosopher Nietzsche, who makes it the target of a vicious satire, but also in Grove's female characters.

More specifically, though, Grove emphasizes the feminization and sexualization of discursive resistance. In all three novels, it is the women who are linked to linguistic flexibility and experimentation, opposing and poking holes in "the word of the father." This is first explored in *Maurermeister Ihles Haus*, in which Grove opposes the German patriarch's inflexible language of authority with the linguistic flexibility and exuberance of his daughter, Susie Ihle, a contrast that becomes a pattern for the Canadian prairie novels as well. In the first paragraph, the reader sees her as an eleven-year-old leaping over ropes and chains in her little Baltic home town at the sea coast, ready to set into motion whatever is static: "The hazy stillness on the water ... demanded almost to be shattered" (*MI* 13). As Susie and her friend stalk two bourgeois lovers and call them names, it is significantly by manipulating language that the two girls disrupt the conventions and the order of the little Baltic sea town: Susie takes delight in word plays and punning, in parodically imitating the school headmaster's Saxon dialect, and, above all, in offending bourgeois respectability with sexual equivocation.[10] Even in the

---

8 Friedrich Nietzsche, *Die Fröhliche Wissenschaft*, in *Nietzsche* (Frankfurt: Fischer, 1957) 104; *The Gay Science*, trans. Walter Kaufmann (New York: Vintage, 1974) 161.

9 German *wider* = against, contrary to, in opposition to.

10 Hidden behind shrubbery, Susie and her friend Betty shout to the lovers: "Ihr sollt euch vermäääählen" (*MI* 12), "You ought to get ma-a-a-ried" (*MI* 16), and later, getting carried away by their prank, they give their earlier sentence a more overtly sexual twist: "Ihr sollt euch vermehren!!" (*MI* 13), "Ought to reproduce" (*MI* 17). Unfortunately, the joke is somewhat lost in the English translation, as the words "vermählen" and "vermehren" rhyme in German but not in the translation. Susie and Betty also play on Karl Schade's name, calling him "Kahl" (= bald) Schade.

first chapter, Susie enjoys creating her own linguistic carnival in which she becomes linked to subversive laughter ("Lachen") and giggling ("Kichern"). This playfulness is particularly important since "the au thoritative discourse," as Bakhtin describes it, permits no play with the context framing it, no play with its borders, no gradual and flexible tran sitions, no spontaneously creative stylizing variants on it."[11]

Susie's exuberant play with signifiers – her pleasure with words, puns and name-calling – is, to apply Julia Kristeva's terminology, a "maniacal eroticization of speech," as if she were "gulping it down, sucking on it, delighting in all the aspects of an oral eroticization and a narcissistic safety belt which this kind of non-communicative, exhibitionistic, and fortifying use of speech entails." This "play with signifiers" is typical for a "borderlander," a person who lacks a sense of home and of boundaries.[12] Thus Susie's language is both a reflection of her own position and a tool that shapes her relationship with her father as one of continual (border-line) resistance, a position that refuses ultimate assimilation. Living in her father's house but destined to leave it for somebody else's house, Susie is a threshold person who finds herself "betwixt and between the positions assigned and arrayed by law," as Lynda Boose describes the precarious position of the daughter-figure in a patriarchal family.[13]

Just as the daughter's liminal status endows her with "the special power of the weak," to use Boose's words, so Susie's favourite linguistic strategy of subversion is the principle of negativity, even lying: "All we have to do is keep saying no" (*MI* 18), she tells her girlfriend when their pranks become uncovered. When accused of calling names, "Susie col-lected herself quickly: 'That's a dirty lie,' she said, loudly and indig-nantly" (*MI* 1819). Here, the manipulation of language is a strategy that is directed against another woman, as it is often used as a weapon against her girlfriends, at the same time that it serves as a strategy to deal with a tyrannical patriarchal power at home.

And yet, psychologically bound to the father-figure, the rebelling daughter is frequently "seduced" into submission to "the father's word." Grove's conceptualization of the father-daughter relationship as a deeply sexualized one has to be seen in the context of the emerging psycho-

---

11 Bakhtin 343.

12 Julia Kristeva, "Within the Microcosm of 'The Talking Cure,'" trans. Thomas Gora and Margaret Waller, *Interpreting Lacan: Psychiatry and the Humanities*, Vol. 6, ed. Joseph H. Smith and William Kerrigan (New Haven: Yale UP, 1983) 42.

13 Boose 67.

analysis and women's growing challenge of patriarchal prerogatives from the turn of the century on. Foucault has noted that at a time when psychoanalysis allowed incestuous desires to be articulated in language as a means of normalization, "preparations were being made to undo those reprehensible proximities in other social sectors." Consequently, the social attitude toward incest was marked by fascinating contradictions: "on the one hand, the father was elevated into an object of compulsory love, but on the other hand, if he was a loved one, he was at the same time a fallen one in the eyes of the law" (*HS* 130).

We find a similar ideological contradiction in Grove's sexualization of the father-daughter relationship in his naturalist fiction. On the one hand, he presents daughter-figures rebelling against the patriarchal order of their homes, searching for new languages, articulating their sexual rights, and developing new forms of independent living, thus reflecting the social increase in women's powers and rights in the early twentieth century. On the other hand, these same daughter-figures are frequently caught in an Oedipal relationship with the father. While consciously recognizing and rejecting the father's tyrannical power, they are also tied to the father-figure through their psychological disposition. Resolved to rebel and carve out their own lives, these daughters are deterministically bound in naturalist circles of repetition, internalizing the father's rule and law while simultaneously rebelling against it. In *fin-de-siècle* Germany, Grove witnessed women's growing demand for new rights, and after immigrating to Canada he was faced with Manitoba's strong women's movement, which gained for women the right to vote in provincial elections in 1916, when Grove was teaching in the province. Considering these fundamental changes for women, it is significant that Grove's German and Canadian fiction should become a field on which psychological determinants are shown to limit these new rights, further enchaining the daughter in the conventional patriarchal framework. If Grove's exploration of the daughter's condition is a critical reflection of patriarchy's power to endure in the face of legal and social changes, it also reflects naturalism's continued enchainment of the rebelling female within its secure (male) boundaries.

Interiorized (and assimilated) into the individual psyche, the sexualized relationships of power in *Maurermeister* are inscribed within the privacy and secrecy of the family home, whose space is represented as a psychical and sexualized landscape. According to Christine Froula,

the relations of literary daughters and fathers resemble in important ways the model developed by Judith Herman and Lisa Hirschman to describe the family situations of incest victims: a dominating, authoritarian father;

an absent, ill, or complicitous mother; and a daughter who, prohibited by her father from speaking about the abuse, is unable to sort out her contradictory feelings of love and terror of him, of desire to end the abuse and fear that if she speaks she will destroy the family structure that is her only security.[14]

In his German and Canadian fiction, Grove not only invokes this incestuous pattern but explores the father's sexualized power in spatial terms whereby the father's house takes on an uncanny quality in which sexuality and fear, pleasure and bondage become mixed in typically naturalist forms. Indeed, the beginning of *Fanny Essler* (which is the chronological continuation of *Maurermeister*) presents the daughter locked up in her room, in metaphorical bondage, in a state of masochistic waiting that is simultaneously eroticized, as it stimulates the daughter's fantasies about an all-powerful father-figure in the guise of a younger *Märchenprinz*.

"Father-daughter stories are full of literal houses, castles, or gardens in which fathers ... lock up their daughters in the futile attempt to prevent some rival male from stealing them," writes Lynda Boose in her study on the representation of father-daughter relationships.[15] This motif of the daughter's literal and metaphorical enchainment in the father's house lends itself to a naturalist exploration of sexualized "female bondage," and it is introduced by Grove in his two German novels. *Maurermeister* is set in the patriarchal house that gives the work its title. For Susie, a teenage Fanny Essler, the house is more than a simple dungeon: it is imbued with the father's omnipresence, his principle of threatening but equally seductive power. Showing the house, the yard, and her father's shop to her friend Hedwig Ribau, eleven-year-old Susie Ihle ends up sitting in the new family carriage in intimate closeness with her friend: "Hier fühlte man sich geheimnisvoll in Sicherheit. Es war ein Haus im Hause" (*MI* 66) ("They felt secretive and secure. It was a house within a house" [*MI* 68]). On the surface, these sentences evoke the archetypal function of the house-image as a shelter (a facet that John Elliot in *Our Daily Bread* also connotes with his house, when he invites his daughters, who are troubled in their marriages, back to the security of their parental home).

---

14 Christine Froula, "The Daughter's Seduction: Sexual Violence and Literary History," Boose and Flowers 112.

15 Boose 33.

But this sense of the security of the house is instantly subverted. The German phrase "geheimnisvoll in Sicherheit" is more telling than the English translation, in that "*geheim*nisvoll" not only contains the word "heim" (= home) but as a whole word also means the opposite of home, as it denotes secretiveness, at the same time that it is related to "un*heim*lich," the uncanny. "Geheimnisvoll" as a premodifier for "Sicherheit" is an odd collocation in German verging on the oxymoronic, as it appears deliberately to undermine the sense of "Sicherheit" in the rest of the house. The phrase suggests the presence of a potential intruder and disturber of peace who is not somebody outside the house, but somebody *in* the larger house itself, namely, the father-figure. Not surprisingly, the novel describes several scenes where the father intrudes suddenly and violently into his daughter's space, where he makes entrances that are like assaults on her body. Just as Elliot's daughter Gladys confesses as an adult woman, "I am afraid of him [her father] ... Just as mother was,"[16] so the scene in which Susie is "geheimnisvoll in Sicherheit" is preceded, significantly, by a chapter that describes Master Ihle's violent entrance into the house that forces Susie and her sister to hide in the wardrobe to escape the father's wrath.

Indeed, it is the adverb "unheimlich" (uncanny) that Grove uses when the father enters the house, to indicate that then the "heimisch" quality becomes negated. The closeness with the father is so threatening that it becomes "un-heimlich" for the daughter. Given this textual play on the absence of "Heim" and the novel's title with its emphasis on the house, the novel underscores the separation between "Haus" and "Heim," a distinction that Martin Heidegger emphasizes some decades later when he asks rhetorically: "do the houses in themselves hold any guarantee that *dwelling* occurs in them?"[17] For Heidegger, "dwelling" ("wohnen") means to live in peace, to be at home, a sense that Susie experiences only in the house "within the house," where she discovers her own home,

---

16   Frederick Philip Grove, *Our Daily Bread* (Toronto: Macmillan, 1928) 285; further references to this novel will appear in the text, abbreviated *ODB*. In *Our Daily Bread*, Grove gives the motif of the tyrannical, wrathful father an interesting twist, since it is only very late in the novel that Elliot's wrath surfaces. In the beginning of the novel, he is introduced to the reader as "a thinker, [who] had lived a life of introspection, dreams, and ideas" (*ODB* 5); it is in the middle of the novel that we witness the first explosive, hateful attack on his son Arthur who refuses to become a farmer.

17   Martin Heidegger, "Building Dwelling Thinking," *Basic Writings*, J. Glenn Gray, ed. (New York: Harper & Row, 1977) 324.

that is, her body and her language, in the intimacy with her girlfriend whose language Susie admires and mimics.

In *Maurermeister,* the eruption of the patriarch's sexualized power in the midst of the family home is only insinuated, but not fully developed as a motif. (Mrs. Ihle goes to her children for protection, occasionally sleeping in her daughter's room to avoid being sexually assaulted by her intoxicated husband.) Grove's early Canadian novel *Settlers of the Marsh,* however, develops this motif further, presenting a mother figure who is brutally victimized, assaulted, and ultimately destroyed by the father-figure. On her farm in the bush country of northern Manitoba, Mrs. Amundsen is subjected to repeated rapes that are followed by unwanted pregnancies and self-inflicted abortions (at a time when even contraceptive devices were illegal in Canada). While nineteenth-century naturalist fiction frequently conceptualized female sexuality in terms of prostitution, Grove's fiction not only parodies this obsession (in *Fanny Essler*) but, more importantly, his Canadian fiction critically turns the exploration of sexualized power to rape (even rape in marriage), which has become a predominant concern in twentieth-century feminism. In the following scene, the daughter, Ellen Amundsen, becomes a witness of her father's assault, which is almost like an attack on her own body:

> Suddenly I heard mother's voice mixed with groans, Oh John, don't.
> I will not repeat the things my father said. An abyss opened as I lay there. The vile, jesting, jocular urgency of it; the words he used to that skeleton and ghost of a woman... In order to save mother, I was tempted to betray that I heard. Shame held me back ...[18]

The brutal reality of this sex act provides a parodic comment on Freud's description of the child's traumatic shock when witnessing "the primal scene," the (normal) intercourse between the parents, which, according to Freud, the child often (mis)reads as an act of violence. In Grove's novel, in contrast, the graphic nature of the rapist sexuality is shocking for the reader, as it is traumatic for the adolescent witness, signalling, through the daughter's critical perspective, a perversion of the "primal scene" and the eruption of sexualized violence in the midst of supposedly stable family life.

It was probably the outspoken feminist critique of Elsa von Freytag-Loringhoven that provided the raw material for the motif of

---

18 Frederick Philip Grove, *Settlers of the Marsh,* New Canadian Library (1925; Toronto: McClelland & Stewart, 1984) 112. Ellipses are in the text. Further references will appear in the text, abbreviated *S.*

sexualized violence in Grove's German and Canadian novels. In her autobiography, the Baroness introduces the real-life prototype for Grove's patriarchs in her own father, whom she describes as "meanly cruel," sentimental, and "inclined to boss in the family." In fact, she accuses her father of being responsible for her mother's "dreadful death by cancer of the womb," since it is caused by her father's "thoughtless mental as well as physical conduct, that of a soverign [*sic*] yet entirely uncultured male brute" (*A* 1). Since the daughter is confronted with the reality of her mother's sexual subjugation, the patriarch's power is established in his sexual right to the mother's body; and the father's sexualized power enters the daughter's space when she becomes a witness to the violation of the mother's body. In Grove's fiction it is, significantly, always the females, never the males, who witness such traumatic acts of sexual abuse and thus are forced to recognize the limits of their resistance in the material reality of their own (female) bodies.

Moreover, the daughter's physical limits echo her linguistic limits, so that it should come as no surprise that her discursive relationship with her father is characterized by silence and secrecy. As Foucault has observed, "silence and secrecy are a shelter for power, anchoring its prohibitions" (*HS* 101). Also, examining "The Daughter's Seduction: Sexual Violence and Literary History," Christine Froula has noted that the cultural text "dictates to males and females alike the necessity of silencing woman's speech when it threatens the father's power"; this silencing, in turn, ensures "that the cultural daughter remains a daughter, her power suppressed and muted, while the father, his power protected, makes culture and history in his own image."[19]

Ellen Amundsen is a case in point for such an entrapment in silence. While her solidarity with her victimized mother is accompanied by a rejection of the rapist father, she can only whisper her opposition to his sexualized violence while her father is alive. Moreover, her feelings are contradictory and confused, as the many ellipses in her confession indicate. Just as Susie is resentful about helping and protecting her mother, so Ellen is not capable of "saving" her mother by revealing herself as a witness of the rape. Not daring to shame the father, she remains silent, thus co-opting with the father's image as the omnipotent head of the family and the sole upholder of an abstract law. Before his death, she mimics the role of the obedient daughter, fulfilling his desires to the letter.

---

19 Boose and Flowers 112.

We are reminded here of what Luce Irigaray, Jane Gallop, and Christine Froula have criticized as the daughter's (or the father's) seduction. It was, to be sure, Freud who first noted that almost all of his female patients told stories of having been seduced by their father, a phenomenon that Freud recognized as a sexual fantasy, as an expression of the female Oedipus complex. In her critique of Freud, however, Luce Irigaray notes that "the law organizes and arranges the world of fantasy at least as much as it forbids, interprets, and symbolizes it."[20] In other words, it is the patriarchal law that encourages the daughter's fantasies of seduction, which in turn ensure her (pleasurable) submission to the patriarch. Jane Gallop emphasizes with Luce Irigaray how much the daughter's status, power, and identity are dependent on the sexualized terms of the patriarchal law: "If the phallus is the standard of value, then the Father, possessor of the phallus, must desire the daughter in order to give her value."[21] Given this culturally inscribed psychoanalytic text, it should come as no surprise that the patriarchal daughter's desire for her father is desperate: "the only redemption of her value as a girl would be to seduce the father, to draw from him the mark if not the admission of some interest."[22] And the only way to seduce the father is "to avoid scaring him away, is to please him, and to please him one must submit to his law, which prescribes any sexual relation."[23] This explains why Susie continues to admire her father despite his tyrannical excess and why Ellen Amundsen submits to her father's law without questioning it openly. For both daughters, submission to the father is deterministically assured.

While Susie rebels openly against her mother, she oscillates discursively between silence and eulogy in relation to her father. An expert manipulator of signifiers outside the house, Susie is often silenced when she enters the literal house and rebels openly against her father: "'If you don't shut your trap this instant,' Mr. Ihle flew at her with menace in his voice, 'I'll give you what for'" (*MI* 102). To the reader Ihle appears very much like the comic stock figure of the ridiculously wrathful tyrant, as E. D. Blodgett has suggested; for his wife and the children, though, the threat is real enough: "What should I do?," Mrs. Ihle asks, "When I say anything he just hits me" (*MI* 49). While Susie's voice of *Widerstand*, of

---

20 Luce Irigaray, *Speculum of the Other Woman*, trans. Gillian Gill (Ithaca: Cornell UP, 1985) 38.

21 Jane Gallop, "The Father's Seduction," Boose and Flowers 102.

22 Luce Irigaray, quoted in Gallop 102.

23 Gallop 102.

resistance and protest, is developed in dialogue with her mother, this language of *Widerstand* is paradoxically *not* directed against the father whose tyrannies she resents but against her mother, whom Susie accuses of being impotent, of not being able to protect herself or her children: "You are just as frightened of him as we are" (*MI* 49), she tells her mother accusingly, confirming Irigaray's point that "women's rebellions are never aimed at the paternal function – which is sacred and divine – but at that powerful and then castrated mother, because she had brought a castrated child into the world."[24]

In *Maurermeister Ihles Haus*, Grove's concern is to show the institution-alization of the "father's seduction" in the family and the school system. The school – even a school for "höhere Töchter" with exclusively female teachers – plants the emotional seed for the daughter's identification not with a mother but with a patriarchal father-figure, by giving birth to children's patriotism and arousing the children's "first 'great feelings'" (*MI* 90). In 1888, fourteen-year-old Susie's traumatic emotional reaction to the Kaiser's death signals to what extent she has internalized the idea of a phallic father as the supreme love object:

> This event, the death of the old Emperor, was the first, and it remained the only experience of Susie's entire youth that caused her real and protracted grief. Even when later her mother was suddenly taken from them and died, she did not suffer so immediately and so selflessly as now in the case of this death, which in no way affected her directly. (*MI* 88–89)

In Susie's young life the old Kaiser, in contrast to her father, is the stereotyped, sentimental image of a kindly old man with a white beard who loves flowers above all. This image of the Kaiser, complementing that of her wrathful, erratic, younger, self-made father, works to consti-tute the image of the ideal father in her mind, a fantasy that conjures up strength and power and that partly displaces the mother as a figure of positive identification. The death of this male icon of power is traumatic because it implies the death of the fantasy image of the phallic father, which Susie has cathected with deepest emotions.

But what about the mother's power?, we may ask, turning to an icon that is omnipresent in Grove's German and Canadian fiction. The mother is often deeply complicitous with the power structures that subjugate her, but to say that the mother is deterministically bound by the patriar-chal structures is not enough. Grove's mother-figure leaves her daugh-ter very vulnerable, occasionally even participating in the father's

---

24 Irigaray, *Speculum*, 106.

"seduction" of the daughter, by supporting the institutional structures discourses, and practices that predetermine the daughter's subjugation Mrs. Ihle, for example, carries with her a romanticized version of patriarchal power by desperately holding on to the image of her husband before her marriage, a sexualized fantasy of male power that never dies in her life, although she finds the man she lives with repugnant and ridiculous. Also, while she counteracts Susie's fantasy of the Kaiser by taking her to the cemetery to visit the grave of the maternal grandmother, Mrs. Ihle also perpetuates the male version of the family history in her daughter's life. In Mrs. Ihle's stories, the paternal grandmother, for example, emerges as a negative figure, a stereotypical castrating woman: "The old woman, though; she made your grandfather's life such hell that once, when he was drunk, he tried to beat the old woman to death with an axe" (*MI* 44). Not only has Bertha Ihle swallowed her husband's version of his mother as "a devil incarnate," but her story of her husband's origins presents the wife as the scapegoat who is responsible for both marital disputes and her husband's violence. A victim of her husband's assaults, Bertha discloses in her story that she has deeply internalized her victimizer's rationalization, namely, that it is the woman who is responsible when she is attacked by her husband.

Grove's fictional mother-figures emerge as truly naturalist figures of disillusionment and pathos, echoing both Zola's Gervaise Macquart (in *L'Assommoir*) and Maupassant's Jeanne (in *Une Vie*). Lorraine McMullen has argued that Grove stereotypes the Canadian pioneer woman in the role of Earth Mother, who is "passive, obedient, hardworking, [and a] breeder of large families."[25] And yet, submission to the patriarch does not necessarily mean that these women are weak or impotent. In *Our Daily Bread*, Grove introduces Martha Elliot as a powerful pioneer-matriarch, with much of the novel's language suggesting that she is the one who quietly dominates in her Manitoban homestead as a mother-queen: "Mrs. Elliot sat enthroned while Cathleen combed her hair, Isabel buttoned her shoes, and Henrietta laid out her dark-grey silks" (*ODB* 15). Admiring his wife's "quiet majesty" (*ODB* 264), her husband adopts the guise of the queen's humble servant and gets the carriage ready. Indeed, John Elliot and his eldest son John recognize that she, not Elliot, is the one with the power to hold the family together, and as if to prove them right, the family indeed disintegrates shortly after Martha's death. Yet *Our Daily Bread* does not celebrate the power of

---

25 McMullen 67.

matriarchy, but critically draws attention to the fact that Martha Elliot's power is not in ultimate contradiction with its apparent opposite, namely, patriarchy. Martha's matriarchal powers complement her husband's patriarchal domination in the family as they are appropriated by (and ultimately serve) John Elliot's territorial dream, supporting the determining structure of the patriarchal family.

In this context, it is significant that the patriarchal households in Grove's German and Canadian fiction are modelled on the classical Greek *oikos*, based on a European model that Grove translates into a Canadian context. The *oikos* is generally characterized by a dissymmetry in the relationship between husband and wife, as Foucault's analysis of Xenophon's *Oeconomicus* shows. Although the wife is a key figure in the management of the Greek (and Grovian) *oikos*, it is the husband who governs and guides the wife, as she becomes the "*synergos* he needs for the reasonable practice of economy." For the male, then, marriage implies "being the head of a family, having authority, exercising a power whose locus of application was in the 'home.'"[26] Appropriating this Greek model to conceptualize the entrapments of both the German bourgeois wife and the Canadian pioneer woman, Grove highlights the naturalist assimilation of women within patriarchal structures.

But while Grove insists on the women's enslavement as the "reality principle" of their lives, he also shows the opposite: it is the mothers who lay the seed for the daughters' resistance. When faced with death, Bertha Ihle, Martha Elliot and Mrs. Amundsen resist and break the established social, economic, and discursive patterns of the family *oikos*. Martha Elliot and Bertha Ihle, for instance, become what the German text describes as "'wunderlich,'" peculiar or odd, a term that encodes the women's disruption of "normalcy." In both cases, the women react against the patriarchal structures of their households by deliberately excluding their husbands and children from their lives. Slamming doors and making loud scenes with her husband, Mrs. Ihle openly rebels against her husband's oppression by appropriating his own tyrannical strategies, while Mrs. Elliot – Bartleby-like – quietly refuses any further (sexual) intimacies and personal contacts with her husband. Both husbands are impotent and baffled when faced with their wives' rebellion, as their language of command inevitably collapses: "Mr. Ihle countered these scenes simply by going out of the house, muttering and perturbed" (*MI* 97).

---

26 Michel Foucault, *The Use of Pleasure*, trans. Robert Hurley (New York: Vintage, 1986) 155, 151.

Nevertheless, just as any "carnivalesque" freedom is temporary, so a simple disruption of normalcy does not bring about genuine change in the family institution. Grove highlights Foucault's point that a simple reversal of the power relation does not lead to liberation but often perpetuates the structure of a power relation that can easily be reversed again: the nature of the power play itself does not change. The two rebelling wives do not manage to break out of the textual boundaries of naturalism, but are quickly recontained within predictable patterns: Mrs. Ihle assuming the role of the naturalist "madwoman" who eventually dies in a mental institution, and Mrs. Elliot finding herself entrapped in the role of the naturalist diseased female, confronted with the disintegration of her own body.

Dying of cancer, Martha Elliot struggles with new ways of articulating her rebellion against the patriarch's rule, trying to challenge the entrapping patterns of her family's lives. But her limits are mirrored in the inevitability of her own death: "she was turning and twisting in agony," the narrator writes, "Little sounds, like grunts, escaped her contorted mouth in staccato sequence" (*ODB* 115). Dying of abdominal cancer, she is reduced to a naturalist body of pain that she can escape only by transforming it through morphine into what John Elliot perceives as "a shapeless mass of relaxed muscle" (*ODB* 117). Conscious of her entrapment, Martha Elliot makes a metaphorical connection between her naturalist death and the deterministic course of her life with John Elliot. In a confessional scene (so typical for Grove's fiction), she tries to articulate her entrapment and her new skepticism by communicating it to Gladys, her eldest daughter:

> Oh, she [Martha] cried, I don't even know any longer whether there's a God or not. If there is, I don't care. Come here, listen. I want to whisper to you. You may think I've had so many children because I was fond of them. No! They just came. Because I lived an evil life with your father. Look at me! – And she suddenly bared her body: a terrible sight! (*ODB* 133)

On the surface, this expression of a naturalist entrapment in sexuality and her bitter self-condemnation as "the harlot of Babylon" may be seen as a result of sexual repressions that inevitably link sex with guilt and retributive punishment. However, this confession and Martha's rejection of her husband also "push against" the boundaries of the genre, in that they signal a moment of *anagnorisis* – Martha's recognition of her deep complicity with John Elliot's deterministic life course: after all, her sexuality was ruled by his commission to "Bear children" (*ODB* 183). Thus Martha's sexual language of self-condemnation is the closest she comes to expressing a mother's feeling of guilt for having borne ten children not for her own (or for the children's) sake, but as tools for Elliot's territorial dream of expansion.

Yet Martha does not manage to find a solidarity with her daughters, nor does she manage to formulate her newly found wisdom and her condemnation of Elliot's dream in an effective, resisting language. She rebels against Elliot by refusing to have him near her in the last months of her life, but is incapable of telling him what she accuses him of. After a long period of silence, she can only communicate her legacy to her children by falling back to the coherence of her "old" language that is ruled by the demands of the patriarchal *oikos*. Trying to warn two of her children not to lock themselves into the prisonhouse of doomed marriages, she tells her oldest son that his fiancée is "no farmer's wife," as she tells her daughter Isabel that her chosen partner lacks the proper "descent." Her language is ineffective as a true warning. Martha, then, remains caught in the naturalist prisonhouse of language, unable to prevent the cycle of entrapment in the next generation.

The mother's lack of an oppositional language and her aborted efforts at rebellion in the face of death anticipate the fate of her daughters; the recontainment of rebellion in the next generation takes a variety of different forms. While in *Maurermeister*, the father is presented as a static tyrant-figure, who in a last act of revenge tries to assault his daughter, the tyrant-father in *Our Daily Bread* eventually emerges as a figure of pathos who is supplanted by his powerful daughters. In *Our Daily Bread*, Grove deliberately characterizes Elliot as "a Lear of the prairies" to suggest that the daughters' continued neglect of an aging and senile father-figure can be seen as an act of passive aggression in which the women take their "revenge" for the emotional abuse they have suffered.

Yet despite these apparent reversals in power, Grove emphasizes that the changes are illusory. While most of Martha Elliot's daughters attempt to resist the notion of a patriarchal marriage, they remain entrapped in the same old snares. The androgynous Henrietta, for example, negotiates a contract so that she will at least keep her financial independence in her marriage, but her language of patriarchal resistance inevitably slips into the discourse of female prostitution, as Pete can only have her "provided [he] can pay the price" (*ODB* 62). Once they are married, their relationship turns into a continual power struggle in which Henrietta eventually asserts herself as a tyrannical "master of the house" and thus as the double of her father. Cathleen speaks the language of "a new ideal of manhood" (*ODB* 45), but only to subject her own discourse to this new master's discourse. Isabel, like her namesake Isabel Archer, adopts a discourse of romantic love, selflessly giving her "virgin love" to redeem her husband-to-be whom everyone else despises, only to find out that there is no redemption in marriage. Margaret, however, is somewhat different, presenting the most challenging alternative of the Elliot sisters. Refusing to get married, so as not to be subjugated by any man, she speaks in a deliberately patriarchal language. "I'll be my own master while I know my mind'" (*ODB* 110), she tells her brother-in-law when he suggests that a woman's destiny is inevitably marriage and motherhood. Yet her usage of the term "master" subverts the very idea of mastery, since she refuses to be involved in any master-slave relationship. Appropriating a masculine language to resist the patriarchal notion of a woman's destiny as a bearer of children, Margaret manages to walk a very fine line between parodic imitation of and co-optation by the patriarchal language.

In a sense, this is the strategy Susie Ihle attempts to use in her struggle for independence, and yet Susie's language oscillates between Henrietta's master discourse and Margaret's parodic imitation of it. Toward the end of *Maurermeister*, Susie's rebellion against her father becomes more and more open and defiant, but at the same time her own private language of resistance also becomes more "masculine," drawing very strongly on terms that feminist critic Hélène Cixous has identified as belonging to the masculine "economy of the proper": "Sie [Susie] wollte ein eigenes Haus haben: niemanden über sich: ihr eigener Herr sein: wer sie beherrschen wollte, der musste ihr imponieren" (*MI* 243).[27] The language used in this quotation is the discourse of mastering and being mastered, a discourse of ruling and commanding respect, of appropriation and property that lacks the parodic twist that Margaret's language has. Here we might ask with Hélène Cixous:

> If the position of mastery culturally comes back to men, what will become of (our) femininity when we find ourselves in this position?
> When we use a master discourse?[28]

---

27 I am quoting here in the original German because the English translation transforms Susie's obviously masculine discourse in German into feminine terms in English. In the following quotation, I italicize the most problematic words in the translation: "She wanted to have her own *home* ["Haus" evokes a property = house]; nobody over her: to be her own *mistress* [German "Herr" is masculine and is linked to the verb "herrschen" = to rule over]. Whoever wanted *to give her orders* ["beherrschen" not only has the masculine "herr" in it but literally translated means "to rule over"] must *impress* her ["impress" corresponds to the German "beindrucken" which Grove deliberately does not use in the German text; "imponieren" linked to Latin "impono" is a much stronger term and even has a touch of intimidation to it]" (*MI* 238).

28 Cixous, "Sorties," 136.

As Susie adopts the language of patriarchy without any apparent distance from this language, she is in danger of replicating the patriarchy, of accepting the master-slave power structure of her parental home, and is thus in danger of turning into a Henrietta-like character. She is tempted to marry Consul Blume because his title would give her the powerful status of "Frau Konsul," and the only reason she is loath to make the ultimate decision is that the Consul lacks the one thing that would make him a perfect husband (in her eyes): he lacks masculine aggression, or in other words, he refuses to be (like) her father.

The fact that Susie ultimately decides to marry the Consul suggests the end of resistance and the acceptance of a very unsatisfying reality principle. But if the novel presents a naturalist circle of repetition, it simultaneously signals an open-endedness that makes possible a more optimistic (and a more resisting) reading, one that emphasizes Susie's growth and her continued challenge of female containment within naturalist (and male) boundaries. It is during her very last confrontation with her father that Susie (re)discovers the traces of a new feminine voice of resistance, a language that is rooted in her childhood experience. Just as Julia Kristeva stresses the importance of negativity and disruption in relation to the masculine "symbolic order" as the most effective strategy of feminine resistance, so almost all of Susie's sentences in her last fight with her father are negations, a language that resists and exposes her father's hollow truths by simply negating his assertions. Asked to obey her new stepmother, Susie quietly responds by saying: "That's not my mother" (*MI* 240), adding, "My Mama's dead." Here, the new voice and strength of verbal resistance are rooted in her mother's memory, and it is this new voice that prompts Ihle's violent and physical attack, his "iron grip around her throat" (*MI* 241), as if he wants to cut off her new empowered voice.

The daughter's relationship with the father thus has come full circle, in that the father's last act is to turn from the mother's body to the daughter's body as the object on which to inscribe his sexualized power. Indeed, the language describing the father's attack is deliberately rapist: "But at that moment her father's great mass came lunging toward her. He seized her by the hair and flung her to the ground. Susie saw him standing over her, his face bloodshot and swollen" (*MI* 241). But the fact that his grip around her throat signifies a "release" (*MI* 242) to Susie suggests that for the first time in her life she has emotionally distanced herself from her father. The daughter leaves the father's house but also breaks with the predictable father-daughter text, in that her separation is not prompted by a powerful father-rival who claims possession of the daughter.

I do not, however, mean to read the ending in terms of a positive resolution and even less in terms of an ultimate female liberation. Susie's need to *attach* herself to a man is highly problematic, especially since she has barely *detached* herself from her parental home. But Susie has gained a new perspective on her father, and there is hope that she has come to see the Consul's lack of aggression in a different light, after she stops looking at him through her father's censoring eyes. As a rebelling daughter-figure, she does not break out of but remains on the very borders of the naturalist genre, hovering somewhere between rebellion and assimilation.

Though in his early and in his late novels, the mothers' resistance is not very effective, Grove gives this motif a much more radical twist in *Setters of the Marsh*. This novel presents the most explicit descriptions of sexualized violence, just as it presents the most challenging alternative in its exploration of female rebellion. Here the mother's legacy turns into a true discourse of power in her daughter's life. Although deeply victimized and doomed to die, Mrs. Amundsen sheds the romantic complicity of Bertha Ihle and the confusion and despair of Martha Elliot to communicate her legacy in a powerfully feminist text, when she tells her only child, "Make your own life, Ellen, and let nobody make it for you" (*S* 112). At the same time, the task of effecting change – and of breaking out of the naturalist convention of the female's victimization through her sexuality – is placed, once again, on the daughter's shoulders. Ellen, to be sure, embraces this legacy with enthusiasm and conviction, just as she embraces her farm work, consciously refusing the role of farmwife-cum-child-bearer. Androgynous, like Fanny Essler, she exchanges her woman's clothing for male overalls, thus changing roles and displaying a flexibility that is in stark contrast to the rigidity of both her father and her future husband.

Like her mother, Ellen articulates her rebellion against her father's sexualized violence in the form of a sexual confession. She, significantly, confesses to Niels Lindstedt, the novel's protagonist, who is in love with her. Unlike Fanny Essler's confessions, though, Ellen's language has a shocking, disruptive, even traumatic effect on the male listener. Contextualized by Niels's courtship, Ellen's confession assumes a power that Fanny's never had: it turns into what Foucault has termed "an insurrection of subjugated knowledges." She articulates what she has kept silent for years, deliberately destroying the fantasy image of her father. Her story confronts Niels with the reality of her father's sexual assaults, her mother's abortions and eventual death. In a language of authenticity and truth, saturated with naturalist images of torture, pain, and slow bodily disintegration, she disrupts Niels's romanticized ideal of marriage and his fantasy of a home with children. While his romance is best encapsulated in the enormous white house he built for Ellen, she brings his male fantasy down to earth by exposing to him the ugly reality of her mother's marriage and sexuality.

One way of reading the novel is to see Ellen in exclusively sexualized terms, to identify her "sexual repression" as part of a naturalist causal chain that leads to Niels's downfall. And yet such a reading glosses over the novel's feminist subtext. After all, it is Ellen who opens the dialogue, while Niels feels threatened by the implied changes she asks for. He has no words, but runs away in panic, retreating into a discourse of determinism that leads to his marriage (and eventual murder) of Clara Vogel. Those readers who emphasize Ellen's "frigidity" as the causal root of Niels's problem become complicitous with Niels's (and naturalism's) misogynist conception of "normal" sexuality. Such an approach also glosses over the fact that Ellen is pioneering while Niels is backward-bound. The passionate tone of her speech, her plea for friendship, and her desire for change suggest that it is not so much sexual intimacy that she rejects when she declines Niels' marriage proposal, but the patriarchal notion of sexualized power that ruled her mother's life on the family farm. In other words, Ellen's sexual confession is an act of feminist rebellion that does not create Niels's tragic enchainment in a naturalist plot, as the novel's overt text suggests, but that tries to pre-empt it.

Indeed, Ellen's feminist voice of resistance – "No man, whether I liked him or loathed him, was ever to have power over me!" (*S* 112) – goes to the core of Niels's (and naturalism's) sexual misogyny. It is no coincidence that she should "confess" to Niels, since her confession is intended to disrupt the binary divisions of Niels's patriarchal thinking (best encapsulated in his entanglement in the "madonna-whore complex" that determines his relationship with women). In order to achieve change, she must disillusion Niels, since he is, after all, a prototypical representative of patriarchy: he is the "strong man," he is what Reelen is for Fanny Essler, he is the father-ersatz for the daughter-lover, he is, in other words, Amundsen's younger double. Although his sexual repression is opposed to Amundsen's continued rape of his wife, Niels, like Amundsen, conceives of sexuality as an abstract principle, a "natural" right and duty, not as pleasure. Also, Niels is a powerful "empire-builder," like Ellen's father, and shares Amundsen's rigidity and determination in expanding his farm.

Even more importantly, though, Niels doubles Amundsen when he kills his wife in an act of sexualized violence. The novel dwells on Niels's anger, his rage, his "desire to kill, to crush," feelings that precede his murder. This rage is, significantly, prompted by his realization that his wife, Clara Vogel, "did not acknowledge his right to demand: he had no authority over her" (*S* 159). The narrative voice (and the novel's emphasis on Niels's perspective) are deeply complicitous with Niels's sexualized violence, as in the following passage that precedes the murder of Clara: "If at that moment Niels had struck; if he had gone straight to her and torn her finery off her body, sternly, ruthlessly, and ordered her to do menial service on the farm, he would have conquered ..." (*S* 152). The narrative voice presents sexualized violence as a possible solution to Niels's marital problems by invoking the misogynistic cliche that what a woman really wants is to be conquered by a man in an act in which passion merges with aggression.

The novel's plot partly endorses the same misogynistic ideology: Niels can exorcize his problem only by killing Clara, by completing the naturalist plot. In narratological terms, Niels's action is predetermined according to the logic of naturalism's sexual plot. The destruction of the sexualized, prostituted female is a textual inevitability that entails narrative sympathy for the victimizer. It should come as no surprise, then, that Niels's murder of his wife has often been read as an unpremeditated act that belongs to a naturalistic world beyond the character's realm of free will and moral consciousness. When shooting his wife in an act of jealousy, Niels is represented as a character who acts under a compulsion beyond his control: "Irresistibly a clockwork began to move. There was not a spark of consciousness in Niels. He acted entirely under the compulsion of the spring" (*S* 186). He is tied to a woman who is sexually active and whom he has identified as the town prostitute; the murderous act is the logical consequence of the entrapment Niels feels in his marriage. Narrative manipulations, then, prepare the reader to accept Niels's eventual redemption.

And yet, in its treatment of sexualized power, *Settlers of the Marsh* also unravels its ideological contradictions: the novel does not unequivocally affirm this misogynistic vision but deconstructs it through the women's feminist voices. More specifically, Clara Vogel assumes the voice of a new woman, which is deeply unsettling not only for Niels but also for the narrative's ideological cohesion. Like Fanny Essler and Ellen Amundsen, Clara falls in love with the sexualized fantasy image of Niels as "the strong man" but quickly discovers that she has married a puritanical misogynist. She is quick in communicating her disillusioning analysis: "it is that ridiculous man-nature in you," she tells him "You married me. You don't want me any longer. But I am not to belong to any one else. I am to be your property, your slave-property" (*S* 153). Insisting on her sexuality and her independence, Clara, like Ellen, challenges the predictable gender pattern, thus threatening Niels's order of things. In its exploration of sexualized violence in the domestic household, then, the novel inevitably deconstructs itself by juxtaposing Clara Vogel's and Ellen's demands for different female and sexual rights with a male narrative voice that partly condones sexualized violence against women.

Like *Maurermeister*, *Settlers* ends with an overt sense of closure that suggests a deliberate break with pessimistic naturalism and a movement into new generic and ideological transformations. After Niels's "conversion" and release from prison, he is finally reconciled with Ellen. In her feminist reading of the ending, Gaile McGregor has argued that, on a covert level, the ending presents a gender reversal of the Harlequin romance structure, which she identifes as typically Canadian: "Dominant female/submissive male: this would seem to be the only kind of marriage that 'works' in the Canadian context." By the end, so McGregor argues, Niels surrenders to Ellen "his male prerogative of initiation and structuring action."[29] Indeed, it is Ellen who speaks and Niels who listens; it is Ellen who wants "to see wide, open, level spaces" (*S* 215) and thus looks into the future, while he appears to follow her lead.

But in many ways, the novel also undermines this comic solution, turning into what Blodgett has termed "frustrated comedy," or what Baguley has described as the naturalist ending's propensity for "instigating a new (dis)order." While Niels no longer insists on his prerogatives (in fact, he lacks speech, "not [trusting] himself to speak" [*S* 215]), the ending also exposes how much his silences co-opt with patriarchal conventions. The only sin Niels acknowledges and repents by the end is his sexual weakness: "As for the thing that has sent me here [to the prison]. I don't blame myself" (*S* 201). His refusal to repent his murder of Clara creates a problematic gap that suggests that he has not really moved beyond his own (or Amundsen's) misogyny.

Equally problematic is the fact that by the end, Clara's voice of resistance has been effectively silenced, while Ellen has turned away from her mother's legacy. The invocation of comically resolved gender harmony – "No need for words" (*S* 216) – is deeply troubling in light of the fact that throughout the novel powerful speech has been the women's prerogative. Recognizing that her "destiny" is to have children, Ellen turns away from her mother's voice of protest to embrace her "woman's" destiny as a child bearer for the man who is the double of her patriarchal father. Also, the process of forgiveness that makes possible Niels's re-

---

29 Gail McGregor, *The Wacousta Syndrome: Explorations in the Canadian Langscape* (Toronto: U of Toronto P, 1985) 149, 148.

joining of the human community is initiated in the novel by men. Niels is first absolved of his sexualized violence by the prison warden, whose conception of justice relies on the same patriarchal god that Amundsen invoked when raping his wife. Thus, Ellen and Clara's feminist texts in *Settlers of the Marsh* are undercut by the ending's naturalist circularity. The male – patriarchal – reality principle triumphs, with the feminist voices of rebellion safely recontained within the genre's boundaries.

Finally, matters become even more complex when we consider the (auto)biographical subtexts of *Maurermeister Ihles Haus* and *Settlers of the Marsh*. While the German novel traces the childhood of Elsa von Freytag-Loringhoven, the Canadian novel fictionalizes Grove's separation from her, so that Niels becomes a double of the author, who exorcizes the memory of his own wife Elsa by metaphorically "killing" her in his naturalist novel in the figure of Clara Vogel. The naturalist author thus becomes a problematic double of his murderer-protagonist. Similarly, Clara's feminist words are very Elsa-like, as a comparison with Elsa's autobiography reveals. Like Clara, who exposes Niels's misogyny, Elsa criticized her lover FPG as "too limited masculine" and "too strictly conventional," as when she describes, in her memoirs, his lack of humour and his compulsive working habits as well as his "sinister will power," all of which combine to create a "jailer attitude" for Elsa (*A* 94– 110). Like Niels, whose "sexual instincts were dead" (*S* 165) when confronted with Clara's sex drive, Felix told Elsa in Kentucky, "I don't need any woman" (*A* 72), keeping her sexually at a distance. Lastly, Elsa describes in her autobiography the confrontation between her and FPG on a small farm in Kentucky: "it is hard to believe that a glorious castle, built as for life can topple and vanish in disgrace – as it did – shattering into its last shame-bespattered distorted pieces in America! He had to make the experience that true quality in a woman cannot be bullied or bluffed. ... He was as incapable to grant a woman her right to personality as was my father" (*A* 109). Thus the author, FPG, has once again come full circle. From a critic of patriarchal father-figures in his early fiction, Grove increasingly identifies with them; from a defender of the woman's cause, he turns into an authorial silencer of the feminist voice; from a parodic transformer of the naturalist genre, he turns back to it as a haven of traditional male conventions.

"My sympathies were always with the women. Yet I was no sentimentalist; in my books I gave the facts and let them speak for themselves," Grove writes in his (fictionalized) autobiography (*ISM* 224). And so he does, with the effect that the women's voices erupt to contradict the male voices, including the narrative voice. At the same time, however, *Maurermeister*, *Settlers*, and *Our Daily Bread* also illustrate how much

Grove's "facts" encode a male bias. Grove presents us with women who are discursively subversive and playful and who continually undermine and disrupt male self-seriousness, but his naturalism also limits these women's subversive powers. The mother-figures, Martha Elliot, Mrs. Amundsen, and Bertha Ihle, are doomed to die once they break out of discursive normalcy, while the daughters' voices of resistance are safely recontained within male systems of order. Susie Ihle's story ends abruptly once she has found a very precarious voice with which to confront her father, so that the seeds of her discursive resistance are never allowed to grow in the novel. Ellen Amundsen's voice finally co-opts with the patriarchal voice as she embraces the woman's patriarchal destiny – to be a bearer of Niels's children. Margaret Elliot, the most independent woman in *Our Daily Bread*, really lives on the border of the novel; her independence is relegated into the gaps of Grove's text, suggesting that (without Elsa's continued help and stimulus) Grove was either not willing or not capable of writing a woman's parodic mimicking of the patriarchal language. The exploration of women's discursive resistance in *Maurermeister* and *Our Daily Bread* affirms Grove's deep interest in, and sympathy with, the plight of female characters in the patriarchal household, but the novels also point to his limitations as a male author trying to write the female voice of resistance. Thus, despite the feminist subtexts, these novels force us to recognize the author's own ambivalent nostalgia for patriarchal – and narrative – power structures.

13

Conclusion

In this study I have examined some of the continuities and transformations in naturalism's journey from Europe to Canada and America and from the nineteenth to the twentieth century. As a predominantly male genre, naturalism continued its preoccupation with the female's "problematic" sexuality. In an age concerned with the "truth" of the female body, Dreiser and Grove carved out a niche for their fiction by making use of women's new voices, incorporating women's sexual confessions into an already sexualized genre. Thus, they participated in and further stimulated the twentieth-century psychoanalytic and sexological desire to hear the woman's body speak the authentic truth about itself. Yet while energizing the naturalist genre, the women's (feminist) voices often present an unsettling voice of *Widerstand* in these texts. Contradicting male concepts of power as well as the male narrator's standards of biological or behavioural normality, these female voices create the dialogical quality so typical of Dreiser and Grove's naturalism.

The desire to upset taboos and to present an "entropic vision" in naturalist literature has been shown to be often in contradiction with the narrators' and authors' own desire for establishing specifically male

233

systems of order. It is, above all, in his treatment of female sexuality and female rights that the male naturalist writer exposes his desire for "normalizing" the female body. The narrator-author of "Emanuela" speaks for most of Dreiser's fictional narrators (and for most of his male characters) when he claims to disrupt society's Victorian conventions by speaking the truth about sex, a truth that promises to "liberate" the body from repressive social constraints. Yet for most of the female characters this celebrated sexual liberation is an illusion, as their bodies and sexualities are evoked only in terms of a goal that prompts the males to impose their own sexualities and to search in women's bodies for what D.H. Lawrence – another problematic sexual "liberator" – has called the "bedrock of her nature." Insisting on imposing the norms of what they claim to be a "normal" sexuality, Dreiser's narrators and male characters elevate their own, male sexuality as the "true" standard, thereby not only erasing any notion of a plural (women's) sexuality but covertly also marginalizing female sexual activity into the "abnormal." To a large extent, Dreiser's narrators' affirm, even celebrate, a male sexuality, as they affirm the Don Juan philosophy of most of the male characters with all its misogynistic implications. The women's resistance often exposes naturalism's male bias, but as often the female voices are successfully recontained within the boundaries of the male genre, enchained in patterns of subjugation that are reminiscent of nineteenth-century French naturalism.

Exploring the role of discourses, practices, and norms as the privileged psychological and social determinants of their twentieth-century naturalism, Dreiser and Grove's fiction displaced the nineteenth-century emphasis on genetic and hereditary physiology. The authors' twentieth-century naturalism is consonant with Foucault's recognition that discourse is always yoked to power. Their fiction explores how discourses structure relationships of power, how these power relationships in turn "produce" specific forms of discursive resistance and how a resisting discourse can shift once again and become reappropriated by the dominant discourse. Dreiser and Grove's naturalism explores a great variety of oppositional strategies while continually emphasizing the limits of such resistance. In their struggle against seductive (and equally restrictive) forms of patriarchal power, many of the female characters (e.g., Fanny Essler, Susie Ihle, Emanuela) consciously reject the language that others (fathers, lovers, bourgeois society) impose on them, deliberately refusing to be a dutiful daughter, a "seduced" woman, a "prostitute," a "wife," or a traditional "housekeeper." Other resisting female characters appropriate the language of the (male) masters to engage in a ruthless power struggle (e.g., Henrietta Elliot), only to demonstrate that such a strategy perpetuates and energizes the very power principle they set out to subvert. The women's "reverse" discourses, once put into circulation, quickly "run the risk of re-codification, re-colonization" (*P/K* 86). In most cases, the naturalist cycle closes itself, with the male systems of (narrative, generic, and social) order once again in place.

In a work with the suggestive title *Forget Foucault*, Jean Baudrillard has charged that "with Foucault, power remains, despite being pulverized, a *structural* and a polar notion with a perfect genealogy and an inexplicable presence, a notion which cannot be surpassed in spite of a sort of latent denunciation, a notion which is whole in each of its points or microscopic dots."[1] Baudrillard's critique is well taken. Although Foucault insists on power's "nonessential" quality, Foucauldian power often appears as an abstract machine that takes hold of everything, infiltrating the microcosm of the social field. "Everyone today wallows in the molecular as they do in the revolutionary," Baudrillard writes, adding that, "for Foucault, power operates right away like Monod's genetic code," that is, like the "complex spirals of the DNA."[2] Polemical though it may be, Baudrillard's critique could also be voiced against naturalism's conceptualization of power as a network of force relations that cannot be escaped because it reaches into the microcosmic areas of physical bodies – the genetic, physiological body in the nineteenth and the psychological body in the twentieth century. For Foucault and naturalism there is no outside of power, since resistance is always already part of a larger system of power. In naturalism's "equation inevitable," even the individual capitalist superman is but a "giant pygmy," who rises in order to fall, to die, and to be superseded by others. What always stays, though, is the machinery of power itself.

Is it surprising, then, that new historicist Walter Benn Michaels should have drawn the somewhat cynical conclusion that Dreiser's naturalism is inevitably informed by the logic of the marketplace? In other words, is the Dreiserian or Foucauldian world, perhaps, a universe in which the word *resistance* has been emptied of meaning since, ultimately, power cannot be escaped? Michaels frames his interpretation of Dreiser's naturalism by declaring the end of oppositional criticism:

> What exactly did it mean to think of Dreiser as approving (or disapproving) consumer culture? Although transcending your origins in order to evaluate them has been the opening move in cultural criticism at least

---

1 Jean Baudrillard, *Forget Foucault* (New York: Semiotext[e]: 1987) 39.

2 Baudrillard 33–34.

since Jeremiah, it is surely a mistake to take this move at face value: not so much because you can't really transcend your culture but because, if you could, you wouldn't have any terms of evaluation left – except perhaps theological ones. It thus seems wrong to think of the culture you live in as the object of your affections: you don't like it or dislike, you exist in it, and the things you like and dislike exist in it too. Even Bartleby-like refusals of the world remain inextricably linked to it – what could count as a more powerful exercise of the right to freedom of contract than Bartleby's successful refusal to enter into any contracts?[3]

But as Gerald Graff has pointed out in his critique of Michaels's approach, it appears that the critic who professes to distrust transcendental categories ends by adopting the "market" as a transcendental category.[4]

If anything, this study has attempted to highlight that Dreiser's naturalism should not be reduced to a monological voice or a single dominant discourse of power. Even if resistance is shown to have its inevitable limits, the oppositional voices (often the female voices in this male genre) present overt and covert forms of insurrection, contradicting and baffling the dominant (male) voices, challenging the notion of a unified order. It is these oppositional voices that, in turn, make possible a resisting reading that unravels the text from within, highlighting what naturalism chooses to relegate into its margins. Dreiser's naturalism is full of contradictions and tensions: between the male narrators' omniscient voices and the erupting female voices; between the narrators' rejection of conventions and their embracing of (biological notions of) normality; between the female characters' claim for independence and their subjection to male sexual conquering in "normalized" relationships. It is the texts' internal contradictions and tensions that inevitably unravel their inherent gender bias, and thus the texts themselves expose their narrators' and characters' misogyny from within.

In Grove's fiction, the artist is born in the midst of such contradictions, as *In Search of Myself* demonstrates. Writing his fictionalized autobiography, while identifying himself with his "tragic" male protagonists, the narrator is confronted with his own apocalypse: "In this record, I know, I am dying to myself" (*ISM* 387). In *In Search of Myself*, Grove conceptualized writing as an eternal process of self-doubling, whereby

---

3 *The Gold Standard and the Logic of Naturalism: American Literature at the Turn of the Century* (Berkeley: U of California P, 1987) 18–19.

4 Gerald Graff, "Co-optation," *The New Historicism*, ed. H. Aram Veeser (New York: Routledge, 1989) 168–81.

creation becomes a kind of *mise en abîme* in the face of death. In such a *mise en abîme*, "language turns back upon itself," as Foucault writes: "it encounters something like a mirror; and to stop this death which would stop it, it possesses but a single power: that of giving birth to its own image in a play of mirrors that has no limits."[5] Obsessed in his fiction with his (autobiographical, confessional, and simultaneously fictionalized) persona, Grove creates words that are put in the service of his "search" of himself and his male identity. This search, though, returns him inevitably to the secure and predictable male power structures provided by the naturalist genre, a genre Grove originally wanted to leave behind. The (incestuous) doubling of the author in his narrators and characters thus leads him back to a doubling of the naturalist conventions and the same stock figures.

Grove's conceptualizing of problematic female sexuality and patriarchal power structures has as much to do with cultural realities in Germany and Canada as it does with the author's own ideological contradictions. Just as Dreiser was deeply implicated in the popular and sentimental tradition that he tried so hard to overcome, so Grove was involved in undoing and simultaneously holding on to naturalism's sexual boundaries. His challenge of the "nature of naturalism" is reflected in his exploration of sexual impersonations, cross-dressing, and androgyny. But Grove's (somewhat contradictory) shaping of the genre has to be seen as an ambivalent gesture, growing out of his own sense of sexual and creative crisis. Faced with a strong female competition in Canada (where many bestselling authors were women), Grove reacted in many ways defensively, trying to hold on to naturalism's traditional sexual/textual boundaries. Grove was intent on erecting boundaries between his male realism (which, much to the author's chagrin, never produced a bestseller) and Canada's romance literature by women (which was successful in the marketplace, as the example of Lucy Maud Montgomery shows). Having to compete with such overwhelmingly popular successes of what he considered to be a female genre, Grove appropriated the realist treatment of sexuality as his – *male* – domain and prerogative. This may explain his deep jealousy and defensiveness when faced with the success of Martha Ostenso's naturalist novel, *Wild Geese* (1925), which coincided with the publication of his *Settlers of the Marsh*. Claiming that "only trash wins a prize," Grove reveals how deeply

---

5 Michel Foucault, "Language to Infinity," *Language, Counter-Memory, Practice*, trans. and ed. Donald F. Bouchard (Ithaca: Cornell UP, 1988) 54.

he felt threatened by the success of the twenty-five-year-old female writer who dared tread on what he considered to be "male territory" – the realistic representation of sexuality in Canadian fiction. "How could a young girl know anything of the fierce antagonisms that discharge themselves in sex,"[6] he wrote, implicitly "charging" his own discourse with the tropes of his own phallic prerogatives.

Martha Ostenso, of course, was serious competition. *Wild Geese* takes its roots in the male genre, presenting a Grovian father figure in old Caleb, who tyrannizes his family, especially the daughters, on his farm on the Canadian prairies. At the same time, Ostenso was also committed to "feminizing" the male naturalist genre from within, by giving the women stronger voices. Thus, the ending of *Wild Geese* presents an interesting twist in the naturalist genre: nature participates in the destruction of the male family tyrant, so that "the nature of naturalism" is made to serve a female vision of justice and order. Although Ostenso shared Grove's view of the mother's complicity in the daughter's victimization, the women in the novel emerge as survivor figures, quietly triumphing after Caleb's death.

Even before F. P. Grove's death in 1948, another Manitoban writer, Gabrielle Roy, further continued this "feminization" of Canadian naturalism. In her classic, *The Tin Flute* (1945), sexuality continues to be the realm through which the female body is seduced, exploited, subjugated, and victimized. But the emphasis is, like Ostenso's, on the women's capacity to survive. From Grove's father figure, Roy moves the mother, Rose-Anna Lacasse, into the centre of the naturalist universe. Indeed, the narrative voice itself becomes feminized. Roy's narrator is no longer in a position of male superiority, but is, as Patricia Smart writes, "much better evoked by Rose-Anna Lacasse's image of God – a somewhat harassed mother at the beck and call of all her children/characters at the same time, trying to soothe their pain with her loving attentiveness."[7]

While these two Canadian examples show further possibilities of "feminizing" the genre from within, Grove and Dreiser have to be credited with questioning, criticizing, even deconstructing the genre's male convention in the early twentieth century. But the two male naturalist-realists also reinscribed these male conventions anew into the genre, thus perpetuating its "maleness" in the twentieth century. It is these conventions that became "canonized" as the specifically American and Canadian forms of naturalism. Dreiser's canonization as "the" Ameri-

---

6 Quoted in Makow 41.

7 Patricia Smart, *Writing in the Father's House* (Toronto: U of Toronto P, 1991) 161.

can naturalist and city writer was assured after his publication of *An American Tragedy*; Grove's canonization as the realist historiographer of Canadian prairie-pioneer life was not far behind. But Grove's overt assertion that on the pioneer farm "woman is a slave," as he defended his position in *In Search of Myself*, is not only contradicted by his own writing, but was also challenged by contemporary women realists, such as Willa Cather, who celebrated the female as a strong pioneer figure in *O Pioneers!* (1913).

Lastly, and perhaps most ironically, as naturalist writers Dreiser and Grove found themselves caught in naturalist circles of their own. Both writers carried the symptoms of their sexual/textual tensions and crises inscribed on their bodies: Dreiser suffered from chronic headaches, stomach upsets, and neurothenia, while Grove obsessively bemoaned his bodily failings in his autobiographical writing. While Dreiser's crisis frequently found its expression in bouts of writer's block, Grove's found an outlet for his tension in an obsessive commitment to writing – he was and remained a "workaholic" throughout his life. In their naturalist fiction, they inscribe the "threat" of the new woman but also exorcize this threat through naturalist strategies: the strong, stubbornly rebelling woman is often doomed to die (e.g., Roberta Alden, Clara Vogel, Martha Elliot), while the newly empowered woman is frequently "tamed" through more sophisticated "normalizing" practices (Carrie Meeber, Fanny Essler). And yet the new woman's body, sexuality, and voice constitute a threat in the context of male naturalism that is only barely contained, as she continually "spills" over the boundaries of their narratives, confronting and challenging the male narrative voice with a different kind of truth.

In Grove's case, this "feminizing" of the genre from within energized the author's creative process. The new woman's power and threatening sexuality necessitated more and more words, spirals of sexual confessions, stories of sexual entrapment and victimization, which allowed the author to recontain the female body and to assert his male voice of authority and his male vision of order in his naturalist fiction. Thus, it should come as no surprise that Grove's own life was characterized by a private renunciation of sexuality "for the sake of art"; this "antisexuality" in his personal life is reflected both in his autobiography, *In Search of Myself*, and in Elsa's memoirs. Conversely, Dreiser's personal history was that of a Don Juan womanizer, which made him a double of his male characters, as he, like his male characters, tried to "conquer" the female body through his phallic power. This doubling of his male characters, however, is a dangerous venture for any naturalist author, since the power of his character is always already limited, his downfall from superior height prescribed by the logic of naturalist conventions. The authorial role thus becomes slippery, hovering uneasily on the border of the genre, confronting the author with his own fears and failings. These elements are not radically new in the twentieth century; the male fear of feminization was a characteristic of nineteenth-century French naturalism. But this crisis becomes more overt as the narrators and authors become more conscious of narrative contradictions. Thus the version of male naturalism that emerges in this twentieth-century tension is one that simultaneously questions and affirms, appropriates and rewrites, deconstructs and reconstructs the nineteenth-century naturalist connection between male power and the female's sexual "nature."

Bibliography

Select Bibliography on Sexuality and Power in Foucault, Feminism and Other Theory

Apter, Emily. *Feminizing the Fetish: Psychoanalysis and Narrative Obsession in Turn-of-the-Century France*. Ithaca: Cornell UP, 1991.

Bakhtin, Mikhail M. *The Dialogic Imagination: Four Essays*. Trans. Caryl Emerson and Michael Holquist. Austin: U of Texas P, 1981.

——. *Problems of Dostoevsky's Poetics*. Trans. Caryl Emerson. Minneapolis: U of Minnesota P, 1987.

Banner, Lois W. *American Beauty*. New York: Alfred Knopf, 1983.

Barzilai, Shuli. "Borders of Language: Kristeva's Critique of Lacan." *PMLA* 106 (1991): 294–305.

Baudrillard, Jean. *Forget Foucault*. New York: Semiotext(e), 1987.

Beauvoir, Simone de. *The Second Sex*. Ed. and trans. H. M. Parshley. New York: Vintage Books, 1974.

Berger, John, et al. *Ways of Seeing*. London: BBC and Penguin, 1981.

241

Boose, Lynda E. "The Father's House and the Daughter in It: The Structures of Western Culture's Daughter-Father Relationship." Boose and Flowers 19–74.

Boose, Lynda, and Betty S. Flowers, ed. *Daughters and Fathers*. Baltimore & London: Johns Hopkins UP, 1989.

Bordo, Susan. "Anorexia Nervosa: Psychopathology as the Crystallization of Culture." *The Philosophical Forum* 17 (1985–86): 73–103.

Carter, Angela. *The Sadeian Woman: An Exercise in Cultural History*. London: Virago, 1979.

Cixous, Hélène. "The Laugh of the Medusa." Marks and de Courtivron 245–64.

——. "Sorties: Out and Out: Attacks/Ways Out/Forays." *The Newly Born Woman*. Hélène Cixous and Catherine Clément. Trans. Betsy Wing. Minneapolis: U of Minnesota P, 1988. 61–132.

Coward, Rosalind. *Female Desire*. London: Granada, 1984.

Deleuze, Gilles. *Foucault*. Minneapolis: U of Minnesota P, 1988.

Diamond, Irene, and Lee Quinby, ed. *Feminism and Foucault: Reflections on Resistance*. Boston: Northeastern UP, 1988.

Dijkstra Bram. *Idols of Perversity: Fantasies of Feminine Evil in Fin-de-Siècle Culture*. New York & Oxford: Oxford UP, 1986.

Dock Smiley, Terry. *Women in the "Encyclopédie": A Compendium*. Maryland: José Porrúa Turanzas, 1983.

Dreyfus, Hubert, and Paul Rabinow. *Michel Foucault: Beyond Structuralism and Hermeneutics*. Chicago: U of Chicago P, 1983.

Dubinsky, Karen. "'Maidenly Girls' or 'Designing Women'? The Crime of Seduction in Turn-of-the-Century Ontario." *Gender Conflicts: New Essays in Women's History*. Ed. Franca Iacovetta and Mariana Valverde. Toronto: U Toronto P, 1992.

DuBois, Ellen Carol, and Linda Gordon. "Seeking Ecstasy on the Battlefield: Danger and Pleasure in Nineteenth Century Feminist Sexual Thought." *Pleasure and Danger: Exploring Female Sexuality*. Ed. Carole S. Vance. Boston: Routledge & Kegan Paul, 1984. 31–49.

During, Simon. *Foucault and Literature: Towards a Genealogy of Writing*. London & New York: Routledge, 1992.

Felski, Rita. *Beyond Feminist Aesthetics: Feminist Literature and Social Change*. Cambridge, MA: Harvard UP, 1989.

Fetterley, Judith. *The Resisting Reader: A Feminist Approach to American Fiction*. Bloomington: Indiana University Press, 1978.

Foucault, Michel. *Discipline and Punish: The Birth of the Prison*. Trans. Alan Sheridan. New York: Vintage Books, 1979.

——. "The Subject and Power." Dreyfus and Rabinow 208–26.

——. "On the Genealogy of Ethics: An Overview of Work in Progress." Dreyfus and Rabinow 229–52.

——. *Foucault Live (Interviews, 1966–84)*. New York: Semiotext[e], 1989.

——. *Language, Countermemory, Practice*. Ithaca: Cornell UP, 1988.

——. *Politics, Philosophy, Culture: Interviews and Other Writings 1977–1984*. New York: Routledge, 1988.

——. *Power/Knowledge: Selected Interviews and Other Writings 1972–1977*. New York: Pantheon Books, 1980.

——. "The Ethic of Care for the Self as a Practice of Freedom: An Interview with Michel Foucault on January 20, 1984." *The Final Foucault*. Trans. J. D. Gauthier. Ed. James Bernauer and David Rasmussen. Cambridge, MA & London: MIT Press, 1988. 1–20.

——. *The History of Sexuality, Vol. 1: An Introduction*. Trans. Robert Hurley. New York: Vintage, 1980.

——. *The History of Sexuality, Vol. 2: The Use of Pleasure*. Trans. Robert Hurley. New York: Vintage, 1986.

——. *The Order of Things: An Archaeology of the Human Sciences*. New York: Vintage, 1973.

——. "The Political Technology of Individuals." *Technologies of the Self: A Seminar with Michel Foucault*. Ed. Luther H. Martin et al., Amherst: U of Massachusetts P, 1988. 145–62.

Freud, Sigmund. *Civilization and Its Discontents*. Trans. Joan Riviere. Ed. James Strachey. London: Hogarth Press & Institute of Psycho-Analysis, 1979.

——. *The Basic Writings of Sigmund Freud*. Ed. and trans. A. A. Brill. New York: Random House, 1938.

——. *Gesammelte Werke*. Chronologisch geordnet. Frankfurt: Fischer Verlag, 1941.

Froula, Christine. "The Daughter's Seduction: Sexual Violence and Literary History." Boose and Flowers 111–135.

Gallop, Jane. *Reading Lacan*. Ithaca & London: Cornell UP, 1988.

——. "The Father's Seduction." Boose and Flowers 97–110.

Girard, René. *Deceit, Desire, and the Novel: Self and Other in Literary Structure*. Trans. Yvonne Freccero. Baltimore & London: Johns Hopkins UP, 1976.

Glicksberg, Charles I. *The Sexual Revolution in Modern American Literature*. The Hague: Martinus Nijhoff, 1971.

Graff, Gerald. "Co-optation." *The New Historicism*. Ed. Aram Veeser. New York: Routledge, 1989. 168–81.

Haug, Frigga, et al. *Female Sexualization: A Collective Work of Memory*. Trans. Erica Carter. London: Verso, 1987.

Hauser, Kornelia. "Sexuality and Power." Haug et al. 185–230.

Heidegger, Martin. "Building Dwelling Thinking." *Basic Writings*. Ed. J. Glenn Gray. New York: Harper & Row, 1977. 319–39.

Heller, Peter. "A Quarrel Over Bisexuality." *The Turn of the Century: German Literature and Art, 1890–1915*. Ed. Gerald Chapple and Hans Schulte. Bonn: Bouvier Verlag, 1981. 87-117.

Hutton, Patrick H. "Foucault, Freud, and the Technologies of the Self." *Technologies of the Self, A Seminar with Michel Foucault*. Ed. Luther H. Martin et al. Amherst: U of Massachusetts P, 1988. 121–44.

Irigaray, Luce. *Ce sexe qui n'en est pas un*. Paris: Les Éditons de Minuit, 1977. Rpt. *This Sex Which Is Not One*. Trans. Catherine Porter with Carolyn Burke. Ithaca: Cornell UP, 1985.

——. "Luce Irigaray." Interview. *French Philosophers in Conversation*. Ed. Raoul Mortley. London & New York: Marthy, 1991. 62–78.

——. *Speculum of the Other Woman*. Trans. Gillian C. Gil. Ithaca: Cornell UP, 1989.

Jaeger, Patricia, and Beth Kowaleski-Wallace, ed. *Refiguring the Father: New Feminist Readings of Patriarchy*. Carbondale: Southern Illinois UP, 1989.

Kristeva, Julia. "La femme, ce n'est jamais ca" [Woman can never be defined]. Interview. *Tel Qel* (Autumn 1974). Rpt. Marks and Courtivron 137–41.

——. "Within the Microcosm of 'The Talking Cure.'" *Interpreting Lacan*. Trans. Thomas Gora and Margaret Waller. Ed. Joseph H. Smith and William Kerrigan. New Haven: Yale UP, 1983. 33–48.

Kulessa, Hanne. "Nachwort." *Tagebuch einer Verlorenen*. Margarete Böhme. Frankfurt: Suhrkamp, 1989.

Lacan, Jacques. *Écrits: A Selection*. Trans. Alan Sheridan. New York & London: Norton, 1977.

Lang, Ursel. "The Hair Project." Haug et al. 91–112.

Laplanche, Jean, and J. B. Pontalis. *The Language of Psycho-Analysis*. Trans. Donald Nicholson-Smith. New York: Norton, 1973.

Lydon, Mary. "Foucault and Feminism: A Romance of Many Dimensions." Diamond and Quinby. 135–47.

Marks, Elaine, and Isabelle de Courtivron, ed. *New French Feminisms: An Anthology*. New York: Schocken Books, 1981.

Martin, Biddy. "Feminism, Criticism, and Foucault." *New German Critique* 27 (1982): 3–30.

McNay, Lois. *Foucault and Feminism: Power, Gender and the Self*. Cambridge: Polity Press, 1992.

Mencken, H. L. "Puritanism as a Literary Force." *A Book of Prefaces*. New York: Alfred Knopf, 1917. 195–283.

Moi, Toril. *Sexual/Textual Politics: Feminist Literary Theory*. London & New York: Methuen, 1985.

Nietzsche, Friedrich. *Die Fröhliche Wissenschaft.* In *Nietzsche.* Frankfurt: Fischer, 1957. 93–131. Rpt. *The Gay Science.* Trans. Walter Kaufmann. New York: Vintage, 1974.

Perkins Gilman, Charlotte. *The Yellow Wallpaper.* Old Westbury, NY: Feminist Press, 1973.

Pykett, Lyn. *The 'Improper' Feminine, The Women's Sensation Novel and the New Woman Writing.* London and New York: Routledge, 1992.

Ricci, N. P. "The End/s of Woman." *Canadian Journal of Political and Social Theory/Revue canadienne de théorie politique et sociale* 11 (1987): 11–27.

Rubin, Gayle. "Thinking Sex: Notes for a Radical Theory of the Politics of Sexuality." *Pleasure and Danger.* Ed. Carole Vance. Boston: Routledge & Kegan Paul, 1984.

Sartre, Jean-Paul. *Being and Nothingness: A Phenomenological Essay on Ontology.* Trans. Hazel Barnes. New York: Washington Square P, 1966.

Showalter, Elaine. *Sexual Anarchy: Gender and Culture at the Fin de Siècle.* New York: Penguin, 1990.

Smart, Carol, ed. *Regulating Womanhood: Historical Essays on Marriage, Motherhood, and Sexuality.* London: Routledge, 1992.

Trilling, Lionel. *Freud and the Crisis of Our Culture.* Boston: Beacon Press, 1955.

Warner, Marina. *Alone of All Her Sex: The Myth and the Cult of the Virgin Mary.* New York: Vintage, 1983.

Weedon, Chris. *Feminist Practice and Poststructuralist Theory.* Oxford: Basil Blackwell, 1987.

Wilson, Elizabeth. *The Sphinx in the City: Urban Life, the Control of Disorder, and Women.* London: Virago, 1991.

Select Bibliography on Naturalism (exluding Dreiser and Grove)

Baguley, David. *Naturalist Fiction: The Entropic Vision.* Cambridge: Cambridge UP, 1990.

——. "The Nature of Naturalism."Nelson 13–26.

——. "The Lure of the Naturalist Text." *Canadian Review of Comparative Literature* 19 (1992): 273–80.

Bahr, Hermann. "Der Naturalismus als Zwischenakt." *Naturalismus, Die deutsche Literatur: Ein Abriß in Text und Darstellung, Band 12.* Ed. Walter Schmähling. Stuttgart: Philipp Reclam, 1977. 104–05.

——. *Zur Überwindung des Naturalismus, Theoretische Schriften 1887–1904.* Ed. Gotthart Wunberg. Stuttgart: W. Kohlhammer Verlag, 1968.

Bell, David F. *Models of Power: Politics and Economics in Zola's "Rougon Macquart."* Lincoln & London: U of Nebraska P, 1988.

Berg, William J. *The Visual Novel: Emile Zola and the Art of His Times.* Pennsylvania: Pennsylvania State UP, 1992.

Bernheimer, Charles. *Figures of Ill Repute: Representing Prostitution in Nineteenth-Century France.* Cambridge, MA: Harvard UP, 1989.

Cargill, Oscar. *Intellectual America: Ideas on the March.* New York: Macmillan, 1941.

Chevrel, Yves. *Le naturalisme.* Paris: Presses Universitaires de France, 1982.

——. "Toward an Aesthetic of the Naturalist Novel." Nelson 46–65.

——. "Le Roman Naturaliste: Un défi à la littérature populaire?" *Richesse du Roman Populaire.* Actes du colloque international de Pont à Mousson. Ed. Reneé Guise and Hans-Jörg Neuschäfer. Sarrebruck, Nancy: Centre de Recherche sur le roman populaire, 1986. 37–53.

Conder, John. *Naturalism in American Fiction.* Lexington: UP of Kentucky, 1984.

Fischer, Jens Malte. *Fin-de-siècle: Kommentar zu einer Epoche.* München: Winkler Verlag, 1978.

Fisher, Philip. *Hard Facts: Setting and Form in the American Novel.* New York: Oxford UP, 1985.

Flaubert, Gustave. *Madame Bovary.* Paris: Le Livre de Poche, 1961.

Frye, Northrop. *Anatomy of Criticism: Four Essays.* Princeton: Princeton UP, 1973.

Furst, Lilian. "Thomas Mann's *Buddenbrooks*: 'The First and Only Naturalist Novel' in Germany?" Nelson 226–44.

Furst, Lilian, and Peter N. Skrine. *Naturalism: The Critical Idiom.* London: Methuen, 1971.

Goncourt, Edmond de, and Jules de Goncourt. *Germinie Lacerteux.* Paris: Charpentier, 1911.

Hamon, Philippe. "The Naturalist Text and the Problem of Reference." Nelson 27–45.

Hapke, Laura. *Girls Who Went Wrong: Prostitutes in American Fiction, 1885–1917*. Bowling Green: Bowling Green State U Popular Press, 1989.

———. *Tales of the Working Girl: Wage-Earning Women in American Literature, 1890-1925*. New York: Twayne, 1992.

Henighan, Tom. *Natural Space in Literature: Imagination and Environment in Nineteenth and Twentieth Century Fiction and Poetry*. Ottawa: Golden Dog Press, 1982.

Howard, June. *Form and History in American Literary Naturalism*. Chapel Hill & London: U of Carolina P, 1985.

Kaplan, Amy. *The Social Construction of American Realism*. 1988; Chicago: U of Chicago P, 1992.

Kolkenbrock-Netz, Jutta. *Fabrikation, Experiment, Schöpfung: Strategien ästhetischer Legitimation im Naturalismus*. Heidelberg: Carl Winter, 1981.

Lukács, Georg. *Realism In Our Time: Literature and the Class Struggle*. Trans. John and Necke Mander. New York: Harper & Row, 1964.

Mahal, Günter. *Naturalismus: Deutsche Literatur im 20. Jahrhundert*. München: Wilhelm Fink Verlag, 1975.

Mann, Thomas. *Buddenbrooks: Verfall einer Familie*. Gesammelte Werke in Einzelbänden. Frankfurt: Fischer Verlag, 1981.

———. *Betrachtungen eines Unpolitischen*. Gesammelte Werke in Einzelbänden. Frankfurt: Fischer Verlag, 1983.

Mencken. H. L. *A Book of Prefaces*. New York: Knopf, 1917.

Mitchell, Lee Clark. *Determined Fictions: American Literary Naturalism*. New York: Columbia UP, 1989.

Münchow, Ursula. *Deutscher Naturalismus*. Berlin: Akademie Verlag, 1968.

Nelson, Brian, ed. *Naturalism in the European Novel: New Critical Perspectives*. New York & Oxford: Berg, 1992.

Neuschäfer, Hans-Jörg. *Populärromane im 19. Jahrhundert*. München: Wilhelm Fink Verlag, 1976.

Norris, Frank. "Zola as a Romantic Writer." *Norris: Novels and Essays*. New York: Library of America, 1986. 1106–08.

Ostenso, Martha. *Wild Geese*, New Canadian Library. Toronto: McClelland & Stewart, 1967.

Parrington, Vernon Louis. "1860–1920: The Beginnings of Critical Realism in America." *Main Currents in American Thought*, Vol. 3. New York: Harcourt, Brace, 1930.

Poirier, Richard. *A World Elsewhere: The Place of Style in American Literature*. London: Chatto & Windus, 1967.

Pykett, Lyn. "Representing the Real: The English Debate about Naturalism, 1884–1900." Nelson 167–188.

Restif de la Bretonne. *Oeuvres*. Genève: Slatkine Reprints, 1978.

Roy, Gabrielle. *The Tin Flute*, New Canadian Library. Trans. Alan Brown. Toronto: McClelland & Stewart, 1993.

Seamon, Roger. "Naturalist Narratives and Their Ideational Context: A Theory of American Naturalist Fiction." *The Canadian Review of American Studies* 19 (1988): 47–64.

Seltzer, Mark. *Bodies and Machines*. New York & London: Routledge, 1992.

——. "*The Princess Casamassima*: Realism and the Fantasy of Surveillance." Sundquist 95–118.

Smart, Patricia. *Writing in the Father's House: The Emergence of the Feminine in the Quebec Literary Tradition*. Toronto: U of Toronto P, 1991.

Spiller, Robert E. *The Cycle of American Literature: An Essay in Historical Criticism*. 1955; New York: Mentor, 1956.

Sundquist, Eric J., ed. *American Realism: New Essays*. Baltimore & London: Johns Hopkins UP, 1982.

Theobald, Margret. "Der Mythos Großkaufhaus im Romanwerk Emile Zolas." Unpublished (Staatsexamen) diss. Saarbrücken: Universität des Saarlandes, 1988.

Walcutt, Charles Child. *American Literary Naturalism: A Divided Stream*. Minneapolis: U of Minnesota P, 1956.

Wharton, Edith. *The House of Mirth*. 1905; New York: Penguin, 1986.

Zola, Émile. *Au Bonheur des Dames*. Livre de Poche 228. Paris: Fasquelle, 1981.

——. *Thérèse Raquin*. Livre de Poche 34. Paris: Fasquelle, n.d.

——. *L'Assommoir*.Livre de Poche 97. Paris: Fasquelle, 1983.

——. *Nana. Les Rougon-Macquart*, Vol. 2. Ed. Henri Mitterand. Paris: Galli-mard, 1961.

——. *Germinal*. 1885; Livre de Poche 145. Paris: Fasquelle, 1968.

——. *Le Roman expérimental*. 1880. Paris: Garnier Flammarion, 1971.

Select Bibliography on Theodore Dreiser

Bowlby, Rachel. *Just Looking: Consumer Culture in Dreiser, Gissing and Zola.* New York & London: Methuen, 1985.

Church, Joseph. "Minnie's Dreams in *Sister Carrie.*" *College Literature* 14 (1987): 183–87.

Conrad, Peter. *The Art of the City: Views and Versions of New York.* New York: Oxford UP, 1984.

Dreiser, Theodore. *A Gallery of Women,* 2 vols. New York: Horace Liveright, 1929.

——. *American Diaries: 1902–1926.* Ed. Thomas P. Riggio. Philadelphia: U of Pennsylvania, 1982.

——. *An American Tragedy.* 1925; New York & Scarborough: Signet, New American Library, 1981.

——. *Dawn.* New York: Horace Liveright, 1931.

——. *Jennie Gerhardt.* 1911; Cleveland & New York: Dell, 1963.

——. *Notes on Life.* Ed. Marguerite Tjader and John J. McAleer. Alabama: U of Alabama P, 1974.

——. *Selected Magazine Articles of Theodore Dreiser: Life and Art in the American 1890s.* Ed. Yoshinobu Hakutani. Rutherford: Fairleigh Dickinson UP, 1985.

——. *Sister Carrie.* 1900; New York: Modern Library, 1961.

——. *Sister Carrie.* Unexpurgated ed. 1981. Ed. Neda Westlake et al., Harmondsworth: Penguin, 1983.

——. *The Bulwark.* Garden City: Doubleday, 1946.

——. *The "Genius."* New York: John Lane, 1915.

——. *Theodore Dreiser: A Selection of Uncollected Prose.* Ed. Donald Pizer. Detroit: Wayne State UP, 1977.

——. *Trilogy of Desire, Vol. 1: The Financier.* New York: Thomas Y. Crowell, 1974.

——. *Trilogy of Desire, Vol. 2: The Titan.* New York: Thomas Y. Crowell, 1974.

——. *Trilogy of Desire, Vol. 3: The Stoic.* New York: Thomas Y. Crowell, 1974.

——. *Twelve Men.* New York: Boni & Liveright, 1919.

Drescher-Schröder, Christa. *Das Bild Chicagos in der Cowperwood-Trilogie Theodore Dreisers mit besonderer Berücksichtigung von "The Titan."* Frankfurt: Rita G. Fischer Verlag, 1980.

Fiedler, Leslie A. "Dreiser and the Sentimental Novel." *Dreiser: A Collection of Critical Essays.* Ed. John Lydenberg. Englewood Cliffs: Prentice-Hall, 1971. 45–51.

Fisher Fishkin, Shelley. "From Fact to Fiction: *An American Tragedy.*" *Theodore Dreiser's "An American Tragedy."* Ed. Harold Bloom. New York: Chelsea House, 1988. 103–26.

Freedman, William A. "A Look at Dreiser as Artist: The Motif of Circularity in *Sister Carrie.*" *Modern Fiction Studies* 8 (1962): 384–92.

Gerber, Philip L. *Theodore Dreiser.* Twayne's United States Authors Series. New Haven: New Haven College and UP, 1964.

——. "A Star is Born: 'Celebrity' in *Sister Carrie.*" *Dreiser Studies* 19 (1988): 2–25.

——. "The Financier Himself: Dreiser and C.T. Yerkes." *PMLA* 88 (1973): 112–21.

Gerbstein, Sheldon N. "Dreiser's Victorian Vamp." *Sister Carrie.* Theodore Dreiser. New York: Norton, 1970.

Gogol, Miriam. "Dreiser's Search for a 'Religion of Life': A Psychoanalytic Reading." *Dreiser Studies* 21 (1990): 21–30.

——, ed. *Theodore Dreiser: Beyond Naturalism.* New York: New York UP, 1995.

Hochman, Barbara. "Goethe's *Faust*: A Leitmotif in Dreiser's *The "Genius.*" *The Dreiser Newsletter* 16 (1985): 1–12.

Hovey, Richard, and Ralph S. Ruth. "Dreiser's *The "Genius*": Motivation and Structure." *Hartford Studies in Literature* 2 (1970): 169–83.

Hussman, Lawrence. *Dreiser and His Fiction: A Twentieth Century Quest.* Philadelphia: U of Pennsylvania P, 1983.

——. "The Fate of the Fallen Woman in *Maggie* and *Sister Carrie.*" *The Image of the Prostitute in Modern Literature.* Ed. Pierre L. Horn and Mary Beth Pringle. New York: Frederick Ungar, 1984. 91–100.

Kwiat, Joseph. "Dreiser and the Graphic Artist." *American Quarterly* 3 (1951): 127–41.

Lehan, Richard. *Theodore Dreiser: His World and His Novels.* Carbondale & Edwardsville: Southern Illinois UP, 1969.

——. "The City, the Self, and Narrative Discourse." In *New Essays on "Sister Carrie.*" Ed. Donald Pizer. Cambridge: Cambridge UP, 1991. 65–85.

Lingeman, Richard. *Theodore Dreiser, Vol. 1: At the Gates of the City 1871–1907.* New York: G.P. Putnam's Sons, 1986.

——. *Theodore Dreiser, Vol. 2: An American Journey 1908–1945.* New York: G. P. Putnam's Sons, 1990.

Lydenberg, John, ed. *Dreiser: A Collection of Critical Essays.* Englewood Cliffs: Prentice-Hall, 1971.

Matheson, Terence J. "The Two Faces of Sister Carrie: The Characterization of Dreiser's First Heroine." *Ariel* 11 (1980): 71–85.

Matthiessen, F.O. *Theodore Dreiser.* New York: William Sloane, 1951.

Mencken, H.L. "Theodore Dreiser." *A Book of Prefaces* 65–148.

Michaels, Walter Benn. *The Gold Standard and the Logic of Naturalism: American Literature at the Turn of the Century.* Berkeley: U of California P, 1987.

——. "Dreiser's *Financier*: The Man of Business as a Man of Letters." Sundquist 278–95.

——. "*Sister Carrie*'s Popular Economy." *Critical Inquiry* 7 (1980): 373–90.

——. "Critical Response, Fictitious Dealing: A Reply to Leo Bersani." *Critical Inquiry* 8 (1981): 165–71.

Mizruchi, Susan L. *The Power of Historical Knowledge: Narrating the Past in Hawthorne, James, and Dreiser*. Princeton: Princeton UP, 1988.

Moers, Ellen. *Two Dreisers: The Man and the Novelist as Revealed in His Two Most Important Works, "Sister Carrie" and "An American Tragedy."* New York: Viking Press, 1969.

Mukherjee, Arun. *The Gospel of Wealth in the American Novel*. London: Croom Helm, 1987.

O'Neill, John. "The Disproportion of Sadness: Dreiser's *The Financier* and *The Titan*." *Modern Fiction Studies* 23 (1977): 409–22.

Orlov, Paul. "The Subversion of the Self: Anti-Naturalistic Crux in *An American Tragedy*." *Modern Fiction Studies* 23 (1977): 457–72.

Petrey, Sandy. "The Language of Realism, The Language of False Consciousness: A Reading of *Sister Carrie*." *Novel* 10 (1976): 101–13.

Pizer, Donald. *The Novels of Theodore Dreiser: A Critical Study*. Minneapolis: U of Minnesota P, 1976.

——. *Twentieth-Century American Literary Naturalism: An Interpretation*. Carbondale & Edwardsville: Southern Illinois UP, 1982.

——, ed. *Critical Essays on Theodore Dreiser*. Boston: G.K. Hall, 1981.

——, ed. *New Essays on "Sister Carrie."* Cambridge: Cambridge UP, 1991.

Powys, John Cowper. "Modern Fiction." *Sex in the Arts: A Symposium*. Ed. John Francis McDermott and Kendall B. Taft. New York: Harper & Brothers, 1932. 34–63.

Roberts, Sidney B. "Portrait of a Robber Baron: Charles T. Yerkes." *Business History Review* 35 (1961): 344–71.

Rusch, Frederic E. "Dreiser's Introduction to Freudianism." *Dreiser Studies* 18 (1987): 34–38.

Sherman, Stuart P. "The Barbaric Naturalism of Mr. Dreiser." *The Nation* 101 (1915): 648–50. Rpt. Lydenberg 63–72.

Wallace, Jack E. "The Comic Voice in Dreiser's Cowperwood Narrative." *American Literature* 53 (1981): 56–71.

Woloch, Nancy. *Early American Women, A Documentary History 1600–1900.* Belmont, CA: Wadsworth, 1992.

Select Bibliography on Frederick Philip Grove

Ayre, Robert. "A Solitary Giant." *Canadian Forum* 12 (1932): 255–57. Rpt. Pacey 17–24.

Bader, Rudolf. "Frederick Philip Grove and Naturalism Reconsidered." *Gaining Ground: European Critics on Canadian Literature.* Ed. Robert Kroetsch and Reingard M. Nischik. Edmonton: NeWest, 1985. 222–33.

Bailey, Nancy I. "F. P. G. and the Empty House." *Journal of Canadian Fiction* 31–32 (1981): 177–93.

Blodgett, E. D. *Configuration: Essays on Canadian Literatures.* Toronto: Essays on Canadian Writing P, 1982.

——. "Grove's Female Picaresque." *Canadian Literature* 106 (1985), 152–54.

Böhme, Margarete. *Tagebuch einer Verlorenen.* Frankfurt: Suhrkamp, 1989.

Chapple, Gerald, and Hans H. Schulte, ed. *The Turn of the Century: German Literature and Art, 1890–1915.* Bonn: Bouvier Verlag, 1981.

Craig, Terrence. "Frederick Philip Grove und der "fremde" Einwanderer im kanadischen Westen." *Deutschkanadisches Jahrbuch* 9. Ed. Gerhard Friesen and Karin Gürttler. Toronto: Historical Society of Mecklenburg Upper Canada, 1986. 141–51.

Darling, Michael. "A Mask for All Occasions: The Identity of FPG." *Essays on Canadian Writing* 1 (1974): 50–53.

DeVore, Lynn. "The Backgrounds of *Nightwood*: Robin, Felix, and Nora." *Journal of Modern Literature* 10 (1983): 71–90.

Divay, Gaby. "Felix Paul Greve's Fanny Essler Novel and Poems: His or Hers?" Unpublished ms.

Freytag-Loringhoven, Elsa, Baroness von. "Autobiography." Djuna Barnes Collection. University of Maryland Archives.

Frye, Northrop. "Canadian Dreiser." *The Canadian Forum* (1948), 121–22. Rpt. Pacey 186–87.

——. *The Bush Garden: Essays on the Canadian Imagination.* Toronto: Anansi, 1971.

Gide, André. "Conversation with a German Several Years Before the War." Trans. Blanche A. Price. *Pretexts: Reflections on Literature and Morality.* Ed. Justin O'Brien. London: Secker & Warburg, 1959. 234–42.

Greve, Felix Paul. *Wanderungen.* Munich: Littauer, 1902.

——. *Fanny Eßler: Ein Roman.* Stuttgart: Axel Juncker Verlag, 1905. Rpt. *Fanny Essler*, 2 vols. Trans. Christine Helmers et al. Ottawa: Oberon, 1984.

——. *Maurermeister Ihles Haus*. Karl Schnabel: Berlin, 1906. Rpt. *The Master Mason's House*. Ed. A. W. Riley and Douglas Spettigue. Trans. Paul P. Gubbins. Ottawa: Oberon, 1976.

Grove, Frederick Philip. *A Search for America: The Odyssey of an Immigrant*. 1927; New Canadian Library, Toronto: McClelland & Stewart, 1971.

——. *Fruits of the Earth*. 1933. New Canadian Library, Toronto: McClelland & Stewart, 1965.

——. *In Search of Myself*. Toronto: Macmillan, 1946.

——. *It Needs to Be Said*. ... Toronto: Macmillan, 1929.

——. "Jane Atkinson." Grove Collection. University of Manitoba Archives, Winnipeg. Box 13. Folders 1–8.

——. *Our Daily Bread*. Toronto: Macmillan, 1928.

——. *Over Prairie Trails*. 1922; New Canadian Library, Toronto: McClelland & Steward, 1970.

——. *Settlers of the Marsh*. 1925; New Canadian Library, Toronto: McClelland & Stewart, 1984.

——. *Tales from the Margin: The Selected Short Stories of Frederick Philip Grove*. Ed. Desmond Pacey. Toronto: Ryerson, 1971.

——. *The Letters of Frederick Philip Grove*. Ed. Desmond Pacey. Toronto & Buffalo: U of Toronto P, 1976.

——. *The Master of the Mill*. 1944; Toronto: Macmillan, 1945.

——. *Two Generations: A Story of Present-Day Ontario*. Toronto: Ryerson, 1939.

——. "Two Lives: The Story of an Ontario Farm," Grove Collection, University of Manitoba Archives, Winnipeg. Box 12. Folders 5–7.

Hardt, Ernst. *Briefe an Ernst Hardt: Eine Auswahl aus den Jahren 1998-1947*. Ed. Jochen Meyer. Marbach: Deutsches Literaturarchiv, 1975.

Heidenreich, Rosmarin. "The Search for FPG." *Canadian Literature* 80 (1979): 63–70.

Hjartarson, Paul. "Design and Truth in Grove's *In Search of Myself*." *Canadian Literature* 90 (1981): 73–92.

——, ed. *A Stranger to My Time: Essays by and about Frederick Philip Grove*. Edmonton: NeWest, 1986.

——. "Of Greve, Grove, and Other Strangers: The Autobiographies of the Baroness Elsa von Freytag-Loringhoven. Hjartarson, *A Stranger to My Time*, 269–84.

——. "The Self, Its Discourse, and the Other: The Autobiographies of Frederick Philip Grove and the Baroness Elsa von Freytag-Loringhoven." *Reflections: Autobiography and Canadian Literature*. Ed. Klaus P. Stich. Ottawa: U of Ottawa P, 1988.

Hürlimann, Martin. *Berlin: Königsresidenz-Reichshauptstadt-Neubeginn*. Zürich: Atlantis, 1981.

Kaye, Frances W. "Hamlin Garland and Frederick Philip Grove: Self-Concious Chroniclers of the Pioneers." *Canadian Review of American Studies* 10 (1979): 31–39.

Keith, W. J. "F. P. Grove's 'Difficult' Novel: *The Master of the Mill*." *Ariel* 4 (1973): 34–48.

——. "Grove's Search For America." *Canadian Literature* 59 (1974): 57–66.

Knilli, Friedrich, and Michael Nerlich, ed. *Medium Metropole: Berlin, Paris, New York*. Heidelberg: Carl Winter Universitätsverlag, 1986.

Knönagel, Axel. *Nietzschean Philosophy in the Works of Frederick Philip Grove*. Frankfurt: Peter Lang, 1990.

Kroetsch, Robert. "The Grammar of Silence: Narrative Pattern in Ethnic Writing." *Canadian Literature* 106 (1985): 65–74.

Mathews, Robin. "F. P. Grove: An Important Version of *The Master of the Mill* Discovered." *Studies in Canadian Literature* 7 (1982): 241–57.

Makow, Henry. "Grove's 'Garbled Extract': The Bibliographical Origins of *Settlers of the Marsh*." *Modern Times*. Vol. 3: The Canadian Novel. Ed. John Moss. Toronto: New Canada Publications, 1982. 38–54.

McGregor, Gaile. *The Wacousta Syndrome: Exporations in the Canadian Langscape* [*sic*]. Toronto: U of Toronto P, 1985.

McMullen, Lorraine. "Women in Grove's Novels." Nause 67–76.

McMullin, Stanley E. "Grove and the Promised Land." *Canadian Literature* 49 (1971): 10–19.

——. "Evolution versus Revolution: Grove's Perception of History."Nause 77–88.

Mitchell, Beverley. "The 'Message' and the 'Inevitable From' in *The Master of the Mill*." *Journal of Canadian Fiction* 3 (1974): 74–79.

Moss, John. *Sex and Violence in the Canadian Novel*. Toronto: McClelland & Stewart, 1977.

Nadel, Ira Bruce."'Canada Made Me' and Canadian Autobiography." *Canadian Literature* 101 (1984): 69–77.

Nause, John, ed. *The Grove Symposium*. Reappraisals: Canadian Writers Series. Ottawa: U of Ottawa P, 1974.

Pacey, Desmond. *Frederick Philip Grove*. Toronto: Ryerson, 1945.

——, ed. *Frederick Philip Grove: Critical Views of Canadian Writers*. Toronto: Ryerson, 1970.

Pache, Walter. "Der Fall Grove-Vorleben und Nachleben des Schriftstellers Felix Paul Greve." *Deutschkanadisches Jahrbuch* 5 (1979): 121–35.

Riley, Anthony W. "The Case of Greve/Grove: The European Roots of a Canadian Writer." *The Old World and The New: Literary Perspectives of German-speaking Canadians*. Ed. Walter E. Riedel. Toronto: U of Toronto P, 1984. 37–58.

——. "The German Novels of Frederick Philip Grove."Nause 55–66.

Spettigue, Douglas O. *FPG: The European Years*. Ottawa: Oberon, 1973.

——. *Frederick Philip Grove*. Toronto: Copp Clark, 1969.

——. "Fanny Essler and the Master." Hjartarson 47–64.

——. "Felix, Elsa, André Gide and Others: Some Unpublished Letters of F. P. Greve." *Canadian Literature* 134 (1991): 9–39.

Sproxton, Birk. "Grove's Unpublished MAN and Its Relation to *The Master of the Mill*."Nause 35–54.

Sterner, Gabriele. *Art Nouveau: An Art of Transition – From Individualism to Mass Society*. Trans. Frederick G. Peters and Diana S. Peters. New York: Barron's, 1982.

Stich, K. P. "Beckwith's 'Mark Twain' and The Dating of Grove's *A Search for America*." *Canadian Literature* 127 (1990): 183–85.

——. "F.P.G.: Over German Trails." Review of *The Master Mason's House*. *Essays on Canadian Writing* 6 (1977): 148–51.

——. "Grove's New World Bluff." *Canadian Literature* 90 (1981): 111–23.

——. "Grove's 'Stella.'" *Canadian Literature* 113-14 (1987): 258–62.

——. "The Memory of Masters in Grove's Self-Portraits." *Etudes Canadiennes/ Canadian Studies* 12 (1982): 153–64.

Stobie, Margaret. *Frederick Philip Grove*. New York: Twayne, 1973.

——. "'Frederick Philip Grove' and the Canadianism Movement." *Studies in the Novel* 4 (1972): 173–85.

Sutherland, Ronald. *Second Image: Comparative Studies in Quebec/Canadian Literature*. Toronto: New Press, 1971.

——. "What was Frederick Philip Grove?" Nause 1–11.

Willey, Thomas. "Thomas Mann's Munich." Chapple and Schulte 477–91.

Wilson, Jennie. "A Comparative Study of Frederick Philip Grove and Theodore Dreiser." Master's thesis. U of New Brunswick, 1962.

Index